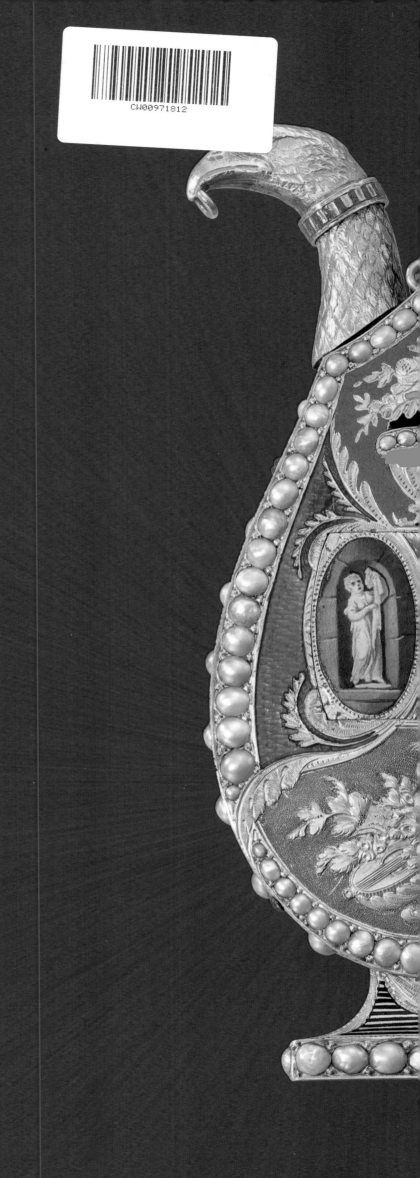

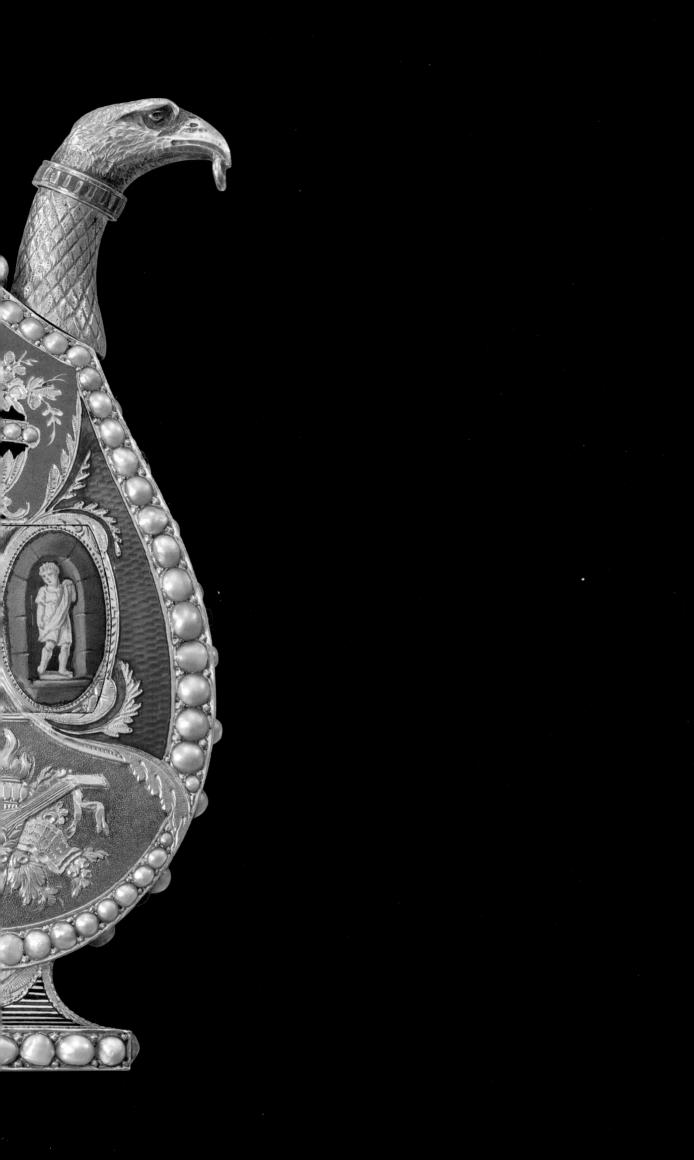

A Voyage Through Time

The Masis Collection of Horological Masterpieces

CREDIT

Editor
D. Masis

Photography
Clarissa Bruce

Design
Duman Media Ltd

Colour Separation
Savas Tunali

Printing - Binding
Promat A.S.

Published in 2020 by
Unicorn, an imprint of Unicorn Publishing Group
5 Newburgh Street
London
W1F 7RG
www.unicornpublishing.org

CONTENT

Foreword
D. Masis

What started with a chance phone call was to become a magnificent obsession - a forty-five-year epic journey of both collecting and learning that has evolved into my watch collection as you see it now. The eventual realizations of a long-held ambition to publish this book allows me to share with a wider audience the exceptional beauty and craftsmanship of these wonders of the watchmaker's and goldsmith's art.

Back in 1979, a close jeweller friend of mine based in the Closed Bazaar of Istanbul telephoned me and said "Hurry up, come immediately!." I always had an interest in old jewellery and objects of virtue and used to wander around the bazaar hunting for them in my spare time and so I went directly to his shop.When I entered, I saw several silver pocket watches on the counter.He said "You will buy this collection". Until that day I had no particular interest in pocket watches or in silver objects generally but he insisted so much that I couldn't even bargain on the price. I paid what he asked and came home. I now had fifty-three silver pocket watches spread out on the dining table mostly with old Turkish numerals on the dials, and was trying to understand what I had actually bought. At that moment, suddenly one of them started ringing (a clockwatch as I discovered later) which immediately fascinated me, I started opening more of the cases and to my surprise there they were, centuries old mechanical marvels, some of them still in working condition.

From that day I was hooked but realised I had much to learn because in those days I knew nothing about horology. I bought several books and read and read. The more I read, the more captivating and fascinating the world of pocket watches appeared to me.

As my interest became more serious, not to mention expensive, I decided to attend the major watch auctions held in London at the great houses of Sotheby's and Christie's. My first mentor in these early days of my collecting was Tina Millar of Sothebys, I will never forget her generous help and guidance at that formative stage which fired my enthusiasm even further. Through Tina, I met the great English watchmaker and Breguet authority George Daniels, who, after seing my Breguet minute repeater said "Dick, you have the best piece for the foundation of a serious collection - now get on with it!" These characteristically direct words from a master watchmaker whom I had always admired deeply excited me very much. From this point I started buying and buying almost non-stop. At one point, the collection numbered some 863 pocket watches and had started to get out of control, so I decided that it must have a focus and direction - would I go for mechanical complexity or concentrate on craftsmanship and beauty? I decided on the latter. The pieces to be found in this book have been carefully chosen by the writer to represent not only the highlights of my collection, but to illustrate to the reader the sheer diversity and enormous skill of watchmakers, jewellers, enamellers and lapidaries over a period of well over four hundred years.

Today when I look at these beautiful pocket watches I see art, beauty, taste, wonderful workmanship and the incredible amount of time and work that was put into them.Then I turn my head and look at wristwatches and I wonder where did it all go? wristwatches are industrial pieces in my opinion and I ask myself why people collect them, perhaps only for speculative reasons.I cannot imagine myself gaining any enjoyment in having two hundred wristwatches, nor feeling any satisfaction looking at them.I don't use a wristwatch because my telephone gives me the right time anyway. About 35 years ago, Osvaldo Patrizzi came to visit me in İstanbul, he was travelling from India and had just bought a collection of pocket watches there.He said to me "Dick, I am having problems in finding enough pocket watches in the world, I think I will start auctions for wristwatches as well'. He did, and the rest is history. A few years ago, a gentleman was sitting next to me in an auction bidding for a wristwatch. In all the excitement, I couldn't help myself asking him why he had paid so much for, in my opinion, an ugly looking piece like that! He said "The dial is a different colour", this is not something I can identify with in my collecting, on the contrary, the more I look at wristwatches the deeper my appreciation of pocket watches becomes.

My wish for the future is that in due course my family will continue to take the same interest and delight in pocket watches that I have over the past four decades, perhaps building and enhancing the collection to be passed down to future generations.

I would like to thank my wife and my children who have helped me so much in this long venture, sleepless nights following Hong Kong sales, locking myself in my room for hours, spending hours looking at the same watch instead of having dinner with them. My gratitude specially to my wife who spent hours helping me organise the collection and helped with every detail during the whole journey. Finally, my thanks to all the great watchmakers and craftsmen down the centuries - because of them and their splendid creations I have had a wonderful 45 years!.

My special thanks extend to Sabine Kegel and specially to Richard Chadwick whose devoted work has enabled this book to be brought to completion.

Introduction
R. Chadwick

Having spent the last thirty years of my working life with one or other of the major auction houses, I had been aware of the existence of the Masis watch collection for many years, and also the driven passion of its owner to assemble one of the world's great horological treasuries.

However, it was not until I was approached with the suggestion to write this book and then given the opportunity to see the collection in its entirety that I fully realised the sheer quality, range and unparalleled variety of the assembled watches.

What Dick Masis has achieved over the last forty years is truly remarkable. He has also approached the collecting of watches in a thoroughly unique way. His collecting philosophy is that any watch under consideration for acquisition must first and foremost be an object of artistic beauty and should display excellence of craftsmanship in whichever medium it is made.

The collection spans a period of over four hundred years of the watchmaker's art, beginning with some of the earliest surviving portable timepieces made in Germany in the late 16th century. From this earliest time, watches were revered as rare and precious objects and as befitted their status, the cases made to house these mechanical marvels were largely made in precious metals, often produced by the great gold and silver smithing workshops of the time. The decoration of watch cases developed into a specific art which encompassed a number of highly skilled trades; the gold chaser, enamellist, stone-setter and lapidary all used the watch case as a platform to showcase their art. Indeed, some watch cases are among the greatest European miniature works of art to ever be created.

The Masis collection is particularly rich in examples of gloriously painted Geneva enamels encompassing the work of the Huaud family working in the baroque period, through to those sumptuous Swiss and London made watches that were exported to China and Turkey in the early years of the 19th century. Although the emphasis of the collection is focused upon artistic beauty, it naturally includes some outstanding complicated and historically important watches, notably the earliest known minute repeating watch and the earliest known jump-hour watch.

This book aims to inform the reader not only of the richness and diversity of the Masis collection itself but to adequately display some of the watchmaking masterpieces that have enthralled generations of owners. Through the publication of this work it is hoped that it will encourage wider appreciation of the watchmaker's art.

It only remains for me to thank Dick Masis himself for his trust in allowing me to compile this book of his collection and for his patience and good-humoured encouragement during its development. I would also like to thank my colleague Sabine Kegel of Christie's in Geneva and both Clarissa and Richard of Pearson Bruce UK, whose stunning photography truly brings these objects to life.

CHAPTER 1

PRE-1750

Pre-1750

The earliest small portable timepieces were produced from the early 15th century. These "watches" as they came to be known, were made possible by the invention of the mainspring. A movement fitted with a mainspring in a barrel meant that a pendulum was no longer necessary, and when used in conjunction with a foliot balance and verge escapement the timepiece could be entirely portable. The earliest recorded watchmakers were working in the German cities of Nuremberg and Augsburg and made the first timepieces intended to be worn on the body. Of course, the earliest watches were not worn primarily to tell the time, their accuracy being so erratic that timekeeping was of very minor importance. They were, however, considered to be considerable status symbols, the preserve only of royalty, high clergy, nobility and the very rich. Worn as pieces of jewellery and valued for their fine workmanship and ornamentation, watches at this period were viewed as intriguing mechanical wonders.

The Masis Collection is fortunate to have several excellent late 16th and early 17th century watches, including examples of the earliest German watches with the 'stackfreed' mainspring equaliser, a short-lived alternative to the fusée and also a rare survival of watches with astronomical indications which were functioning scientific instruments able to display the day, date and month calendar, phases of the moon and the seasons.

During the 17th and early 18th centuries, the most expensive watches had cases made from carved rock crystal or decorated with miniature paintings on enamel. The Masis Collection is particularly richly endowed with superlative 17th century watches with examples in both rock crystal and painted enamel cases - incredible miniature works of art in their own right. The technique for painting on enamel was developed in the French city of Blois around 1630, but really blossomed in Geneva largely due to the Huaud family headed by Pierre Huaud, Protestants who had fled France and established themselves in Switzerland in the early 17th century.

The work of the Huauds was always highly prized by European monarchs including Louis XIV of France and the Elector of Brandenburg for whom the Huauds worked by special appointment. This collection includes several important signed examples of their work.

After the invention of the balance spring in 1657, the timekeeping properties of watches improved dramatically, so much so that from about 1690-1700 watches were sufficiently accurate to be fitted for the first time with a minute hand in addition to the single hour hand of pre-balance spring watches.

The distinctive French 'oignon' watches made from late in Louis XIV's reign until the middle of the 18th century echo in miniature the richly decorated baroque style of the period perfectly. Their English counterparts are, as expected, more restrained decoratively whilst exhibiting the very highest standards of workmanship and finishing. An English watch in the Masis Collection which is of particular note is the exceptional quarter repeating silver coach watch made by Daniel Quare around 1690 for the Duke de Luxembourg, one of Louis XIV's most important generals.

Inv. 1080

German

Oval, gilt metal and enamel, two-train, single-hand clockwatch with stackfreed

Unsigned, German, circa 1580

Gilt brass full plate verge movement with square baluster pillars, fixed barrel, G-shaped stackfreed, five-wheel train, second wheel with six-leaf pinion, the rest with five leaves, steel escape wheel, steel two-arm circular foliot with hog's bristle regulator, small brass S-shaped cock secured by a screw, striking from a fixed barrel with five-wheel train, governor pinion with brass cylindrical weight, striking on a shallow circular bell inside the back of the case, the barrels engraved with scrolls

Silver dial decorated with translucent blue and green enamel resembling cloisonné and forming a rosette, mounted in the centre of the gilt brass oval plate decorated with arabesques, champlevé Roman hour chapter ring with stars for half-hours, aperture at the bottom to set the striking, iron tulip hand

Three-part case, the back cover pierced and engraved with arabesque and serpent decoration, the band engraved in relief, the hinged front cover

63 x 46 mm.

Provenance: The collection of The Lord Sandberg CBE

Published in: The Sandberg Watch Collection, Terence Camerer Cuss, 1998, pages 32-33.

C. Jeanenne Bell G.G. Collectors Encyclopedia of Pendant and Pocket Watches (Page 11)

This watch is one of the rare surviving 16th-century watches with an enamelled dial.

The stackfreed works by regulating the power from the mainspring. This is usually achieved by the action of the stackfreed spring on a cam mounted directly or indirectly to the barrel arbour. The constant change of the radius of the cam regulates the power transmitted to the wheel train. In this watch, the unusual shape of the stackfreed spring is an interesting example of the development of early German horology.

The stackfreed was almost certainly invented in Nuremberg in the 16th century and seems to have been limited to southern Germany. Its advantage over the early fusée was that it required less height and hence allowed the manufacture of flatter watches. The stackfreed was, however, a very inefficient device since it worked by exerting an opposing friction force on the mainspring. It required more powerful mainsprings and higher gear ratios in watches, which may have introduced more variation in drive force. With the development of narrower, more compact fusées, the stackfreed disappeared from use around 1630.

M.S., possibly Martin Schmidt

Oval, silver and gilt metal, pre-balance spring, single-hand, two-train, hour-striking clockwatch

Signed M.S., possibly Martin Schmidt, Prague, circa 1580.

Oval gilt brass full-plate verge movement with turned column pillars, chain fusée, five-wheel iron train, two-arm iron balance, small brass S-shaped cock secured by a screw, pierced and curved foot, iron striking train with brass fixed barrel engraved with alternating horizontal lines, iron count wheel on the back plate, gilt hammer-striking on round shallow bell mounted inside back cover; stamped on the back plate 'MS' with inverted goblet symbol between the letters

Silver dial with Roman hour numerals with half-hour markers and Zs for 2s, inner 24-hour Arabic hour numerals from 13 to 24, a narrow quarter-hour ring between the Roman and Arabic chapters, the centre engraved with a flower vase with a bird on top, pin-hole for adjusting striking at 9 o'clock, blued steel single hand

Three-part case with hinged gilt metal covers, both pierced and engraved with a Gothic rosette, the front to allow for reading of the dial, the back with a bell for sound, the silver band engraved with floral decoration, swivel pendant with loose ring, small gilt finial at the bottom

71 x 50 mm.

Provenance: The collection of The Lord Sandberg CBE

Published in: The Sandberg Watch Collection, Terence Camerer Cuss, 1998, pages 30-31.

C. Jeanenne Bell G.G. Collectors Encyclopedia of Pendant and Pocket Watches (page 10)

This watch is of the type once known as a 'Nürnberg egg'. The name was coined in the 18th century, when it was assumed that the earliest German watches were always of that shape. The assumption probably stemmed from a 1590 German translation of Rabelais' Gargantua-Pantagruel, where the word 'Ueurlein' (little clock) appeared as 'Eyrlein' (little egg) and from then on early oval watches were named 'Nürnberg eggs'. See: Watches, G.H. Baillie, London, 1929, p.61.

The present watch uses the more efficient fusée and chain system to even out the power of the mainspring, rather than the stackfreed device more commonly found in German watches of the late 16th century. The fusée went on to become the standard mainspring equalizer in European timepieces, the less satisfactory stackfreed was used exclusively in some German timepieces but disappeared completely after about 1630.

Inv. 1334

The Fingask Castle Watch
French

Small octagonal faceted rock crystal and gilded brass single-hand pendant watch with watch key cast with a crown and sceptre and initials 'M.R' signed D. du Chemin à Rouen

Watch unsigned, probably Northern France, circa 1630 and later.

Later 18th-century full plate gilt brass verge movement with chain fusée

Gilded chapter ring with Roman numerals, applied on a gilt brass dial plate, blued-steel single hand.

Octagonal case with gilt band and bezel, the back carved from a single piece of rock crystal, hinged front cover set with a similar panel of rock crystal

31.8 mm. length.

This diminutive rock crystal watch is among the surviving relics that have long been traditionally associated with Mary, Queen of Scots (1542-1587). Once part of the collection of Stuart relics at Fingask Castle in Scotland, this watch descended through the Threipland family with the story that it had belonged to the ill-fated Queen of Scots, being at some time given to the family by Lord Seton. Naturally, with historical artifacts dating back over four hundred years, the line between fact and fiction tends to blur. Remarkable for its tiny size, the style of construction indicates a date of manufacture in the first half of the 17th century, probably in Northern France between 1620 and 1640, therefore it could not have existed within Mary's lifetime. The accompanying watch key signed 'D. du Chemin à Rouen' is decorated with a crown and sceptre and the initials 'M.R' supposedly for 'Maria Regina', but appears to be of later date. In the late 19th century, while investigating the provenance of the famous 'Mary, Queen of Scots' skull watch, (collection of the Worshipful Company of Clockmakers), reputedly given by Mary to her lady-in-waiting, Mary Seton, the Reverend Henry Leonard Nelthropp believed that "ownership of the jewels, dresses and furniture belonging to Queen Mary has proved beyond doubt that watches were not among her valuables". However, some credence can be given to the Seton family connection because the Setons were in the immediate circle of courtiers attending the Queen of Scots. As with Mary herself, the watch is of French origin (its original movement may well have been signed by its maker). All taken into consideration, it is therefore easy to see how the family tradition surrounding the watch had come about. It is possible that the "Lord Seton" who by repute gave the watch to the Threipland family, was either the 2nd or 3rd Earl of Winton who were adult at around the time the watch was made. Robert Seton, 2nd Earl of Winton (1585-1634), a devoted Catholic and supporter of the Stuarts all his life, or his younger brother, George Seton, 3rd Earl of Winton (1584-1650), a staunch Royalist and Cavalier. Their father, Robert Seton, 1st Earl of Winton (1553-1603) was one of the Scottish peers who had supported Mary, Queen of Scots.

Of course, the watch could have entered the Threipland collection in the 18th century, sold to them as a relic with the story already attached. However, regardless of the accuracy of its reputed history, this watch is a fascinating historic object, long revered in the possession of one family and believed for centuries to be a direct link with Mary, Queen of Scots.

Actual Size

Provenance: Mr and Mrs Mark Murray Threipland, Fingask Castle; sold on the premises, Christie's, 26-28 April 1993, lot 1276.

Literature: Relics of the House of Stuart, John Skelton & St. John Hope, London, 1890, Plate XVIII.

Exhibited: The Royal House of Stuart, London 1889, No. 328.

Fingask Castle, Rait, By Perth, was purchased by Sir Stewart Threipland in 1783 and was to house many portraits and relics displaying Threipland loyalty to the Jacobite cause. Some of these were lent by William Murray Threipland to the 1889 'Exhibition of the Royal House of Stuart', held at the New Gallery, London.

14th Earl of Kintore

Simon Gribelin

Early engraved silver and gilt-brass pre-balance spring single-hand pendant watch with incomplete integral sundial and compass

Signed S. Gribelin, Bloys (Blois) with a flower, circa 1620

Keywound oval gilt verge movement with four vase-shaped pillars, fusée (lacking gut line), steel balance with pierced and engraved pinned balance cock and set up cover (ratchet and set up wheel lacking)

Engraved gilt dial applied with an engraved Roman chapter ring, with central scene of the Flood, with 'Jehovah' inscribed in Hebrew above, flanked by figures emblematic of Life and Death and with memento mori symbols below, single blued steel hand

Oval case with engraved silver band with vignettes depicting the Evangelists, cast foliate stem with suspension loop, the silver front cover engraved to its outside with central scene of Adam and Eve with the serpent and with four further scenes from Genesis, and to the inside with a foliate band, the silver rear cover engraved to its outside with central scene of the Resurrection and with four further scenes from the New Testament, and to the inside engraved for a compass and sundial

6.5 cm. long; 3.8 cm. wide

Provenance: Formerly the property of the 14th Earl of Kintore.

Simon Gribelin is recorded in Blois from 1588, as married in 1593 and dying after 1633.

Literature: E. von Bassermann-Jordan & H. von Bertele, Uhren, Braunschweig, 1969, p.122

Von Bassermann-Jordan illustrates an oval pocket watch by Robert Grinkin of London with similar sprig engraving to the inside cover.

An octagonal watch, also by Grinkin, and engraved with a scene depicting the baptism of Christ was sold anonymously, Sotheby's Geneva, 13 November 2007, lot 70.

An oval engraved silver and gilt watch by Salomon Chesnon of Blois, its inner case also with compass and sundial, was sold anonymously, Sotheby's New York, 16 November 2008.

See also, an oval watch with sundial and compass, its exterior case simply patinated, by Etienne Papon of Gien (a town further along the Loire from Blois), sold anonymously, Christie's London, 5 July 2002, lot 17.

Inv. 1212

François Masseron

Early gilt-brass and rock crystal pre-balance spring single-hand pendant watch

Signed F. Masseron, Paris, circa 1640

Keywound hinged gilt full plate verge movement with round baluster pillars, chain fusée, short wheel train, two-arm balance without spring, irregular pierced and engraved cock secured by a screw, ratchet-wheel mainspring set-up with click decorated en-suite to the cock

Silver dial with Roman numerals and half-hour markers, centre engraved with a village in a mountainous landscape, single tulip hand

Lobed circular two-piece case, the bezels chased with a simple foliate pattern, the back carved from a piece of rock crystal with twelve segments, the rock crystal front cover carved to match, tulip pendant and loose ring pendant, small baluster finial

47 mm. overall length.

Provenance: Fine Watches from the Atwood Collection, Sotheby's New York, December 11th, 1986, lot 21.

Literature: J. F. Hayward, English Watches, pl. II.

Once part of the legendary collection of Seth Atwood, owner of the Time Museum of Rockford, Illinois, U.S.A. This watch is an exceptional example of a mid-17th century rock crystal cased pendant watch dating from before the advent of the balance spring.

When it was made, this watch would have been regarded as a great curiosity and a rare and expensive treasure. On 5th January 1650, Constantijn Huygens wrote of his excitement at buying such a watch in Geneva. In a letter to his brother Christiaan Huygens, he informs him that he had just bought a watch "à la mode with a case of rock crystal that permitted a view of the movement such as one would see if the case were made of ice".

A watch with an almost identical rock crystal case by Benjamin Hill dating from the mid-17th century is in the collection of the Victoria and Albert Museum, London (Inv. 209-1908).

Another almost identical watch by Jean Rousseau dating from circa 1650 is in the Metropolitan Museum of Art, New York, the gift of J. Pierpont Morgan (accession no. 17.190.1014).

François Masseron is recorded as working in Paris in 1652.

Inv. 1855

Sebald Schwarz

Silver cruciform pre-balance spring single-hand watch

Signed Seb. Schwarz, Nurnberg, circa 1620

Keywound verge movement of riveted and pinned construction, cruciform plates, gut fusée, short train, early pierced and engraved single-footed balance cock, balance without spring, worm and wheel set up

Silver dial with brass chapter ring with Roman numerals and half-hour markers,the dial plate engraved with Adam and Eve and Cain and Abel, single iron hand

Cruciform pierced and engraved silver case decorated with the crucifixion of Christ amid scrolling foliage and a memento mori below, the back with soldiers turning away from Christ, the sides with two apostles, loose ring pendant

50mm. wide., 65 mm. length.

Sebald Schwarz is recorded in Jürgen Abeler's book Meister der Uhrmacherkunstas working at the end of the 16th and beginning of the 17th centuries. A silver encased wooden clock by Sebald Schwarz was in the collection of the Mathematisch-Physikalischen Salon, Dresden, before World War II.

27

Inv. 1626

Louis Prévost.

Early gilt metal pair case astronomical single-hand watch with date and months calendar, age and phase of the moon and periods of the day and night, zodiac and seasons indications

Signed Louys Prevost, the case attributed to Jonas Arpin, circa 1685

Keywound gilt finished verge movement, chain fusée, pierced and engraved scroll and foliage decorated balance cock and foot, large three arm balance, vase-shaped pillars

Chased gilt dial, three subsidiary dials with engraved silver rings, blued steel index pointers and centred by rosettes, indicating lunar age with inner revolving engraved star and moon phase disc, date and time, three apertures for the signs of the zodiac, times of the day, days of the month and corresponding season

Plain circular inner case, finely engraved scroll and foliage decorated outer case

57 mm. diam.

Louys or Louis Prévost was active in Saumur, France, becoming a watchmaker in 1660. He subsequently emigrated to Geneva, presumably to escape persecution after the revocation of the Edict of Nantes.

A very similar watch with outer case signed 'L.ARPIN.FECIT' was in the Sandberg Collection and is published in the book of the Sandberg Collection, pp. 126-127.

Jonas Arpin is recorded working as a chaser in the second half of the 17th century.

The present watch is a fine example of a so-called 'montre à mouvement de lune' or "watch with moon movement" as they were called in the 17th century.

These watches were the successors of the astronomical clocks and spheres made in 16th century Germany and France. Spheres were astronomical clocks on which, thanks to an ingenious device, one could follow the cycles of the stars and their passing through the different signs of the zodiac. The first sphere was made in 1504 by Julien Coudray of Blois, watchmaker of Louis XII and François I. Table clocks with astronomical indications manufactured thereafter were common devices in the 16th century.

The first astronomical pocket watch appeared in the early 17th century and is attributed to Anthoine Arlaud, made bourgeois of Geneva in 1617 and who trained in 1626, the French watchmaker Anthoine Dagoneau in the manufacture of "watches with alarm clocks and celestial movements".

Examples of these extraordinary timepieces can be found in the world's most important museums and collections, notably the Louvre in Paris, the Patek Philippe Museum in Geneva and London's Victoria & Albert Museum and the British Museum.

Inv. 1076

Jacob Bauman

Silver and varicoloured gold repoussé four-train quarter repeating and striking coach watch with date and alarm

Signed Jacob Bauman, Augspurg, No. 3, circa 1730

Keywound four-train verge movement, chain fusée, finely chased, engraved and pierced scroll decorated balance cock, repeating, striking and alarm on four hammers onto a bell, Striking/Not lever in the band

White enamel dial with Roman numerals, outer Arabic five-minute numerals and date indication with central hand, central alarm disc with single hand

Circular large pierced, chased and engraved scroll and applied varicoloured gold floral decorated case, the reverse centred by a chased, embossed biblical scene in high relief, repeating activated by depressing a button in the band, gimballed pendant

115 mm. diam.

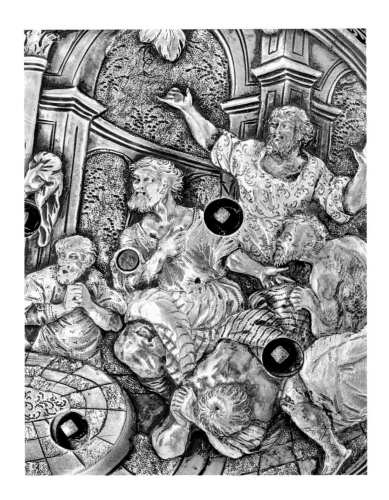

Actual Size

It is exceptional to find a coach watch with varicolored gold decoration. This watch, an extremely fine example of its type with beautifully made repoussé case, shows many of the characteristics of those watches made in Friedberg for makers across Europe.

Friedberg watchmakers specialized in the production of repeating and striking watches. From the beginning of the 18th century, they were making watches and coach watches with quarter, half quarter and even minute repeating mechanisms and selling them all over Europe. The cases, often of very high quality, were produced in Augsburg and the movements were made in the style of the country for which they were destined. Some of them were signed by their makers, some bear signatures of eminent French and English makers (perhaps at their request, when they were retailing them), still others bear the signature of their makers, written backwards, together with the names of cities in which they were intended to be sold. Until the discovery of a large quantity of ebauches, blancs and completed movements which had never been cased, and their study by Sebastian Whitestone, these watches were wrongly attributed to unrecorded makers from different European countries.

See: German watches, Christian Pfeiffer Belli, Antiquorum Vox Magazine, Spring 2006, p. 14.

Pierre Belon

Small gold and turquoise enamel pre-balance spring single-hand pendant watch

Signed P. Belon à Paris, circa 1650

Keywound gilded full plate verge movement, decoratively pierced balance cock and long foot engraved with flowers and foliage, flat steel balance, fusée now with woven wire line, urn shaped pillars

Enamel on gold dial with white chapter ring with black and gilded Roman numerals with half hour divisions between, turquoise centre, gold tulip hand

Circular case entirely overlaid with turquoise enamel, raised semi-roundels of white enamel with black highlights interspersed with shaded orange roundels, the back centred with a flower in matching enamel tones, the round pendant similarly decorated, centre of the inside back with stylised black enamel flower, bezel with gold tags for crystal retention

34mm. diam.

This extremely beautiful and rare small pendant watch is one of a rarified group of mid-17th century turquoise enamelled watches made for the French royal court. The few surviving examples of this type, of which the present watch is one of the smallest and most exquisite, are associated closely with Louis XIV and his family. Indeed, only the royal family and the grandest of aristocrats would have been able to possess such a valuable object. Furthermore, the watchmaker Pierre Belon had privileged access to the King and Queen in his capacity as the official royal watchmaker.

The distinctive turquoise enamel used as the dominant colour has its origins in the French city of Blois in the first half of the 17th century. However, the design and techniques employed in the making of this watch would indicate that it is probably the work of the Geneva enamellist Pierre Huaud I (1612 -1680), son of a French goldsmith who emigrated to Geneva in 1630 and who had in fact been apprenticed in Blois.

Pierre Huaud I's work often includes small flowers as minor or major decoration, always with orange examples, which were apparently never used by his sons. Frequent use of this vivid orange pigment combined with use of turquoise enamel as a ground colour is closely associated with Huaud's technique.

Actual Size

Inv. 1656

Thomas Swetman

Gilt-metal verge clockwatch with jade bell made for the Japanese market

Signed Tho. Swetman, London, no. 4540, circa 1750

Keywound gilt-finished verge movement, pierced and engraved balance cock, elaborately pierced and engraved pillars, small spring barrel for the strike via a single steel hammer on the jade bell

Gilt circular dial with movable steel Japanese chapters revolving in a clockwise fashion, pierced blued steel hand

Circular drum-form elaborate foliate pierced and engraved case

55mm. diam.

This watch was made in London specifically for the Japanese market and as such it is both exceptionally rare and significant in the history of watchmaking. Only a handful of English watches for export to Japan are known from the 18th century, it is quite likely they were made as diplomatic gifts. The present watch is a most ambitious and superbly crafted example with the exceptional feature of a jade bell. It was perhaps intended as a gift for the Emperor himself.

The history of the relationship between Japan and England began in 1600 with the arrival of William Adams. However, in 1673, the shogunate found it unacceptable that King Charles II had married Catherine of Braganza, who was from Portugal, and favoured the Roman Catholic Church. Trade then ceased generally until the 19th century. During the Sakoku period (1641–1853), there were no formal relations between England and Japan, with the Dutch serving as intermediaries.

Provenance:

The Albert Odmark Collection of Important Clocks and Watches.

G.H. Baillie records a Thomas Swetman working in London circa 1750.

Inv. 1657

Jean Rousseau

Gold and painted on enamel pre-balance spring single-hand watch

Signed Rousseau, circa 1660

Keywound verge movement, engraved and pierced foliate decorated balance cock, steel two arm balance, ratchet and wheel regulation

Silver dial with Roman numerals, later inner gilt ring with engraved foliage, single blued steel hand

Circular case with polychrome painted on enamel pastoral vignettes to the band, the back with a scene depicting the Holy Family and St John the Baptist as a child, the interior with a painted pastoral scene, the front cover with a scene depicting St John, the Virgin Mary and child, and a further pastoral scene to the inside, ring pendant and seven piece hinge

36mm. diam.

Provenance:

By repute, this watch had remained in the previous owner's family for many generations, possibly as far back as the 1790s.

The exhibition displayed horological masterpieces from the 17th century as a tribute to the Rousseau watchmaking dynasty. Thirty rare timepieces from the collections of the Patek Philippe Museum, prominent museums and private collections, they celebrated the extraordinary manufacturing expertise of the Geneva workshops that "from the 17th century onwards made the City of Calvin the cradle of fine watchmaking".

Jean Rousseau

Jean Rousseau the younger (1606-1684) was an eminent watchmaker and Master of the Clockmakers' Company of Geneva. He was the great-grandfather of the philosopher Jean-Jacques Rousseau. He was known for making form watches and complicated pieces such as clockwatches, alarm watches and astronomical watches. Among his apprentices were some of Geneva's best watchmakers including Isaac Bordier and Amédée Marchand.

Exhibited:

Patek Philippe Museum, Geneva 'Timepieces Signed Rousseau', 11th May to 13th October 2012.

Baltazar Martinot

Early gilt-metal and painted on enamel single-hand oignon watch

Signed Baltazar Martinot à Paris, the enamel by Andre Mussard, circa 1710

Keywound gilt-finished full plate verge movement, Egyptian pillars, chain fusée, Louis XIV cock pierced and engraved, mock pendulum aperture

Engraved gilt brass dial, white enamel cartouches, Roman numerals, single hand

Circular hinged enamel case, the reverse with finely polychrome enamel scene of the Madonna and child with St. Anne, the band with engraved geometric pattern with polychrome enamel landscape, signed Mussard Pinxit

56mm diam.

Andre Mussard was born in Geneva, probably a brother of the famous Jean V. Mussard (1681-1754), one of the most celebrated enamel painters of the period. In 1740 André was working in La Haye (The Hague) where he stayed until 1758. Much influenced by the style of the Frères Huaud, his best-known subjects are amongst others the Roman Charity and religious scenes. Works by the Mussards can be found in the world's most celebrated museums and collections. The Bath Museum in England has a portrait by André signed Andreas Mussard anno 1751.

Baltazar Martinot was clockmaker to Anne of Austria and then King Louis XIV. Born in Rouen in 1636 and died in 1716. He settled in Paris around 1680.

The Martinot family was a very famous French watchmaking dynasty of the 17th and 18th centuries. The son of Balthazar the elder, Balthazar l'aine was also a watchmaker,; his brothers, all watchmakers, were Claude, Etienne, and Gilles.

Martinot

Gilt brass and painted on enamel single-hand large oignon watch

Signed Martinot à Paris, the enamel painting in the manner of Les frères Huaut, circa 1700

Keywound fire-gilt verge movement, divided Egyptian pillars, three-arm brass balance, blued steel balance spring, chain fusée, balance cock mounted with a finely painted polychrome enamel portrait of a lady, rack and pinion regulator

Gilded brass cartouche dial with blue Roman numerals on white enamel reserves, inner annular white enamel half-hour and quarter-hour chapter ring, single blued steel hand

Circular case, hinged bezel decorated with a finely painted on enamel continuous countryside landscape scene with figures walking, the reverse with a painted polychrome enamel portrait of a young lady playing the lute, border decorated to match the bezel, loose ring pendant

59 mm. diam.

Baltazar Martinot was clockmaker to Anne of Austria and then King Louis XIV. Born in Rouen in 1636 and died in 1716. He settled in Paris around 1680.

The Martinot family was a very famous French watchmaking dynasty of the 17th and 18th centuries. The son of Balthazar the elder, Balthazar l'aine was also a watchmaker; his brothers, all watchmakers, were Claude, Etienne, and Gilles.

The Earliest Known Surviving Minute Repeating Watch

Inv. 1324

Benedikt Fürstenfelder

Gold and carnelian-set pair case minute repeating watch

Signed B. Fürstenfeldr Fecit, early 18th century

Keywound verge movement with chain fusée, pierced and engraved balance cock decorated with foliate scrolls and strapwork, incomplete minute repeating mechanism formerly activated by depressing the pendant, blued regulation dial

Unique gold champlevé dial with Roman numerals, outer Arabic five-minute numerals and additional narrow minute chapter numbered 1-14 in each quarter-hour sector

Circular cases, the outer case with symmetrical pierced foliate scroll strapwork panels between four polished and shaped carnelian panels each mounted with a central gold head, perhaps representing the four continents, larger central panel mounted with a cast figure perhaps representing Africa, pierced inner case

47 mm. diam.

The discovery of this highly significant watch in 2009 provided incontrovertible evidence that minute repeating mechanisms had existed in watches at a far earlier date than was previously thought.

The eminent horologist Sebastian Whitestone has conducted extensive research on the subject of the first known use of the minute repeater in watches and had suggested in 1993 that the earliest use of the mechanism may not have been by the London maker Thomas Mudge in the mid-18th century, but a maker or makers in Friedberg in Upper Bavaria nearly half a century before. In light of the emergence of the present previously unknown watch, he finally had proof that his theory had been correct. However, the tantalizing question remained as to whether the Friedberg makers, in particular Benedikt Fürstenfelder, were the inventors of minute repeating or did it already exist?. Had they used as their inspiration an even earlier minute repeating watch by one of the great English makers such as Thomas Tompion or Daniel Quare, of which no surviving examples are known. Whatever the answer to this question, the present watch is, to date, the earliest known minute repeating watch in the world.

In an article in the December 2010 edition of Antiquarian Horology entitled 'Minute Repeating in Tompion's Lifetime' he set out his findings.

Minute Repeating in Tompion's Lifetime
By Sebastian Whitestone
First published in Antiquarian Horology, December 2010

An article in the Winter 1993 edition of this journal re-dated the known introduction of the minute repeating watch to around the first decade of the 18th century in Bavaria. That article attributed the earliest surviving example to Benedikt Furstenfelder of Friedberg and predicted that closer examination of German repeaters would reveal further examples attesting to a forgotten monopoly centred on that town. A watch has now emerged confirming the attribution and fulfilling the prediction. In so doing it pushes back the date of invention to within the lifetime of the most celebrated baroque watchmaker, Thomas Tompion, against whose known production this innovation is here measured.

A watch has now emerged confirming the attribution and fulfilling the prediction. In so doing it pushes back the date of invention to within the lifetime of the most celebrated baroque watchmaker, Thomas Tompion, against whose known production this innovation is here measured.

Late, somewhat the worse for wear and consequently misunderstood, a nevertheless unimpeachable witness confirms an extraordinary premise. The witness is an incomplete German watch (the present watch). The premise is that for half a century, the ultimate specification of baroque watchmaking was the monopoly of an unheard-of community a thousand miles away from the centre of excellence and invention. The watch was unknown seventeen years ago when an article in this journal re-dated the introduction of minute repeating from the middle of the 18th century in London to around the first decade of that century in Upper Bavaria (note 1). Transferring the laurels of priority from the great London watchmakers Thomas Mudge and John Ellicott to an earlier and much less distinguished generation in Friedberg was controversial.

Curators of horology in England and America had dismissed the proposition prior to its publication. Their view was echoed by a review of the article in Germany suggesting that the cited minute repeating mechanisms could be later modifications (note 2). After a long wait for further evidence, a pocket watch has now emerged that disproves that criticism. Before considering this watch, it should be remembered that a peculiar feature of early 18th-century German pocket watches, especially those from Friedberg, is that they were often engraved or re-engraved with false London signatures and also signed with the names of other European metropolitan makers.

The earliest minute repeating watch described in the above-mentioned article was an early 18th-century silver pair cased watch inscribed 'Marquch, London'. This watch was attributed in that article to Benedikt Fürstenfelder, noting that the signature 'Matqiich' situated alongside a removed maker's name, appeared to derive from a partial re-engraving of the place name Aichach. Fürstenfelder was one of the very few watchmakers who worked around that time in Aichach, which lies ten miles from Friedberg across the river Lech from Augsburg. He had left Aichach permanently by 1710 (note 3), which, if the signature attribution is correct and the repeating mechanism original, establishes minute repeating in Tompion's lifetime and raises the possibility that this triumph of baroque watchmaking was known to its greatest exponent.

Incontrovertible Evidence In mid-2009 a watch (the present watch), signed 'B Füfstenfeldr fecit', appeared on the open market (note 4), described as a quarter repeater. The watch has a gold outer case set with cornelian panels between pierced interlaced scrolls. The verge movement is typical of continental watches made in the first half of the 18th century. The absence of C-scroll borders on the case decoration, the piercing of the balance cock foot and the angular rigidity of the interlaced strap-work are all early features that suggest the watch was made in the first quarter of the 18th century. In fact, there is no decorative or mechanical element which precludes a date of manufacture at the beginning of that century or the end of the preceding one. With much of its repeating work missing, the watch would appear to be an unlikely candidate for pre-eminence in the history of that mechanism. However, it has a unique gold champlevé dial where each minute is numbered 1-14 four times in a narrow chapter between the conventional outer minute circle and the inner hour circle. The 15* minute is marked with a star at the hour and 1-3 at the relevant quarter. This calibration has only one explanation: it shows the actual hammer blows of minute repeating. Since gold champlevé dials of this sort are impossible to fake convincingly and were soon out of fashion, there can be no doubt that this watch was originally designed and made as a minute repeater during, or just before, the first quarter of the 18th century. Fortunately, traces of the minute repeating remain. The idea that these traces could be later additions is dismissed by its unique dial. Bearing the signature of Benedikt Fürstenfelder and containing traces of the otherwise unique repeating system found in the 'Marquch', the watch corroborates the attribution of the 'Marquch' watch and, with its four relatives (note 5), validates the proposition that, throughout the first half of the eighteenth century, minute repeating watches were the monopoly of Friedberg.

The Repeating Mechanism

In spite of the lack of much of the Fürstenfelder repeating mechanism, enough of it is left to be certain that it repeated the minutes. It may be seen that it originally contained the unusual feature of a single cam minute snail revolving every fifteen minutes (geared 4:1 with the hour wheel), just as the 'Marquch' watch has, the only other known example. Comparison with the repeating work of the 'Marquch' shows clearly how the Fürstenfelder repeating was set out and what is missing. The 'Marquch' operates as follows: The pendant pushes on the repeating rack which has a chain attached to the end. The other end of the chain is wound around a pulley on the arbour of the repeating spring situated under the hour rack wheel between the plates, and in now unwinding, winds the repeating spring. The rack moves until the pin meets the hour snail and the hour rack-wheel turns, moving the correct number of its teeth past a loose pallet on the hammer arbour. The quarter rack is situated above the hour rack-wheel (which is between the plates) and is pivoted under tension from a spring. As the hour rack rotates, a cam on its arbour is turned away from a pin on the quarter rack, to fall until the tongue hits the quarter snail. The minute rack is, like the quarter rack, 'broken' i.e. it is in two parts pivoted. Because it is also jointed just above that point, it jackknifes when the tail is no longer locking the cam. This happens when the cam is turned anticlockwise with the hour rack-wheel as the repeating spring is wound. The tongue falls on to one of the fourteen steps of the minute snail. The repeating spring is now fully wound and the watch ready to repeat. The teeth on the hour rack-wheel now return (clockwise), each one moving the hammer arbour via its one-way pallet. After the hours come the quarters, with double strokes made by the tail of the quarter rack on the same hammer arbour and pallet. Lastly, the minutes are struck by the minute rack-wheel set above the hour rack-wheel and under the minute cam. The number of minutes is governed by the level at which the minute rack tail engages the returning minute cam. Whichever step of the 14 on the cam meets the rack tail, it will straighten the rack, lifting the tongue off the minute snail and bringing the rack back against the pin. At this point the rack is rigid again, the tail still locked in the cam which now cannot revolve anymore. Thus, the whole train is stopped. There is no 'all or nothing' piece.

The mechanism of the Fürstenfelder had a very similar layout and operated in the same manner. The one difference is that it has an 'all or nothing' piece above the hour snail and star wheel. The repeating rack is pushed till the pin meets the hour snail. Although the hour wheel, quarter rack, minute snail and minute rack are missing, the minute snail pivot hole may still be seen. The original steel minute rack-wheel survives with 14 teeth in the 'Marquch' diagram this wheel is unmarked but just visible above the plate). The one-way hammer pallet may be seen. The steel hour rack-wheel survives and is hidden between the plates. The quarter snail can also be seen.

The Maker

Benedikt Fürstenfelder was born in Aichach on 2 January 1680. On 8 August 1707, he married Magdalena Gastl von Laimering and had two children before moving to Friedberg. He appears in the Friedberg parish registers from 1710, having a further thirteen children in the following fifteen years with a second wife, Helene. He died in Friedberg in 1754 as senator of their Higher Council. Two of his sons, Johannes and Matthias Benedikt, became watchmakers. Apart from the Marqiich watch there is a large silver coach watch bearing Furstenfelder's Aichach signature, which is illustrated in the first article (note 1). There is a table clock and a pocket watch in the Victorian & Albert Museum, London and a hexagonal table clock in the Poldi Pezzoli, Milan. A palatial Chinese lacquer clock with matching table containing a movement by him was made for the Residenz in Munich and is now in the Bayerisches Nationalmuseum. A small hexagonal table clock with minute repeating is illustrated in Alan Lloyd who gave it an erroneous date and place of manufacture, confusing Friedberg with Freiberg in Saxony (note 6). This mechanism was mentioned in Wadsworth's comprehensive review of repeating watches but he doubted it could have worked in a watch (note 7). In this clock Fürstenfelder uses the conventional four cam minute snail. From surviving material, it would seem most likely that Fürstenfelder's main speciality, like that of his fellow watchmakers in Friedberg, was coach watches in fine silver or silver gilt repousse cases. A number of these watches struck the quarter hour as well as having repeating and alarm. These coach watches were retailed by other makers all over Europe and especially in Paris, Dresden, Vienna and Prague. Unlike many of his confrères, it would seem from his surviving work that Fürstenfelder was above the practice of disguising his name or engraving it next to a false place of manufacture. In the case of the 'Marqiich' watch the original signature was later altered. However, Joseph Spiegel signed himself both 'Legeips, London' and 'Miroir, Paris'. Other likely aliases were: 'Strigner, London' for Jakob Strixner, 'Ysorb' for Johann Paul Brosy and 'Renpaurg, London' for Paul Gottfried Graupner. These signatures are not re-engravings and were no doubt done at the behest of travelling watch sellers of the type mentioned by Leutmann who warns us that such people carry 'London' watches that 'have never seen London' (note 8).

The need for minute repeating

The main reason why Friedberg developed a particular expertise in watch repeating mechanisms may have been its speciality of coach watch manufacture. These 'Kutschenuhren' were placed in a special receptacle in coaches and were normally fitted with quarter repeating. One can imagine the difficulty of reading a watch dial in a dimly lit, shaking coach where bored minds frequently turned to the journey time. However, watch repeating wasn't invented in Germany but in England and France. It seems likely that it was independently invented by Quare and Barlow in London and also by Gloria in Rouen, around 1686 (note 9). These watches were clearly derived from the clocks that were carried to the bedside at night and whose cords, when pulled, gave the time to the nearest quarter without the need to light a candle. Presumably the repeating watch fulfilled the same function at night as the bedside clock. One can only speculate as to whether, during the day, repeating was used more for display than for necessity. But even the latter use can scarcely have required further refinement to indicate minutes, unless it included the timing of short periods in which some special action had to be contained. Normal activity, however, was synchronised to medium-sized divisions of the solar day and not fine divisions of a mean hour. The need, if there was one, for minute repeating is very

likely to have come that it presented to challenge may have well as technical. In elsewhere, labour was religious devotion and or those that exceeded were twice blessed.

from the challenge watchmakers. This been religious as Catholic Friedberg as considered a form of supererogatory works, r e q u i r e m e n t s , But whatever the

challenge, once it had been met and the first minute repeater performed to an audience, then no doubt it resonated in an acquisitive and competitive market that loved novelty and theatrics. And what a sensation it must have caused with its maximum (assuming a single blow at the quarter) of twenty-nine strikes of the bell instead of just fifteen for a normal quarter repeater.

History repeats itself

This is the second time that Antiquarian Horology has pushed back the introduction of minute repearing by nearly half a century, on each occasion rescuing existing examples from obloquy. Illustrated on the front cover of the journal for December 1961 was a photograph of a large minute repeating clock-watch by Thomas Mudge, No. 407, then belonging to the dealer Malcolm Gardiner. Unaware of other Mudge minute repeaters, leading horologists of that time condemned the minute repeating work as a later addition. This extraordinary view prevailed for nine years. Then, on a hot summer's day in 1970, the collector Cecil (Sam) Clutton, possibly aided by a thinning of watch oil in the warm tempetatures, finally persuaded the Duke of Wellington's Mudge, No. 318 to repeat, which in living memory it had refused to do. To his and the duke's surprise it repeated the minutes; a fact duly reported in this journal when Mudge 407 was finally exonerated and Mudge 318 accorded the distinction of being the earliest known minute repeater (note 10). Most readers nowadays, even without the benefit of hindsight, may well consider it inconceivable that any watch could be later modified or upgraded to minute repeating.

There would be insufficient room and, even were it to be possible, insufficient reward for the considerable work involved. However, it is not only the mechanism itself but also the historical references to it that have received implausible interpretation. Minute repeating was mentioned by Derham" in 1696 (note 11) and by Thiout (note 12) in 1741. Both texts were taken to refer to hypothetical and not actual mechanisms. In the case of the Thiout reference, this interpretation was derived from a mistranslation of the original French (note 13). However, from then on it was sustained by a singular implausibility, i.e. that Thiout would attempt to describe and illustrate in detail a mechanical refinement that never existed (note 14).

Minute repeating in England The mention of Minute repeating in Derham was only of a subclassification of repeating in general. This subclassification presumably included half quarter repeating and tenminute repeating, although surviving 17th-century examples of both these systems are extremely rare. This scarce legacy may not reflect their true number three hundred years ago. Perhaps Derham was alluding only to ten-minute repeating.

However, it must surely be right to keep an open mind as to whether minute repeating already existed in 1696. The receding date put on its introduction well illustrates the perils in mechanical history of deriving too rigid a notion of what might have existed from what remains. Nothing is more expendable than that which ceases to function nor more vulnerable than a mechanism deprived of the protection of its precious metal case. In that double jeopardy for the pocket watch, the minute repeater is additionally at risk if we assume that, the more complicated the design, the more likely it is to fail. Tompion becomes relevant here because we know more about his manufacture than that of any other watchmaker of the time. His posthumous celebrity ensured that his watches had a relatively high survival rate but even so that is probably less than 10 per cent on an estimated production of over six thousand (note 15). How certain can we be that among more than five thousand missing Tompion watches there is not a minute repeater? The survival rate of other makers such as Quare may be as little 2 per cent which is hardly sufficient evidence upon which to exclude the possibility of his making minute repeating. When considering minute repeating as a possibly English innovation one has to take into account not only that it was first mentioned in England but also that, unlike London makers at the end of the 17th century, Friedberg's craftsmen seemed to be imitating rather than inventing. Five known German examples compared to none anywhere else before the middle of the century would seem to suggest an extraordinarily long lasting monopoly. This is all the more remarkable given Friedberg's provincial setting and the baroque appetite for virtuosity and sensation. But was Friedberg's original inspiration a Tompion, Quare or Barlow, or was it, as his distinctive dial and mechanism suggest, a young maker from up the road who dared to outdo them?

1. Sebastian Whitestone, 'A Minute Repeating Watch Circa 1715 Friedberg's Ingenuity in a Biased Market', 21/ 2 (Winter 1993), 145-157.

2. Norbert Enders, 'Anmerkungen des Ubersetzers', Uhren MIA (1994), 23-24. Enders points out that C.F. Vogel's Practischer Unterricht von Taschenuhren (Leipzig, 1774) thoroughly covers watch repeating, including quarter and halfquarter repeating, with no mention of minute repeating. His other objections are rebutted by this author in Uhren 17/4, 24-25.

3. Adelheid Riolini-Unger, *Friedberger Uhren* (Friedberg 1993), p. 163. The parish records of Friedberg contain many references to Benedikt Furstenfelder from 1710 onward, leaving no doubt that he had permanently left Aichach by that time.

4. The watch was dated circa 1730 which, in this author's view, is at the very end of a stretched forty-year possibility.

5. Apart from the 'Marquch' watch, the other three Friedberg minute repeaters are:

(1) A small table clock also by Fürstenfelder (private collection, formerly in The Time Museum, Rockford, Illinois); the mechanism is the size of those found in large coach watches.

(2) A watch movement signed 'Lekceh, London' which is a known signature of Johann Heckel of Friedberg; (private collection, illustrated in A. Chapiro, 'Montres Primitives Avec Repetition à Minutes'. ANCAHA Bulletin 1988, 21).

(3) A silver striking coach watch signed Andreas Pfab, Dresden' (private collection, illustrated in Karl Langer, 'Die Erste Minutenrepetition', Uhren 1989, 26) which is very much in the Friedberg style and probably made there and retailed in Dresden. Pfab was not known as a watchmaker. Enders (see note 2) suggests the Pfab could be Swiss on account of the Swiss enamel dial but this ignores the fact that watches of all nationalities came with Swiss enamelling since the days of Huaud. Enamelling was an imported element at the time.

Heckel died in 1743, Fürstenfelder in 1754 and Pfab in 1755, around the beginning of Ellicott and Mudge minute repeating, and showing that we are dealing with a different generation. The above four examples are fully described in the author's previous article (note 1).

6. H. Alan Lloyd, *Some Outstanding Clocks over 700 Years* (London, 1958), p. 100.

7. Francis Wadsworth, 'A History of Repeating Watches', *Antiquarian Horology* 4/12 (September 1965) to 5/3 (June 1966).

8. J. Leutmann, *Vollstandiger Nachricht von den Uhren* (Magdeburg 1717 and 1772), p. 85.

9. A. Chapiro, 'Les Oignons Louis XIV", *Intercbron Journal* l (Paris 1980), 46-48.

10. Cecil Clutton, Letter, *Antiquarian Horology* 7/1 (December 1970), 72.

11. William Derham, *The Artificial Clockmaker* (London, 1696), p. 106: "Lhe clocks [ie timekeepers; clocks or watches] I shall now speake of are such as by pulling of a string etc do strike the hour, quarter or minute at any time of the day or night'.

12. Antoine Thiout, *Traite de L'Horlogerie, Mechanique et Practique* (Paris, 1741), p. 365: 'Although watches have been made on this principle [ie minute repeaters] and no doubt not dissimilar to this design '. The design to which Thiout refers is a detailed illustration possibly derived from a verbal description or rough sketch of a minute repeating mechanism with 'all or nothing' piece and four cam minute snail.

13. Wadsworth (see note 7) states that minute repeating watches 'were not made before about 1750', (page 365), misinterpreting Thiout, as argued earlier by the present author (see note 1).

14. Arm Simon, 'A Pre-1750 Minute Repeater', Antiquarian Horology 19/5 (Autumn 1991), 525. Simon describes a minute repeater by Ellicott which he dates to 1747. With regard to Thiout's reference he concludes that minute repeating watches 'obviously had not been made at that time...'.

15. Jeremy Evans, Thomas Tompion at the Dial and Three Crowns (Wadhurst 2006). Evans' checklist contains some six hundred Tompion watches and he has suggested that total production of watches was probably well over six thousand.

Acknowledgment

I wish to thank Simon Bull from whose peerless eye the Fürstenfelder finally failed to hide.

The author expresses his sincere gratitude to Sebastian Whitestone for his permission to reproduce his article here.

Inv. 1416

King George I Royal Presentation Watch

Johann Jakob Serner

Royal Presentation silver pair case wandering hour watch with painted on enamel portrait of King George I of England (1660-1727)

Signed Joh. Jac. Serner, Lübeck, 232, circa 1720

Keywound verge movement, chain fusée, finely pierced and engraved foliate decorated foot, balance cock set with polychrome painted on enamel portrait of a gentleman

Silver dial decorated with finely engraved foliage, aperture for the Roman wandering hours in the revolving ring, outer silver 60 minutes indication, applied gilt military trophies centred by the oval polychrome painted on enamel portrait of King George I, surmounted by the Royal Crown held by two eagles

Circular plain silver case

52 mm. diam.

This watch is a fine and early example of a Royal presentation watch, set with the portrait of King George I of England (1660-1727), made for his household and given as a gift to a dignitary or friend of his Majesty.

The rare wandering hour dial is a feature to be found only for a few years either side of 1700. Interestingly, George Daniels and Cecil Clutton noted that "a peculiarity of the wandering hour watches is that nearly, if not quite all, surviving English specimens have a royal attribution, such as a royal portrait." Although the present watch was made by a German watchmaker, this is quite likely due to the fact that although King George I had ascended the English throne on 1st August 1714, he did not arrive in England from Germany until 18th September that year. It is probable that Serner had already supplied watches to The Elector of Hanover in Germany and that when The Elector became King of England, he continued to patronise him.

Johann Jakob Serner is recorded working in Lübeck in the first quarter of the 18th century. Serner married twice, once in 1702 and for a second time in 1717. He died around 1728.

This watch was loaned and displayed as part of the Historic Royal Palaces exhibition 'Georgians' at Hampton Court Palace from April to November 2014.

Venus & Adonis

Henry Massy

Early large 20K gold and painted on enamel gem-set watch

Signed Henry Massy, London, no. 2595, the case attributed to Les Frères Huaud, circa 1700

Keywound gilt verge movement with divided Egyptian pillars, pierced and engraved winged balance cock, chain fusée

White enamel dial with Roman numerals and large Arabic five-minute numerals, steel hands

Circular case entirely painted on enamel, the band decorated with four vignettes depicting buildings in landscapes, set with jewels and a painted flower head between, the back decorated with a scene of Venus and Adonis with Cupid, the bezel with a continuous landscape, the interior of the back painted with a scene of a castle view with river, a traveller in the foreground

49 mm. diam.

The Geneva enamellers, particularly the Huaud family, were renowned for their distinctive and beautiful style of enamel paintings. Their outstanding work is characterised by their miniaturist style and use of rich and varied colours in contrast to the pastel shades of the French enamellers of Blois. The enamel cases decorated by the Huaud family are highly regarded works of art in their own right.

Pierre Huaud, son of the French goldsmith Jean Huaud and founder of the dynasty, was born in 1612. He moved to Geneva in 1630 and three of his eleven children became also renowned enamellers: Pierre II (1647-1698), Jean-Pierre (1655-1723) and Ami (1657-1724). It is likely that the three brothers trained in the workshop of their father until around 1680 when Pierre II set up his own business. The second son, Jean-Pierre entered into partnership with Ami in 1682. In 1686, with special permission from the council of Geneva, the three Huaud brothers were invited to Berlin where they were appointed enamel painters to the Elector of Brandenburg, a position they held until their return to Geneva in 1700.

Pierre Huaud II died in 1698, the two younger brothers continued working until the death of Jean-Pierre in 1723 and Ami a year later.

The watch cases of the Huauds are usually found with movements made by various English, French, German and Swiss makers to whom they supplied cases at the time.

Henry Massy is recorded working in Charles Street, London, he was free of the Clockmakers' Company from 1692 to 1745. Henry's father Nicolas Massy II, had his workshop in Cranbourn Street in London. He was born in Blois, France and had come to London as a Huguenot refugee. He was free of the Clockmakers' Company from 1682 and died in 1698. Father and son were descendants of the great French watchmaker Nicolas Massy I of Blois, who became master in 1623 and married in the same year. He became a juror in 1646 and died in 1658.

Inv. 1810

Jean-Baptiste Baillon

Gold and painted on enamel watch

Signed J. B. Baillon, Paris, circa 1750

Keywound gilt full plate verge movement with chain fusée, pierced and engraved balance bridge

White enamel dial with Roman numerals and Arabic five minute numerals

Circular case, the back decorated with a polychrome painted on enamel scene depicting a King from antiquity kneeling while swinging an incense burner and preparing to make an offering at a shrine, his sceptre and crown beside him while onlookers watch and female attendants prepare flower garlands, the engraved bezel decorated with enamel flowers

44 mm. diam.

Jean-Baptiste Baillon was, in the words of F. J. Britten, "the richest watchmaker in Europe". One of the most famous watchmakers in Paris in the 18th Century, Baillon became a master watchmaker in 1727, establishing his workshop first on the Place Dauphine and later in the Rue Dauphine. A further manufactory was situated in Saint-Germain-en-Laye, where other watchmakers worked for him, something highly unusual at that period. Baillon was appointed watchmaker to the Queen of France, Maria Leczinska in1738, 'Valet de Chambre de la Reine-Ordinaire Watchmaker' by 1748, 'Premier Valet de Chambre de la Reine', and from about 1770 watchmaker at the court of Queen Marie Antoinette. Baillon held the post of "Premier Valet de Chambre and Valet de Chambre, Watchmaker Ordinaire de la Dauphine" to Marie-Antoinette. He died in 1772.

Inv. 1830

Probably Southern Germany

Early carved ivory oval pre-balance spring single-hand watch with stackfreed

Unsigned, probably Southern Germany, circa 1650

Ivory oval verge movement, pierced and engraved balance cock, stackfreed

Ivory dial plate carved in relief with a scene of the Creation of Man, raised chapter ring with Roman numerals

Oval case carved in high relief, the back showing Adam, Eve and the Serpent at the Tree of Knowledge, the front lid with Adam and Eve's banishment from Eden, the band carved with stylised foliage

With original ivory key.

48 mm wide. 79mm. overall length

Made of ivory rather than the more usual gilt-brass, this watch is an exceptionally rare survival and an important and beautiful 17th century work of art.

Most likely made in Southern Germany, the movement employs the so-called stackfreed, a simple spring loaded cam mechanism used in some of the earliest spring driven watches. Devised to function as a mainspring-equaliser to even out the force of the mainspring over the period from fully wound to unwound and therefore improving timekeeping accuracy. The stackfreed was almost certainly invented in Nuremberg in the 16th century and its use seems having been limited to southern Germany. Its advantage over the early, crude fusée was that it required less space and thus allowed the manufacture of less bulky watches. The term may have been derived from the German expressions "stark" for strong and "Feder" for spring.

In the account of the Creation, on the sixth day, God created Adam and Eve, together with the plants and the animals, Book of Genesis 1:24-31. According to Genesis 2:21-2, Eve was fashioned from one of Adam's ribs while he slept. Adam and Eve lived in the Garden of Eden, or terrestrial paradise. God had warned Adam not to eat the fruit of "the tree of the knowledge of good and evil" but the serpent convinced Eve that she should try one of those fruits (usually represented as an apple or a fig) so that she could become like a god with the knowledge of good and evil. Eve ate the fruit which she shared with Adam. "Then the eyes of both of them were opened and they discovered that they were naked; so they stitched fig-leaves together and made themselves loincloths", (from The Temptation, Gen. 3:1-7). Adam and Eve were expelled from the Garden of Eden, clothed in skins, having lost their immortality (see The Expulsion, Gen. 3:8-24).

Inv. 1374

For the Duke de Luxembourg

Daniel Quare

Silver pair case quarter repeating two-train coach watch with alarm

Signed Daniel Quare Fecit Londini, inner case numbered 609, circa 1690

Keywound two-train verge movement with chain fusée, engraved barrel for the alarm train, large very finely engraved pierced balance cock, large diamond endstone, repeating on a bell inside the back of the case

Silver Champlevé dial with Roman numerals, sunk alarm disc in the centre with Arabic numerals, blued steel tulip and arrow hands

Circular silver cases, the outer case engraved and pierced for sound, elaborately engraved coat of arms of François Henri de Montmorency-Bouteville, Duc de Luxembourg, case maker's punch mark 'GI', large 9-part lateral hinge. Inner case with lateral floral engraving and with mythical creatures, pierced for sound, medallion with grotesque mask, numbered 609

85 mm. diam.

Daniel Quare (c.1647-1724) was a contemporary of Thomas Tompion and one of England's most eminent watch and clock makers and the inventor of the repeating watch. He established himself at St. Martin Le Grand in London and became free of the Clockmakers' Company in 1671 and Master in 1708.

F. J. Britten states in Old Clocks and Watches and their Makers: "Of the few horologists of Tompion's time who can be admitted as his peers, Daniel Quare was perhaps the most notable example".

Daniel Quare was a celebrated maker of clocks, watches and barometers. He began making quarter repeating watches around 1680 and was one of the first clockmakers to make the hour and minute hands work as one. Among his most distinguished patrons were Kings James II and William III.

King George I offered Quare the post of King's Watchmaker. However, like Thomas Tompion, Quare was a Quaker and his strict religious beliefs prevented him from signing the necessary Oath of Allegiance. Nevertheless he enjoyed regular royal patronage and the King allowed him access to the Palace at any time. Quare's reputation was not confined to Britain however, and his royal commissions spanned the continent. Indeed, further evidence of Quare's international success can be seen from the list of guests at his children's weddings which included important members of society from Venice, Portugal, Sweden, Denmark, Prussia and Florence. The exalted provenance of this watch proves the strength of appeal that good English makers, such as Quare, had to the continental aristocratic market.

François Henri de Montmorency-Bouteville, Herzog von Luxembourg-Piney

Born in Paris on 8th January, 1628, his father was François de Montmorency-Bouteville (1600-1627) who had been beheaded in the Place de Grève six months earlier for killing the Maquis de Beuvron in a duel. François Henri was taken in and brought up by his aunt Charlotte de Montmorency, Princess de Condé. In 1661 he married the greatest heiress in France, Madeleine Charlotte de Clermont-Tonnerre, Duchess de Luxembourg-Piney.

As a member of the eminent Montmorency family and a Marshall of France and Luxembourg, Montmorency-Bouteville became one of the the most famous military leaders of the 17th century and one of Louis XIV's most important generals. He is famed as the comrade and successor of the great Condé. His wartime successes, his ferociousness and his splendid comeback after imprisonment in the Bastille gained him the reputation of being in league with the devil. This rumour later turned into the tale of the Duke of Luxembourg which started being spread in pamphlets and books in Holland, France and Germany around 1680. He died in 1695 at Versailles.

Coat of arms of François Henri de Montmorency-Bouteville, Duc de Luxembourg,

Inv. 1208

Roman Charity

Cornelis Uyterweer

An unusual gilt metal and painted on enamel single-handed watch with mock pendulum

Signed C. Uyterweer, Rotterdam, No. 111, circa 1720

Keywound full plate gilt-finished verge movement, chain fusée, large chased and engraved floral decorated cock with an aperture for the mock pendulum, pierced and engraved floral decorated foot

Gilt dial with Roman numerals, single blued steel hand, engraved and inlaid black enamel pastoral scene

Circular case with chased engraved foliate decorated bezel and rim, case polychrome enamelled in the manner of Huaud, pastoral vignettes to the band, framed by foliage and flowers on yellow and blue ground, reverse with a painted polychrome enamel scene depicting the Roman Charity, the interior also decorated with a painted pastoral scene

49 mm. diam.

Cornelis Uyterweer (Rotterdam 1702-1782) was one of the most influential Dutch watch and clock makers of his time. Head of the Rotterdam Clockmaker Association, he also served as Guildmaster on nine occasions between 1749 and 1769, followed by his son Pieter serving on four occasions between 1775 and 1780.

Uyterweer's watches are distinguished by their unusual, decorative balance cocks, often with mock pendulum, and the finely made repoussé cases.

Cornelis Uyterweer's watch no. 480 with similarly decorated silver balance cock and mock pendulum is on permanent exhibition in the Museum Rotterdam.

Other examples of his work can be found in the Dutch Gold, Silver and Clock Museum in Schoonhoven, the Rijksmuseum in Amsterdam, the Museum of the Dutch Clock in Zaandam, Museum 'Het Princessehof' in Leeuwarden and in the Guildhall of London. Roman Charity is the story of a woman, Pero, who secretly breastfeeds her father, Cimon, after he is imprisoned and sentenced to death by starvation. The scene was often represented by artists in the 17th century including Rubens and Caravaggio.

Cleopatra & Mark Antony

Isaac Lenoir

Silver and painted on enamel deskwatch with concealed dial

Signed Lenoir à Lion (Lyon), the case decorated in the manner of Les Frères Huaud, early 18th century

Keywound gilt full plate verge movement with square baluster pillars, pierced and engraved continental type balance cock, chain fusée, silver regulation dial

White enamel dial with Roman numerals and outer Arabic five-minute numerals, pierced gilt hands

Circular case entirely painted on enamel, engraved silver bezels, the back painted with a scene of Cleopatra with the asp, the band with four landscape vignettes, hinged painted on enamel cover decorated with a scene of Mark Antony and his attendants, the interior of the cover and case painted with classical ruins in landscapes

53mm. diam.

This unusual watch with decoration in the manner of the Geneva enamellists Les Frères Huaud was evidently always conceived as a desk or table timepiece. Interestingly, the back of the case is concave in the centre so that the watch is stable when placed on a flat surface, a feature never seen on cases made for pocket watches

The watchmaker Isaac Lenoir of Lyon is recorded working about 1730-35, he became master in 1730.

The Earliest Known Jump-Hour Watch

Inv. 1901

John Bushman

18K gold repoussé pair case jump hour watch with mock pendulum balance

Signed John Bushman, London, movement no. 389, the outer case attributed to Augustin Heckel, inner case with indistinct London hallmarks, circa 1700

Gilded full plate verge movement with chain fusée, divided vase-shaped pillars with pierced galleries, very finely foliate engraved winged balance cock with aperture for the mock pendulum

Gilded silver dial with chased foliate and strapwork repoussé centre, a satyr mask above a cartouche engraved 'London' in the lower half, aperture for the jumping hours at 12, outer champlevé minutes chapter ring with Arabic five-minute numerals, steel poker minute hand

Circular case, the outer repoussé case decorated with a scene of the Rape of Europa, floral and foliate scroll border and bezel, polished inner case

55 mm. diam.

The gold repoussé outer case can be tentatively attributed to Augustin Heckel who was one of the best London case makers of the period.

A pen and ink design by Heckel of this scene of The Rape of Europa, after an engraving by Gerard de Lairesse (1640-1711), is in the collection of the Victoria & Albert Museum in London.

Another watch case by Heckel decorated with an identical scene, the movement signed Thomas Windmills is in the collection of the British Museum.

This watch is the earliest known pocket watch with jumping hours, a mechanism that, apart from this singular example, is not known to have been used in a watch again until the early 19th century. In 1883, the Austrian Joseph Pallweber patented his jump hour watch.

The minutes are indicated by a single hand on the outer chapter ring, the large aperture shows the hours in Roman numerals which are engraved on a rotating silver disc beneath the dial, the hour numerals instantaneously 'jump' exactly on the hour. The mechanism consists of a system of springs and pawls acting on a fixed brass 12-toothed wheel on the back of the hour disc.

John Bushman was a very sophisticated and innovative watchmaker and it is no surprise to see his name as the maker of this historically important watch. A number of Bushman's surviving watches represent a departure from the standard watches of the time. He is particularly associated with the 'wandering hours' system of displaying the time which is found on a few of his watches around 1700. Clearly related stylistically to and a variation of his 'wandering hours' watches, the present watch is an almost certainly unique piece which pre-dates all other known jump hour watches by at least 100 years, it is therefore of great significance in the history and development of watchmaking.

Jump hour disc

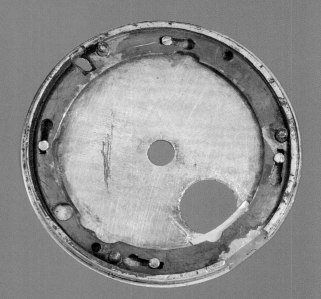

Reverse of dial

Under dial work

John Bushman(1661-1722)

Born in Augsburg, he was the son of the renowned clockmaker Johann Bushmann II. He moved to London in about 1687 where he worked in St. Martins le Grande, Aldersgate Within in the City. He became a Free Brother of the Clockmakers' Company in 1692, Assistant in 1720.

His will in the Public Records Office is dated 10th December 1722.

Inv. 1852

Daniel Grignion

Gold and painted on enamel watch

Signed Dl. Grignion, London, no. 309, the enamel by Les deux frères Huaud, circa 1690

Keywound gilt-finished verge movement with chain fusée, pierced and engraved balance cock and foot

White enamel dial with Roman numerals, the centre decorated with a polychrome enamel scene depicting Mercury and Venus

Circular gold case entirely painted on enamel, the back with polychrome enamel scene of Roman Charity, the band with four polychrome enamel idyllic landscapes with architecture, each with a blue and yellow enamel geometric design surround, small yellow enamel plaque reading 'Les deux frères Huaud/ Peintre de Son A. E.à Berlin', the interior with polychrome enamel landscape with a gentleman, gold bezel engraved with a repeated foliate pattern

39mm. diam.

The signature 'Les deux frères Huaud/ Peintre de Son A. E.àBerlin' on the enamel shows that it was painted by the two younger Huaud brothers, Jean-Pierre and Ami, when working in partnership as official enamel painters to the Elector of Brandenburg between 1686 and 1700. "Peintre de Son A.E. àBerlin" translates as 'painter to his Highness the Elector in Berlin' (Frederick III, Elector of Brandenburg, 1657-1713).

The Geneva enamellers, particularly the Huaud family, were renowned for their distinctive and beautiful style of enamel paintings. Their outstanding work is characterised by their miniaturist style and use of rich and varied colours in contrast to the pastel shades of the French enamellers of Blois. The enamel cases decorated by the Huaud family are highly regarded works of art in their own right.

Pierre Huaud, son of the French goldsmith Jean Huaud and founder of the dynasty, was born in 1612. He moved to Geneva in 1630 and three of his eleven children became also renowned enamellers: Pierre II (1647-1698), Jean-Pierre (1655-1723) and Ami (1657-1724). It is likely that the three brothers trained in the workshop of their father until around 1680 when Pierre II set up his own business. The second son, Jean-Pierre entered into partnership with Ami in 1682. In 1686, with special permission from the council of Geneva, the three Huaud brothers were invited to Berlin where they were appointed enamel painters to the Elector of Brandenburg, a position they held until their return to Geneva in 1700.

Pierre Huaud II died in 1698, the two younger brothers continued working until the death of Jean-Pierre in 1723 and Ami a year later.

The watch cases of the Huauds are usually found with movements made by various English, French, German and Swiss makers to whom they supplied cases at the time.

Daniel Grignion(1684-1763), a native of France worked in London. Grignion& Son, the firm he started at the 'King's Arms and Dial' in Great Russell Street, Covent Garden, with Daniel and son Thomas Grignion as partners. They described themselves as finishers for the late Daniel Quare. Thomas is credited with making technical improvements to the cylinder escapement.

Roman Charity is the story of a woman, Pero, who secretly breastfeeds her father, Cimon, after he is imprisoned and sentenced to death by starvation. The scene was often represented by artists in the 17th century including Rubens and Caravaggio.

Joseph Norris

21K gold and painted on enamel single-hand watch with early hairspring

Signed Joseph Norris, Amsterdam, the enamel signed Huaud le puis né fecit, circa 1685

Keywound full plate gilded brass verge movement with chain fusée, pierced vase pillars, steel balance with early blued steel flat hairspring, pierced and engraved gilded cock with irregular foot

Polychrome painted on enamel dial with Roman numerals on a white chapter ring, the centre decorated with a scene of Diana the huntress and Endymion the shepherd, diamond-set silver single hand

Circular case painted on enamel on gold depicting a scene of Eliezer and Rebecca, Eliezer receiving water from Rebecca's ewer so that he can refresh himself, the inside case-back painted with a landscape scene possibly inspired by an engraving by Gabriel Perelle (1603-1677), the band painted with landscape vignettes within scroll borders, signed in a cartouche "Huaud / le puis né / fecit", engraved gold bezel

39.5 mm. diam.

This exceptional late 17th century watch is one of the few signed works by Jean-Pierre Huaud (1655-1723) to survive in such remarkably well-preserved condition. Furthermore, it is one of the earliest watch cases painted by him. The enamel painting is brilliantly executed, having a real visual depth and three-dimensional quality to the figures and their costumes. The scene would appear to be taken from the book of Genesis and depicts the moment  *Abraham's trusted servant, Eliezer of Damascus requested to take a sip from Rebecca's jug. The dial is similarly decorated with a finely painted scene of Diana and Endymion within the white Roman chapter ring with half-hour markers. The diamond-set hand further denotes the overall high-status of the watch.*

Although the movement is signed Joseph Norris, Amsterdam, it was almost certainly made in Geneva. In common with other Geneva movements of the period, it would have been supplied unsigned to be then signed by Norris, who would have sold the watch under his own name. The extremely sophisticated movement features unusual pierced vase pillars often seen on Geneva watches as is the particular shape of the single-footed cock.

Joseph (or Josephus) Norris (1649-1727) was born in 1649 in Abington, England. He was apprenticed to his older brother, Edward Norris then, around 1668, he left for Amsterdam with the legendary clockmaker Ahasuerus Fromanteel (1607-1693). He became regarded as the best English watchmaker in Holland. Norris returned to his hometown in 1692 where he died in 1727.

The Huaud (or Huaut) family were the best known enamel painters of their day.

Jean-Pierre Huaud (1655-1723) and his brother Ami Huaud (1657-1724) became partners working in Geneva from 1682 to 1688. The present watch would have been made during this early period of their partnership. Like their older brother, Jean-Pierre Huaud I, they were also appointed painters to the Court of the Elector of Brandenburg in 1686, and went to Berlin where they lived and worked until 1700, at which point they returned to Geneva. Although much of their work was done in partnership, they also often worked alone. Their work was sought after by watchmakers from all over Europe.

Diana & Endymion

According to the legend, Diana used to come and kiss Endymion when he was asleep on the top of the mountain each night. Diana's light touch partly drew Endymion from his slumber and he caught a brief glance of her. Incredulous at her beauty, he attributed it to a dream and began to prefer his dreamlike state over mundane daily routines yet he was never awake when she was present. Through her love, Endymion was granted eternal youth and timeless beauty.

Eliezer & Rebecca

Eliezer of Damascus was probably the same "senior servant" in charge of all Abraham's possessions who, many years later, was commissioned by Abraham to go and find a wife for his son, Isaac. How, though, could Eliezer be sure that the woman he chose would indeed measure up to the standards of the saintly Isaac? To ensure that he would find the young woman, Eliezer came up with a plan. Hence was born the famous "camel test": After his long travels, Eliezer would ask a young maiden for a sip of water, and if she offered to provide water for his camels as well, she would be the one. Eliezer travelled hundreds of miles, where he found Rebecca in the town of Nahor in Mesopotamia. Eliezer had watched her fill a jug of water and place it on her shoulder. He ran over and asked to sip from it. Rebecca told him to drink, but hurriedly removed the jug from her shoulder to her hand and let him drink. When he finished drinking, the jug was not yet empty, and she offered to give the camels water as well. By offering water to Abraham's servant, and crucially offering more water for his camels, Eliezer realized that Rebecca was God's chosen wife for Isaac.

Isaac Gravelle

Gold, painted on enamel and en ronde-bosse enamel pre-balance spring single-hand watch

Signed Isaac Gravelle, the enamel attributed to Pierre Huaud I, circa 1660

Keywound gilt full plate verge movement, turned pillars, chain fusée, scrolling blued steel brackets for the worm and wheel set-up, finely pierced and engraved cock with long foot secured by a single screw

Enamel on gold, white enamel chapter ring with Roman numerals and half-hour markers, inner polychrome enamel wreath of flowers, the centre overlaid with green translucent enamel over a flinqué ground, single hand

Circular case with polychrome enamel band of flowers en ronde-bosse, the centre overlaid with green translucent enamel over a flinqué ground and a central portrait of Minerva in a plumed helmet, the turquiose enamelled inside case back painted with a portrait of Mars in a plumed helmet within a black painted scroll frame, split bezel engraved with a repeated pattern

33 mm. diam.

This exceptional and extremely beautiful watch is one of a very small group of similar enamel watches that can be attributed to the great Geneva enamellist Pierre Huaud I. These watches, combining several different enamelling techniques in a single object, are regarded as some of the finest masterpieces of Geneva enamel to survive from the 17th century.

A tour de force of the enamellers art, the present watch displays several characteristics typical of Pierre Huaud's work, namely: the use of translucent green enamel against a chiselled flinqué ground, the high relief white and polychrome enamel foliate and floral overlay, the bright orange colour used on the costumes. The strong blue ground used on the interior with black foliate decoration is a further characteristic, but can also be found on cases by other contemporary enamellers.

Only one watch case signed P. Huaud pinxit à Genève and definitely attributable to the Pierre Huaud the elder is presently known, the technique and colours employed are remarkably similar to the present watch.

Three other watches with related cases are known to date:

Signed Charles Bobinet, formerly in The Belin Collection

Signed Pieter Visbach, in the Victoria and Albert Museum, London, inventory no. 2370-1855, ex Bernal Collection

Signed Jean Baptiste Duboule, in the Patek Philippe Museum, Geneva

The Geneva enamellers, particularly the Huaud family, were renowned for their distinctive and beautiful style of enamel paintings. Their outstanding work is characterized by their miniaturist style and use of rich and varied colours in contrast to the pastel shades of the French enamellers of Blois. The enamel cases decorated by the Huaud family are highly regarded works of art in their own right.

Actual Size

CHAPTER 2

WATCHES
WITH
CHATELAINE

Watches With Chatelaine

According to the renowned collector Genevieve Cummins, author of the book Chatelaines: *Utility to Glorious Extravagance*, the term 'chatelaine' was not in fact coined until 1828 when it was used describe an accessory 'la chatelaine' in the London magazine *The World of Fashion*. The name was inspired by the female head or 'la chatelaine' of the grand French estate. In use since the Middle Ages, the chatelaine itself originated as a purely practical and useful device from which to suspend everyday items such as scissors, keys, needlework tools, thimbles, etcetera that a lady might need to hand at any one time. The popularity of the chatelaine was largely due to the fact that ladies did not have pockets in their gowns, or carry bags other than very small purses and reticules. Chatelaines were designed to be worn at the waistband and usually have a large metal curved tongue specifically for this purpose.

By the mid-18th century the chatelaine came into its own as not only a convenient practical accessory but the ideal place from which to suspend a watch. As a result, the chatelaine quickly became a statement of fashion. To this end the watchmakers and goldsmiths began to produce chatelaines and their accessories to perfectly match and complement the decoration of the watch itself, the watch and chatelaine were then sold as a complete artistic entity. Most of the great French watchmakers of the day made watches designed en suite to a chatelaine including Le Roy, Lépine and Baillon.

In France, the second half of the 18th century was a period of great stylistic innovation in watch case manufacture. This, coupled with the availability of talented craftsmen able to interpret new styles resulted in some of the most exuberant precious objects ever made in the rococo and neoclassical styles.

Often broken up and sold for their intrinsic value, watches with chatelaines have rarely survived intact to the present day. Few, if any, museums or private collections have such a fine and representative selection of watches with chatelaines as the Masis collection. These examples have been selected to display a wide variety of the different techniques of the goldsmith and enameller and in addition to illustrate how the integral design of the watch and chatelaine form a single and harmonious whole.

Jacques Coulin & Amy Bry

Gold, painted on enamel and gem-set watch with varicoloured gold and painted on enamel chatelaine

Signed Jaq. Coulin & Amy Bry, à Genève, no. 1338, circa 1790

Keywound gilt-finished verge movement with chain fusée, pierced and engraved cock

White enamel dial with Roman numerals, gem-set hands

Circular case finely chased with painted on enamel plaque to the back depicting a classically dressed lady and boy at an altar in a landscape, raised enamelled leaf border, gem-set bezel. Varicoloured gold chatelaine composed of four linked panels decorated with floral and love trophies, cherub and flowers, the upper panel set with an oval painted on enamel portrait of a lady, two chains either side for attaching accessories

42 mm. diam.

The partnership of Jacques Coulin & Amy Bry of Geneva was formed by Jacques Coulin (1744-1812) and Amy Bry (1750-1830) and Jean Flournoy (1727-1811) between 1782 and 1799.

Inv. 1667

Peter Dutens

Gold and cornelian openface watch with matched gilt metal and moss agate châtelaine

Signed Peter Dutens, London, no. 289, circa 1760

Keywound full plate gilt verge movement with chain fuseé, pierced and engraved balance cock

White enamel dial with Roman numerals

Circular case with cornelian-set bezel and case back. Gilt metal and moss agate chatelaine with two chains, the first capped with a key, the second with a fob

33 mm. diam.

Peter Dutensis recorded as working in Leicester Square, London, England, between 1759 and 1765.

The use of the chatelaine originates from the Middle Ages when ornamental hooks were suspended from skirts and everyday items such as watches, purses and thimbles were attached by hooks. Serving dual purposes as utilitarian accessories and decorative ornaments, this particular chatelaine with its beautiful agate panels and ornate hand engraved yellow gilt detailing is a superb example of an 18th century chatelaine.

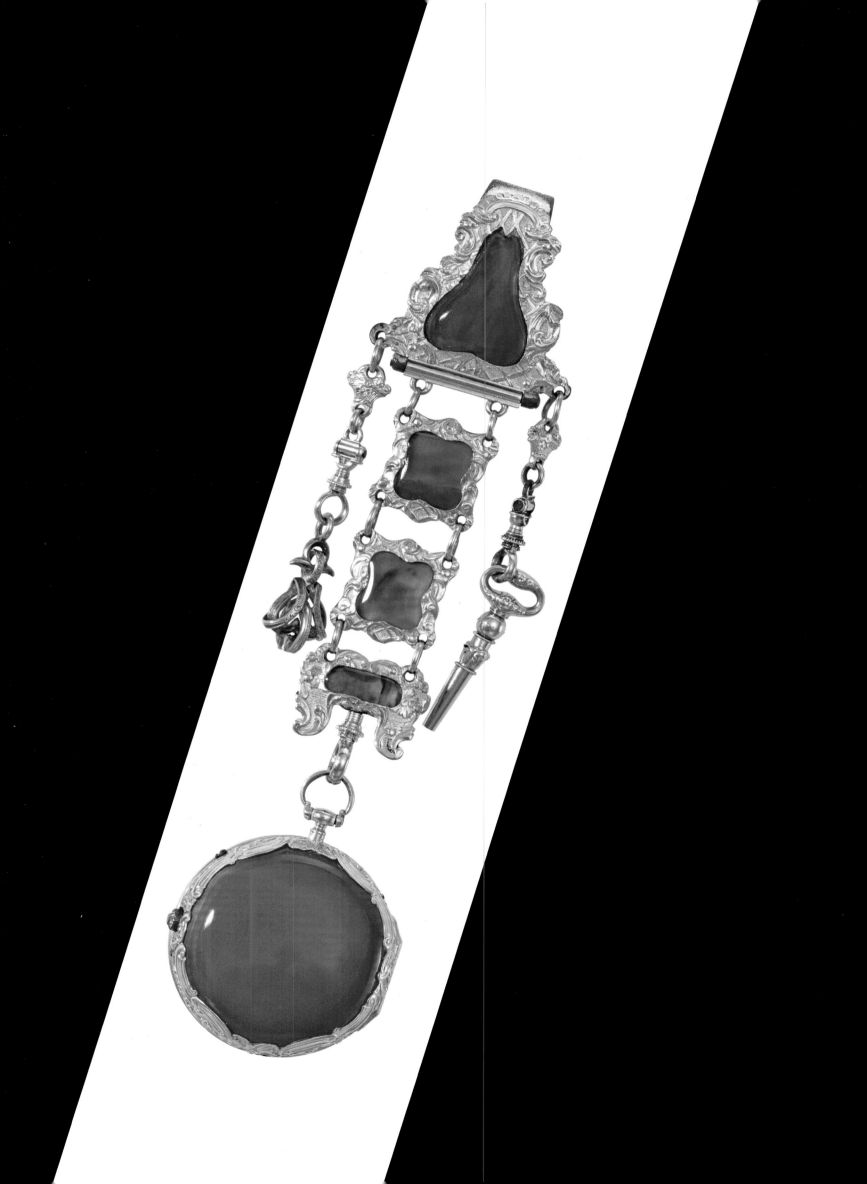

Inv. 1315

Richard Wilder

Gold and painted on enamel quarter repeating pair case watch and a gold and painted on enamel chatelaine

Signed Rich. Wilder, London, no. 1061, circa 1770, the chatelaine with maker's mark PB surmounted by a crown, probably Southern Germany, circa 1750, with the Dutch post-1807 control mark

Keywound gilt-finished verge movement, chain fusée, pierced and engraved cock and foot, diamond endstone, quarter repeating on a bell via two polished steel hammers, dust cover

White enamel dial with Roman numerals

Circular case, pierced and engraved inner case, the outer case decorated with translucent blue enamel, the back with a polychrome enamel scene of two ladies tending their sheep, seated beside a young man serenading and playing musical pipes in a pastoral setting, square-shaped five piece hinge, stamped case maker's HT, quarter repeating activated by depressing the pendant

The chatelaine with shaped triangular hook enamelled en plein with a classical allegory, suspending three shaped square sections similarly enamelled with pastoral scenes in the manner of François Boucher and flanked with chains comprised of oval sections enamelled with flowers on green ground, terminating in a shaped cartouche enamelled with a courting couple and applied with an attachment hook, the two sides with further suspended attachment hooks

49 mm. diam. 115 mm. overall length

A fine example of an English gold and enamel watch made to reflect the fashionable and sophisticated Louis XV French taste of the period. It is complemented by an equally fine gold chatelaine with painted on enamel scenes in the manner of François Boucher.

Although evidently a fine maker, very few watches by Richard Wilder appear to have survived.

Richard Wilder is listed as a clockmaker and watchmaker working at Richmond Buildings, Soho. He was a Liveryman of the Clockmakers' Company in 1776. For a period up to 1775 he was in partnership with John Fladgate working as Fladgate and Wilder.

Inv. 1269

Jean-Antoine Lépine

18K gold and enamel, diamond-set quarter repeating watch with provision for repeating à toc, matching chatelaine and original leather-covered fitted box

Signed L'Épine, Horloger du Roy, à Paris, no. 3891, circa 1775

Keywound gilt-brass full plate verge movement, chain fusée with Harrison's maintaining power, continental pierced and engraved cock, LeRoy-type repeating system, repeating on a bell by depressing the pendant

White enamel dial with Roman numerals, diamond-set half-hour divisions, Arabic five-minute numerals, diamond-set Louis XVI hands

Circular case decorated with translucent orange enamel over engine turning with diamond-set and white enamel star, diamond-set bezel, lever for bell striking or a toc at 6 o'clock. Diamond-set gold and enamel chatelaine stamped "M&P", the decoration matching the back of the watch case

39 mm. diam.

This beautiful and richly decorated watch is exceptional due to the survival of the original matching chatelaine. Furthermore it retains the original box.

Jean-Antoine Lépine (1720-1814)

Now regarded as one of the greatest and most innovative French watchmakers, the son of Jean "The King's Mechanical Expert", he was born at Challex, a village a few kilometers north of Geneva. He arrived in Paris in 1774 and became a workman for André Charles Caron, the King's clockmaker. He married Caron's daughter in 1756 and was himself appointed King's clockmaker around 1765. In 1763, Lépine had invented a new repeating mechanism for watches which was published in 1766. His new caliber invented around 1770 was a revolutionary concept replacing the back plate with bridges. Known as the 'Lépine caliber', its purpose was that the individual parts of the movement could be separately removed for repair and maintenance.

Lépine was also responsible for a number of other inventions, notably the virgule escapement, a simplified version of the double virgule invented by his father-in-law. The virgule was intended to compete with the English cylinder escapement but due to its delicacy and the difficulty of manufacture, it did not generally achieve wider success.

Lépine's other innovations included wolf's tooth wheels intended to reduce friction and a method of keyless winding operated by pumping the pendant. In addition, he also developed a new form of case with hidden hinges and fixed bezel so that the watch was only accessible from the back therefore protecting it from dust and preventing damage to the dial and hands.

Lépine was active in the company until his death at the great age of 93 on 31st May, 1814.

Charles Oudin

18K gold and painted on enamel diamond and pearl-set watch with a three-colour gold and painted on enamel diamond and pearl-set chatelaine

Signed Charles Oudin, Horloger de la Marine, Palais Royal 52, no. 21739, circa 1850

Keyless cylinder movement with wolf's tooth winding

White enamel dial with Roman numerals

Circular case with diamond-set bezels, the back with a painted on enamel panel depicting a young couple in 18th century costume in a landscape, gold chatelaine set with a painted on enamel miniature within a diamond border, diamond-set palmette and pearl-set shell, two chains set with diamonds and pearls

30 mm. diam.

The prestigious French firm of Charles Oudin was always renowned for its elegantly designed and high quality watches which were often adorned with precious stones.

The elder Charles Oudin (1743-1803) and his brother Nicolas both worked for the great Abraham-Louis Breguet. Nicolas's son, Charles Oudin(1768-1840) opened his workshop in the fashionable Palais-Royal area of Paris in 1801 in the Galerie de Pierre, no 65. In 1809, the address is listed as number 52, rue de Richelieu, Palais du Tribunat where the mosaic in the entrance floor, announcing his name and title "Horloger de la Marine Française" can be seen to this day.

Oudin was the watchmaker to the French Emperor and Empress, the Pope, the King and Queen of Spain, and the Imperial Navy.

In 1836, he transferred the business to his son Charles-Raymond. Around 1857, Charles-Raymond sold the firm to a watchmaker named Amédée Charpentier. Charpentier continued to produce watches and clocks under the name 'Oudin-Charpentier'.

Inv. 1598

Swiss

Gold, painted on enamel and pearl-set lady's pendant watch with a gold, enamel and pearl-set chatelaine

Unsigned, circa 1820

Keywound verge movement with chain fusée

White enamel dial with Arabic numerals

Circular case, pearl-set borders to both sides, the front with polychrome painted on enamel depicting a singing lady holding a lyre, the reverse with polychrome painted on enamel putti. Enamel and pearl-set chatelaine, composed of two sections, one enamelled with a lyre and roses and the other with a lady pouring water by a stream, decorated with gold and pearl-set floral swags

30 mm. diam.

Inv. 1436

Hermann Böhm

Renaissance revival Austrian silver-gilt and rock crystal watch and a silver, enamel, pearl, and hardstone-set chatelaine

Signed Hermann Böhm, Vienna, circa 1885

Earlier keywound verge movement, Viennese, circa 1790

Champlevé dial with Roman numerals

Octagonal watch in rock-crystal case. Chatelaine mounted with a fully-modelled enamelled figure of Diana stepping over a doe, against an openwork niche, the hook with champlevé enamel, above cupid-head chains suspending a baroque pearl pendant of an ostrich and a ewer-form perfume flask with hardstone body and chained stopper

22 cm. overall length.

Hermann Böhm (or Boehm) was a skilled goldsmith and enamellist working in Vienna in the late 19th Century. He is widely regarded as one of the leading enamellists in Europe at the time, and his work has greatly contributed to the reputation that Viennese enamel now enjoys.

Böhm worked mainly in the neo-Renaissance, or Renaissance revival style, and was inspired by the Limoges enamellists of the Middle Ages and early Renaissance. He received an award for his exhibit at the 1873 Vienna Exhibition.

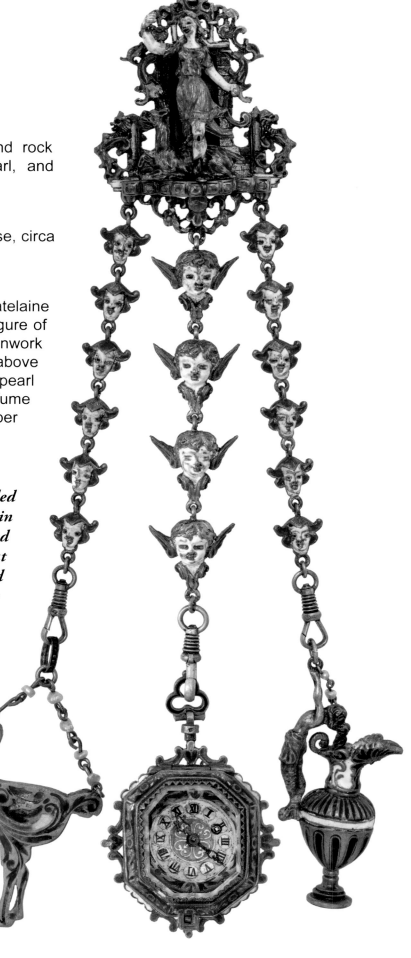

Jean-Baptiste Baillon

Gold, enamel and diamond-set watch with matching gold, enamel and diamond-set chatelaine

Signed J. B. Baillon à Paris, no. 3938, circa 1760

Keywound gilt full plate verge movement with chain fusée, pierced and engraved balance cock

White enamel dial with Arabic numerals

Circular chased repoussé case decorated with scrolls, the back overlaid with enamel in imitation of bloodstone and mounted with a diamond-set flower spray, matching chatelaine with enamel cartouches imitating bloodstone and mounted with diamond-set flower sprays, two side chains supporting an acorn perfume bottle and a bloodstone and gold key

33 mm. diam.

Jean-Baptiste Baillon was, in the words of F. J. Britten, "the richest watchmaker in Europe". One of the most famous watchmakers in Paris in the 18th Century, Baillon became a master watchmaker in 1727, establishing his workshop first on the Place Dauphine and later in the Rue Dauphine. A further manufactory was situated in Saint-Germain-en-Laye, where other watchmakers worked for him, something highly unusual at that period. Baillon was appointed watchmaker to the Queen of France, Maria Leczinska in1738, 'Valet de Chambre de la Reine-Ordinaire Watchmaker' by 1748, "Premier Valet de Chambre de la Reine", and from about 1770 watchmaker at the court of Queen Marie Antoinette. Baillon held the post of "Premier Valet de Chambre and Valet de Chambre, Watchmaker Ordinaire de la Dauphine" to Marie-Antoinette. He died in 1772.

Inv. 1833

Le Bon

18K pink gold and painted on enamel openface watch with matching four-colour gold and painted on enamel chatelaine

Signed Le Bon, no. 722, circa 1810

Keywound gilt-finished full-plate verge movement with chain fusée, pierced and engraved balance cock

White enamel dial with Arabic numerals

Circular case, the bezel decorated with white and blue enamel, the band outlined with opaque white enamel, the back decorated with translucent blue enamel over engine-turning with a polychrome scene of children playing in a landscape beneath an engraved gold tree with two birds, the pendant with opaque light blue and white enamel stamped 'CD' and '725', matching four-colour gold chatelaine decorated with a panel depicting a mother and children with a pet rabbit in a cage and a further panel painted with a basket of flowers

51mm. diam.

The charming painted enamel scene decorating the present watch derives from the type of English genre paintings made by artists from the Royal Academy, such as Joshua Reynolds (1723-1792), Francis Wheatley (1747-1801), William Hamilton (1751-1801), William Redmore Bigg (1755-1828), and others, who specialised in images of romanticised English rural life in the last quarter of the 18th century. Their paintings were engraved and sold as prints which were enormously popular and were used as models for the Genevan enamellers, including Jean-Louis Richter.

Inv. 1813

French

Varicolured gold and painted on enamel gem-set watch with matching varicoloured gold and painted on enamel gem-set chatelaine

Unsigned, circa 1780

Keywound gilt full plate verge movement with chain fusée, pierced and engraved balance cock

White enamel dial with Roman numerals

Circular case, the back set with a polychrome painted on enamel portrait of a lady surrounded by varicoloured gold foliate decoration and a band of blue enamel, matching chatelaine set with six small polychrome painted on enamel portraits of noble ladies, blue enamel ground with varicoloured gold applied foliate decoration, with attached matching key and seal

37 mm. diam.

Inv. 1350

Daniel Vauchez

18K gold, silver and diamond-set painted on enamel watch with diamond-set and painted on enamel chatelaine and original fitted box set with a gold-framed painted on enamel plaque

Signed Vauchez à Paris, circa 1780, the enamel plaque circa 1700

Keywound verge movement, chain fusée, continental pierced and engraved cock

White enamel dial with Roman numerals, Arabic five-minute numerals

Circular case with rose-cut diamond-set bezel, the back set with a painted on enamel portrait of a lady within a diamond-set filigree frame. Chatelaine with three chains joining diamond-set, gold and silver panels, the upper panel depicting an allegory of love, the middle and lower representing music, on each side smaller panels depicting the muses of Geometry and Astronomy, one with a key, the other a seal, the matrix engraved in gothic script J.W. v. B.

38 mm. diam.

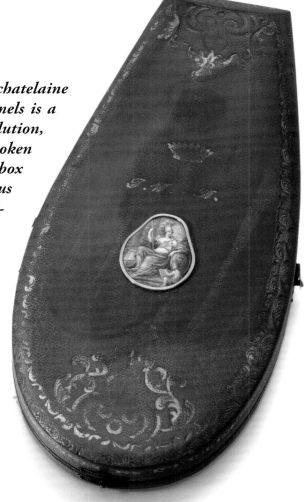

This unusually lavish and very beautiful diamond-set chatelaine fitted with exuberant classical painted on enamel panels is a very rare survival. Dating from before the French Revolution, very few examples have avoided destruction or being broken up for their component parts. The gold-tooled leather box with a coronet and the initials J.W. v. B. of a previous aristocratic owner is interestingly mounted with a gold-framed painted on enamel plaque depicting Minerva, dating from around one hundred years earlier than the watch and chatelaine.

Daniel Vauchez was a watchmaker of high repute. He became Master in 1767 and set up his establishment in the Rue du Petit Lion St. Sauveur from 1769 until 1790. Specializing in decorated watches often set with enamel and stones, most of the pieces were made in Switzerland.

Inv. 1885

Moricand & Comp.

Pink gold and painted on enamel pocket watch set with highly unusual individually diamond-set pearls and a gold and painted on enamel pearl-set chatelaine with key and seal

Signed Moricand & Comp., no. 18321, circa 1790

Keywound full plate verge movement with chain fusée, pierced and chased continental balance cock

White enamel dial with upright Roman numerals, diamond-set hands

Circular case decorated with a polychrome painted on enamel allegory of painting on a translucent royal blue enamel ground, the bezel and border set with pearls, each pearl set with an individual diamond. Gold and pearl-set chatelaine with a painted on enamel panel depicting a reclining lady in a landscape, gold and enamel fob and gold, enamel and pearl-set key

52 mm. diam.

This watch is particularly interesting in terms of its decoration. Both the bezel and the border surrounding the rich translucent blue and painted on enamel panel are set with a row of pearls, as is often seen on a watch of this period and quality. However, the author knows of no other example of a watch where each individual pearl is itself set with a single diamond. The effect is stunning and would have been very labour intensive and required great skill to create.

Christian Moricand (1715-1791) is recorded as a watchmaker who from 1752 to 1755 was associated with his brother Benjamin and the watchmaker François Colladon.

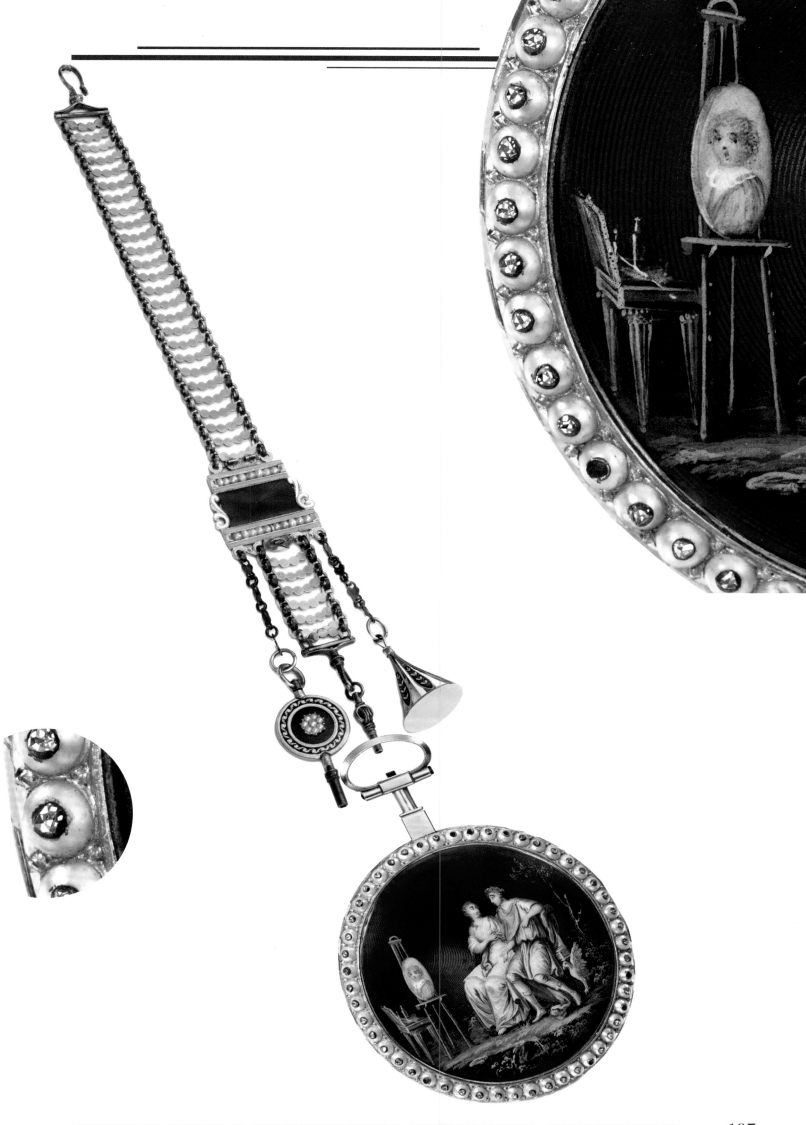

Inv. 1452

Alexander Cumming

22K gold and enamel pair case dumb half-quarter repeating watch with à tact option, with original matching gold and enamel chatelaine

Signed Alexander Cumming, London, no. 765, the cases with London hallmarks for 1769-1770

Keywound full-plate cylinder movement with Cumming's curved teeth of the escape wheel, chain fusée, single footed cock, repeating on a steel block fixed to the case activated by depressing the pendant, gilt-brass dust cap, lever for à tact option in the bezel

White enamel dial with Roman numerals and outer Arabic numerals, signed on the reverse 'PM'

Circular pair case, the outer engine-turned and decorated with translucent blue enamel flowers, the inner case plain polished. Chatelaine with four joined gold and enamel brass-reinforced links each decorated with translucent blue enamel flowers to match the case, gilt spoon, each side with two chains for attaching accessories

49 mm. diam.

Provenance: Collection of Dr. Anton C. R. Dreesmann (1923-2000)

This watch incorporates a very rare form of half-quarter repeating with double rack and double snail without lifting the hammer pushers.

Alexander Cumming (1733-1814) was admitted to the Clockmaker's Company in 1781. He improved the cylinder escapement by including curved teeth on the escape wheel, a feature which can be observed on the present watch. He was also a famous chronometer maker, appointed as expert on Harrison's timepiece by the Act of 1761. In 1766 he published 'The Elements of Clock and watch Work'. He was at the Dial and Three Crowns on Bond Street until 1777, then 12 Clifford Street until 1794 and finally at his shop on Fleet Street, which he kept until his retirement to Pentonville, where he owned property. For some time he worked with his nephew and former apprentice, John Grant.

Inv. 1427

Marie Antoinette & Family

Swiss

18k pink gold, painted on enamel and rose-cut diamond watch with later painted on enamel portraits of Louis XVI and Marie Antoinette, rose-cut diamond and pearl-set chatelaine

Unsigned, the watch circa 1780, the chatelaine and watch enamel circa 1850

Keywound full plate verge movement, pierced and engraved balance cock and foot, rounded pillars

White enamel dial with Roman numerals

Circular case, the back set with a later polychrome enamel panel painted with the portraits of Marie Antionette and Loius XVI of France, black enamel border, enhanced by two diamonds, the bezel and rims with scroll design.

Chatelaine centered by a polychrome enamel plaque with portraits of Marie Antionette and Louis XVI, surrounded by filigree work enhanced by rose-cut diamonds and pearls, three chains, the first with a watch key with polychrome portraits of Marie Antoinette and Louis XVI's children, the Dauphin and Marie Therese Duchesse D'Angouleme, the second a watch fob with polychrome portraits of Louis XV's daughters, Madame Adelaide de France and Madame Victoire de France, the third centered with a red enamel and diamond-set fleur-de-lys with secure hook to attach watch, all three enhanced with filigree work with diamonds and pearls

38mm diam.

Almost certainly a special commission and a magnificent tribute to the former French monarchy, this beautiful jewel-encrusted chatelaine and matching watch commemorates the doomed royal family. The portraits of the King and Queen are accompanied by portraits of the royal children and the Mesdames de France. Louis XVI was the only King of France ever to be executed, and his death brought an end to more than a thousand years of continuous French monarchy.

Provenance

The pendant inscribed with Chicago Museum inventory number 52. 75. 148

The Estate of Leopold Metzenberg (Executive, Sears, Roebuck & Co.)

Gift to the previous owner in 1952

Marie Antoinette

Louis XVI

Dauphin & Marie Therese
Duchesse D'Angouleme

Madame Adelaide de France
& Madame Victoire de France

CHAPTER 3

TURKISH
MARKET

Turkish Market Watches

When Richard Rolt recorded in *A New Dictionary of Trade and Commerce* in 1756, that "Great quantities of watches are exported to Asia, particularly to Turkey; where they serve more for ornaments like pictures in rooms, than for use in pockets."he tells us just how fascinated the Ottomans were with European watches.

The first documented Ottoman interest in watches dates from 1531 when Sultan Süleyman I bought a gold ring watch in Venice, impelling Western ambassadors to present clocks and watches to gain favours. Following the Sultan's lead, it was not long before local officials were receiving the same gifts in addition to the traditional presents of precious textiles. Following a treaty drawn up with Austria in 1547 stipulating the payment of a yearly tribute to the Ottoman Empire to prevent aggression, the quantity of clocks and watches exclusively made for the Ottoman Empire rose considerably and continued even after the termination of the agreement. The first western clock and watchmakers to travel to Turkey at the end of the 16th century were sent to maintain and repair clocks that had been presented as diplomatic gifts to Sultan Murad III.

Dating from the mid-17th century, the Masis Collection is fortunate to have one of the finest and earliest surviving Turkish watches. Made by Bulugat, it was produced in the suburb of Galata in Constantinople which had by that time become an established colony of foreign goldsmiths, watchmakers and engravers.

During the late 18th century and the first half of the 19th century, European watchmakers started to produce watches specifically for the Ottoman market, to the virtual exclusion of their home markets. English makers such as Ralph Gout, George and Edward Prior, James Markwick and Robert Markham and Queen Charlotte's watchmaker Daniel de Saint Leu, catered to Ottoman taste by designing their products with Islamic dials and complicated repeating and striking movements. Because the Ottomans wore their watches on the outside of their clothing and not in a pocket, the makers produced double or triple gold cases with enamel (usually red) decorated with scenes of the Bosphorus or varicoloured gold cases set with diamonds and precious stones.

Even Abraham-Louis Breguet, the most famous watchmaker of all, made watches especially for the Turkish market for which he had a great affinity through his friendship with the Ottoman ambassador to Paris, Esseid Ali Effendi. In the opening years of the 19th century, due to the tumultuous political climate, Turkey was the only great power with a market open to France. Breguet's Turkish market watches were in fact the only watches for which he deviated from his classic style, supplying watches with Turkish numeral dials and exquisitely enamelled cases. This tells us just how important the Turkish market was to him. Indeed, on the advice of Esseid Ali Effendi, Breguet sent the famous French watchmaker Le Roy to Constantinople to become his local agent there.

Inv. 1006

Le Roy

18K gold and painted on enamel and filigree watch made for the Turkish market

Signed Le Roy, circa 1820

Keywound Lépine calibre cylinder movement

White enamel dial with Turkish numerals

Circular case with twelve segments decorated alternately with painted on enamel panels of musical trophies and gold filigree

50 mm. diam.

Inv. 1623

Julien Le Roy

18K gold and painted on enamel quarter-repeating rose-cut diamond and pearl-set pocket watch made for the Islamic market

Signed Julien Le Roy à Paris, circa 1760

Keywound full-plate verge movement with chain fusée, micrometric potence adjustment, pierced and engraved continental balance cock, repeating on a bell activated by depressing the pendant

White enamel dial with Turkish numerals, gold and seed pearl-set Islamic hands

Scallop-edged case, the band engraved and decorated with black champlevé enamel, the bezel with translucent green enamel and gold paillioné flowers set with a rose-cut diamond on each lobe, seed pearl-set border, the back with a painted on enamel scene of a sea battle with an opalescent sunray sky, border decorated to match the bezel

46.5 mm. diam.

Julien Le Roy was one of the most celebrated French watchmakers of his time. Born in Tours in 1686 into a family of five generations of watch and clockmakers, he had already made his first clock by the age of 13. In 1699, he moved to Paris for further training. Together with his brothers, he founded one of the most important clock and watch workshops of the time. Le Roy's reputation was based on his mechanical discoveries, including a special repeating mechanism that improved the precision of watches and clocks. In 1713 he became maître horloger, then juré of his guild. Further appointments followed, including the Directorship of the Société des Arts, but the pinnacle of his achievements was being appointed clockmaker (Horloger Ordinaire du Roi) to King Louis XV in 1739.

Le Roy's workshop also produced a large number of ordinary clocks and watches to satisfy wide public demand. During his life he is known to have made or supervised over 3,500 watches, amounting to an average of one hundred movements a year, or one every three days. In contrast, other workshops only produced between thirty and fifty pieces per year.

Le Roy's extensive clientele included many members of Europe's noble and royal families. He carried on his business from premises in the Rue du Harlay until his death in 1759. His son Pierre (1717-1785), a brilliant clockmaker in his own right, continued until the early 1780s. Examples of Le Roy's work can be found in many major museums, notably the Louvre, Paris, and the Victoria and Albert Museum in London.

Inv. 1869

Julien Le Roy

Gold and painted on enamel gem-set quarter repeating watch made for the Turkish market

Signed Jul'n. Le Roy à Paris, no. 88358, circa 1760

Keywound verge movement with fusée and chain, pierced and chased continental balance cock, repeating on a bell activated by depressing the pendant

White enamel with Turkish numerals

Circular case decorated with blue, red and white champlevé enamel, central painted on enamel musical trophy within a gem-set border, shuttered winding hole

59 mm. diam.

Le Roy

18K gold and painted on enamel watch made for the Turkish market

Signed Le Roy, no. 4435, circa 1820

Keywound Lépine calibre cylinder movement

White enamel dial with Turkish numerals

Circular case decorated with black champlevé enamel, the back with an en grisailles painted on enamel military trophy incorporating Ottoman flags

44 mm. diam.

Basile Charles Le Roy (1765-1839)

Clockmaker to Napoleon, Madame Mere, The King of Westphalia, Princess Pauline Borghese and the Duc de Bourbon. Born and died in Paris. In 1785 he founded the house of Le Roy at thePalais Royale in the Galerie de Pierre, which in 1789 became Le Rue de Egalité. The company was sold around 1845 but name continued to be used until the late 19th century.

Le Roy

18K gold and painted on enamel watch made for the Turkish market

Signed Le Roy, no. 13691, circa 1820

Keywound Lépine calibre cylinder movement, jewelled to the third wheel

White enamel dial with Turkish numerals and signed Le Roy in Turkish script

Circular case decorated with red, green and blue champlevé enamel, the back with a painted on enamel musical trophy on a translucent yellow guilloche background, hinged gold cuvette

48 mm. diam.

Inv. 1077

Markwick Markham Perigal

18K gold and enamel pair case watch made for the Turkish market

Signed Markwick Markham Perigal, London, no. 11854, circa 1780

Keywound gilt-finished verge movement, chain fusée, finely pierced and engraved balance cock and foot, diamond endstone

White enamel dial with Turkish numerals

Circular plain gold inner case, the scalloped outer case with green, red and white champlevé enamel scroll and foliage decorated bezel and rim, the reverse centred by a scalloped painted polychrome enamel scene depicting a seascape and sailing boats, surrounded by a white enamel and translucent scarlet enamel border

39 mm. diam.

James Markwick & Markwick Markham

James Markwick and his son James were both fine watchmakers working in London. The elder was apprenticed on 25th June 1656 to Richard Taylor and subsequently to Edward Gilpin. He became free of the Clockmakers' Company on 6th August 1666. In 1673 he succeeded to the business of Samuel Betts behind the Royal Exchange. His son James Markwick Jr became free of the company in 1692 by patrimony. The younger James Markwick was an eminent maker becoming master of the Clockmakers' Company in 1720, he was one of the first to adopt the use of jewelled bearings in his watches. In later years he was in partnership with his son-in-law Robert Markham who succeeded him using the trading name of Markwick Markham. The company became famous for watches destined for the Turkish market, and towards the end of the 18th century began signing their watches in collaboration with other eminent London watchmakers for their watches intended for the East. The makers associated with Markwick Markham include; Francis Perigal, Peter Upjohn, Story, Borell, Johnson, Recordon and Dupont, all highly reputable watchmakers in their own right.

Francis Perigal was working in New Bond Street in 1770 . Watchmaker to the King. Clockmakers Company 1781, died 1824.

Inv. 1083

Markwick Markham Borell

18K gold, enamel and shagreen triple case two-train hour-striking clockwatch with gold and enamel chain, made for the Turkish market

Signed Markwick Markham Borell, London, no. 21976, circa 1796

Keywound verge movement, finely pierced and engraved balance cock and foot, diamond endstone, striking the hours with two hammers on a bell mounted in the back of the case

White enamel with Turkish numerals

Circular triple case, the outer pierced and gilded, applied shagreen centre with stud decoration, florally engraved polychrome enamel border, diamond-set push piece, 18K gold middle case florally engraved and polychrome enamelled, the centre with a painted on enamel scene of a ship in a calm Mediterranean harbour within a translucent royal blue enamel border, casemaker's punch mark VW (Vale Walker), 18K gold inner case pierced and florally engraved, the pendant set with a large rose-cut diamond

58 mm. diam.

Borell is recorded working in London at the end of the 18th century.

Markwick Markham & Recordon

18K gold and enamel triple case watch made for the Turkish market

Signed Markwick Markham Recordon, London, no. 7062, circa 1800

Keywound verge movement, chain fusée, finely pierced and engraved balance cock and foot, diamond endstone

White enamel with Turkish numerals, gold heart-arrow hands

Circular triple case with scalloped edge, casemaker's punch mark IM, the outer florally engraved and polychrome enamelled, glazed centre, diamond-set push piece, 18K gold middle case florally engraved and polychrome enamelled, the centre with a painted on enamel spray of flowers on a translucent red guilloche enamel background, casemaker's punch mark IM, 18K gold plain inner case, the pendant set with a large rose-cut diamond

52 mm. diam.

Louis Recordon was working in London between 1778 and 1824. Company continued until c.1820.

Inv. 1595

Markwick Markham & Perigal

Markwick Markham Perigal

Gold and painted on enamel triple cased watch made for the Turkish market

Signed Markwick Markham Perigal, London, no. 21808, circa 1800

Keywoundgilt full plate verge movement, fusee and chain, pierced and engraved balance cock

White enamel dial with Turkish numerals

Circular case, polished inner case, case maker's mark IK, central scallop-form case with a polychrome painted on enamel burst of summer flowers against a translucent enamel red ground over engine-turning, surrounded by a ring of white enamel and three-colour gold floral swags, offset diamond-set thumb piece, outer case champlevé enameled with gold, red and green flowers against a yellow and blue ground

50 mm. diam.

Inv. 1022

Swiss

18K gold and enamel pocket compass made for the Turkish market

Unsigned, circa 1820

White enamel dial with points of the compass in Turkish characters, blued and polished steel needle

Circular gold case, the back decorated with painted on enamel flowers on a light green ground, the band, pendant and bow decorated with blue and black champlevé enamel

41 mm. diam.

A considerable rarity, this compass would appear to be the only enamelled pocket compass made especially for the Turkish market known to date. The white enamel dial has Turkish characters for the points of the compass, the case is decorated in a very similar way to a pocket watch and it is indeed quite likely that it may once have been the pair to a matching watch.

The magnetic compass is in fact a Chinese invention, dating from the Qin dynasty (221-206 B.C.). The first such instruments used lodestones to indicate direction, then from the 8th century AD., magnetised needles started to be used for navigation.

Although the compass first originated in China, it was also an instrument in use in the Islamic world and is mentioned in a Persian tale book from 1232. The earliest reference to a compass comes from the Yemeni sultan and astronomer Al-Ashraf in 1282. He appears to be the first to make use of the compass for astronomical purposes. In the 14th century, Middle-Eastern navigators brought the compass into everyday use.

Inv. 1908

Jacques-Frédéric Houriet

Silver pocket Réaumur thermometer with detachable compass made for the Turkish market

Signed ''Tertib-iFrederik el Huriye'' (Jacques-FrédéricHouriet), no. 927, circa 1815

Gilt brass movement with bimetallic curb, rack-and-pinion transmission with coiled return spring, micrometrically adjustable lever mounted at the end of the rack acted upon by the curb

White enamel thermometer dial with Réaumur scales and Turkish indications in gold for degrees of cold, Ice and degrees of heat, blued steel hand. Compass with silvered dial engraved with points of the compass and Turkish indications, the compass may be detached from the case to be used on a flat surface

Circular polished silver case

64mm. diam.

Original leather case

This beautifully conceived instrument is the only known pocket Réaumur thermometer and compass made by Jacques-Frédéric Houriet for the Turkish Market.

One of Houriet's most iconic technical innovations was his own version of the Réaumur thermometer which uses a curved bimetallic strip. Interestingly, it was Houriet's pupil and son-in-law Urban Jürgensen who justly claimed to be the inventor of the metallic pocket thermometer constructed in 1801. The idea was then improved upon by Houriet and it was Houriet who first conceived the idea of fitting a thermometer to watches. This type of thermometer was used for meteorological observations as it could indicate the both hottest degree as well as the coldest possible, unlike a mercury thermometer, which did not go beyond a certain degree of cold. The present thermometer is additionally fitted with a compass which can be detached from the case in order that it can be placed on a flat stable surface.

The bimetallic thermometer device is explained and illustrated by Urban Jürgensen in 'Principes Généraux de l'ExacteMesure du Temps par les Horloges', Copenhagen, 1805.

Jacques-FrédéricHouriet (1743-1830)

A remarkable horologist considered to be the father of Swiss precision watchmaking. He knew or worked with most of the most eminent horologists of his time. His research on compensated balances and the spherical balance spring allowed him to develop and perfect the most precise chronometers of his day. In addition, he successfully solved the problem of the influence of magnetic fields on the rate of chronometers He was apprenticed to his uncle, Daniel Gagnebin, at Renan, and later to the celebrated Abraham-Louis Perrelet, the inventor of the self-winding watch. In 1759, at the age of sixteen, he and his elder brother, an engraver, moved to Paris. Between 1761 and 1768 he studied with some of the leading French horologists, notably Breguet, LeRoy, Berthoud and Romilly and was the first Swiss watchmaker to make tourbillons. Antide Janvier, one of the most eminent horological minds of all time, considered Houriet an "artist worthy of emulation under the double relation of instruction and responsibility."

He is best known for his pioneering work in the construction of marine and pocket chronometers, and in particular for his experiments with isochronism of the hairspring or helical spiral and the effect of gravity or magnetism on the balance and escapement. He supplied a tourbillon chronometer to William Parry for the 1819-21 North Pole Expedition which was especially constructed for anti-magnetic properties. Houriet also trained the Danish watchmaker Urban Jürgensen, on whose work he had a great influence and who became his son-in-law.

Literature:

Frédéric Houriet, The Father of Swiss Chronometry, Jean-Claude Sabrier, 2006

Inv. 1036

Daniel de St. Leu.

18K varicoloured gold and diamond-set large pair case two-train clockwatch made for the Turkish market

Signed Daniel de St. Leu, Watchmaker to Her Majesty, London, no. 21786, circa 1800

Keywound full plate gilt-finished two-train movement, chain fusée, escapement converted to lever, hour, half-hour and quarter striking with two hammers, dust cover

White enamel dial with Turkish numerals, diamond-set half-moon hands

Finely chased floral decorated outer case with military trophies, diamond-set bezel, inner case with finely pierced and engraved decorated band, the top of the pendant set with a large rose-cut diamond

61 mm. diam.

A beautiful example of Daniel de St. Leu's fine craftsmanship, featuring impressive, lavishly decorated gold cases and a self-striking movement.

Daniel de St Leu (active 1753-1797), of Genevan origin, manufactured some of the most exquisite and elaborate watches of the eighteenth century. Gaining royal favour, he was appointed to Queen Charlotte, wife of King George III in 1765, a title he held for the rest of his life since all his watches after this date are either signed 'Sevt. to her Majesty', or 'Watch Maker to her Majesty'.

He also specialized in the manufacture of watches for wealthy Ottoman customers, requesting their watches to be pieces of jewellery, preferably in richly decorated gold cases, occasionally, like the present watch, set with diamonds. During the 18th century, the export of English watches to Turkey operated on a large scale.

R. Rolt records in 'A New Dictionary of Trade and Commerce', 1756, that "Great quantities of watches are exported to Asia, particularly to Turkey; where they serve more for ornaments like pictures in rooms, than for use in pockets."

Inv. 1127

Daniel de St. Leu.

18K gold, enamel, pearl and diamond-set large pair case Grande Sonnerie striking clockwatch made for the Turkish market

Signed Daniel de Saint Leu, Watchmaker to Her Majesty, London, movement no. 1506, circa 1800

Keywound engraved with entwined leaves, chain fusée, finely pierced and engraved balance cock, striking with two hammers on a bell

White enamel dial with Turkish numerals, pearl-set gold hands

Circular case, the outer engraved, pierced and pearl-set, red and blue enamel decoration, the centre with a finely painted scene of naval action between French and Greek ships off the Mediterranean coast, applied crescent moon above set with diamonds, inner case richly florally engraved and pierced

63 mm. diam.

Inv. 1831

Daniel de St. Leu.

18K four-colour gold quarter repeating pair case watch made for the Turkish market

Signed de St. Leu, London, circa 1790

Keywound gilt-finished verge movement with chain fusée, pierced and engraved balance cock, gilt dust cover, quarter repeating on a bell activated by depressing the pendant

White enamel dial with Turkish numerals

Circular case, the inner case pierced and engraved, the four-colour gold outer case chased with foliate scrolls, the back decorated with a military trophy, flowers and foliage

58mm. diam.

Inv. 1063

Etienne Desvignes

18K gold and enamel triple case quarter repeating verge watch made for the Turkish market

Signed Etienne Desvignes, London, case stamped with London date letter for 1813

Keywound verge movement with chain fusée, quarter repeating with two polished steel hammers on a bell activated by depressing the pendant

White enamel dial with Turkish numerals

Circular triple case, the inner decorated with a fine polychrome enamel floral band and bouquet to the back on a translucent guilloche cream enamel ground; scallop-edge middle case decorated to match with flowers on a blue ground; scallop-edge outer case with glazed back and blue, white and translucent scarlet enamel decorated floral bezel and rim

53 mm. diam.

Inv. 1064

Moulinie

18K gold and painted on enamel openface watch made for the Turkish Market

Signed Moulinie AinéàGeneve, no. 3911, circa 1835

Keywound gilt-finished cylinder movement

White enamel dial with Turkish numerals

Circular case decorated with turquoise painted on enamel simulated shagreen, the reverse surrounded by a polychrome enamel painted wreath of flowers centred by a pansy, gilt-metal cuvette

54 mm. diam.

Moulinie Ainé & Cie., watchmakers, were active in Geneva in the first half of the 19th century and specialised in finely enamelled timepieces.

Inv. 1899

Blondel & Melly

Gold and painted on enamel watch made for the Turkish market

Signed Blondel & Melly à Genève, no. 14035, circa 1830.

Keywound gilt bridge-type lever movement jewelled to the third wheel, balance with bimetallic temperature compensation curb

White enamel dial with Turkish numerals, gilt Breguet hands

Circular case finely painted on enamel with a polychrome military trophy amidst spring and summer flowers on a simulated shagreen ground, engraved gold cuvette

50.5 mm. diam.

Blondel & Melly, watchmakers and retailers, were active at Geneva's Quai des Bergues from around 1820 to 1850. The firm specialized in the production of watches for the Turkish market and was renowned for their high quality of their timepieces, embellished with engravings, enamelled motifs, pearl and precious stone settings and others.

Inv. 1863

Blondel & Melly

18K gold and painted on enamel hunter case minute repeating watch made for the Turkish market

Signed Blondel&Melly à Genève, no. 16158, circa 1840

Keywound cylinder movement repeating with two hammers on two gongs activated by a pull-and-twist piston in the pendant

White enamel dial with Turkish numerals

Circular case decorated on each side with painted on enamel military trophies against a translucent pink ground over engine turning, wavy line border decorated with stylised enamel flowers in white and green

51 mm. diam.

For another enamelled watch made by Blondel & Melly for the Turkish market,
see: Technique and History of the Swiss Watch, Eugène Jaquet and Alfred Chapuis, pl. 95.

Front

Back

Blondel & Melly

18K gold and painted on enamel open face watch with an early winding-mechanism, 18K gold Breguet chain and gold and enamel Breguet ratchet winding-key decorated en suite, made for the Turkish market

Signed Blondel & Melly, retailed by Leroy (signature in Arabic characters), no. 13 328, circa 1840

Keywound cylinder movement with unusual early winding system, going barrel, monometallic balance

White enamel dial with Turkish numerals

Circular case with scallop-edge, twelve curved radiating lobed segments and bezel painted on enamel en grisaille on a black background, with alternating flower motifs, allegories of Love, Arts, Music, Geometry and agriculture

50.7 mm. diam.

The movement of this watch is fitted with an early winding system dating from around the early 1840s, when different watchmakers were experimenting with winding mechanisms in the quest for a keyless method of winding a watch.Perhaps the most famous of these was Jean-Adrien Philippe (1815-1894) who patented his keyless winding and hand-setting system in 1845. Louis-Benjamin Audemars (1782-1833) and his sons and Antoine LeCoultre (1803-1881) all experimented with winding systems at this period.

Inv. 1172

Blondel & Melly

18K gold and painted on enamel open face watch with an early winding mechanism, 18K gold and enamel watch made for the Turkish market

Signed Blondel et Melly à Genève, circa 1835

Keywound movement with ruby cylinder escapement

White enamel dial with Turkish numerals

Circular lobed case with enamel decoration in twelve segments painted with flowers, musical, scientific and agricultural trophies, the decoration continuing on to the bezel

53.5 mm. dwiam.

For another enamelled watch made by Blondel & Melly for the Turkish market, see: Technique and History of the Swiss Watch, Eugène Jaquet and Alfred Chapuis, pl. 95.

Swiss

18K gold and painted on enamel quarter repeating jump-hour watch with ruby cylinder escapement, made for the Turkish market

Signed Répétition Breguet, Geneva, case no. 28283, circa 1840

Keywound gilt ruby cylinder movement with 9 jewels, pare-chute suspension on the top pivot, repeating with two hammers on two gongs activated by a pull-and-twist piston in the pendant

Engine turned silvered dial for the minutes with subsidiary seconds, Turkish 15-minute/ seconds numerals, aperture for the jump-hours above with Turkish numerals

Circular case decorated with a finely painted floral love trophy en grisaille, gold and white enamel wavy-line border, the outer border and bezel with champlevé flowers and gold foliage on a black enamel ground, hinged gold cuvette

50 mm. diam.

A very fine and rare example of a jump-hour watch made for the Turkish market. Made in Switzerland but very much in the style of and in homage Breguet, the movement is fitted with a Breguet style ruby cylinder escapement and the balance pivot with a pare-chute shock absorber, both used extensively by Breguet.

Inv. 1875

Battle of the Nile

George Prior

Gold and painted on enamel triple case quarter repeating watch made for the Turkish market

Signed George Prior, London, movement no. 28128, circa 1800

Keywound full plate verge movement with chain fusée, repeating with two hammers on a bell

White enamel dial with Turkish numerals

Circular triple case, the inner case with pierced band and decorated with enamel flowers, the back decorated with a painted on enamel military and nautical trophies and the union flag within a shield against a translucent pink guilloche enamel background, middle case decorated with a finely painted on enamel naval battle scene of three warships flying French and British flags, outer case with glazed back and wavy-line edge decorated with red and blue champlevé enamel flowers with opaque white enamel borders, case maker's punch mark IM for Jonah Mince, diamond and gem-set thumb-pieces

51 mm. diam.

It is thought that the naval battle scene depicted on this watch represents the Battle of the Nile of 1798. After Trafalgar, the battle of the Nile at Aboukir Bay was Nelson's most famous and decisive victory against the French.

George Prior (1765-c.1830)

The son of John Prior of Nessfield (Yorkshire) who was also a clockmaker, George Prior was a leading London maker of watches for the Turkish and Islamic markets in association with his son Edward Prior. He received at least two awards from the Society of Arts for his mechanical timepieces.

The Priors are perhaps the best known of all the English watch and clockmakers who produced wares almost exclusively for the Sultan of the Ottoman Empire and for the lucrative wider Turkish market in the late-18th and first half of the 19th centuries. Watches signed either George Prior or Edward Prior ranged from relatively modest silver cased everyday pocket watches up to superb and hugely expensive gold cased, jewelled or enamelled watches such as the present watch that would have been purchased or presented by the Sultan himself or high-ranking members of the Ottoman court.

The collection at the Dolmabahçe Palace museum displays clocks by the Priors given as gifts to Sultan Abdülhamid II. Further timepieces by George Prior are in the collection of the Topkapi Museum in Istanbul as well as the Victoria & Albert Museum in London.

Inv. 1090

George Prior

18K four-colour gold large quarter repeating pair case watch made for the Turkish market

Signed George Prior, London, no. 15729, circa 1815

Keywound verge movement with foliate engraved decoration, chain fusée, finely pierced and engraved balance cock, ruby endstone, repeating with hammers on a bell in the back of the case activated by depressing the pendant

White enamel dial with Turkish numerals

Circular case, the outer with four-colour gold raised floral decoration and a central vase issuing flowers, inner case richly florally engraved and pierced for sound emission

60 mm. diam.

Inv. 1821

George Prior

Gold and painted on enamel pearl-set pair cased quarter repeating watch made for the Turkish market

Signed George Prior, London, no.99609, enamel painting in the manner of Jean-Louis Richter, circa 1815

Keywound gilt brass full plate verge movement with chain fusée and turned column pillars, pierce and engraved cock incorporating the initials 'GP',repeating on a bell

White enamel dial with Turkish numerals

Circular cases, the outer case with pearl-set bezel, finely painted on enamel cartouche-shaped scene of a ship in a calm bay with harbour-side buildings and mountains in the background, within a red and blue champlevé enamel frame set with split-pearls, the pierced borders with flower decoration in red and white champlevé enamel, plain inner case

64 mm. diam.

Inv. 1817

George Prior

18K gold pair case watch made for the Turkish market

Signed George Prior, London, no. 1427, circa 1810

Keywound verge movement with foliate engraved decoration, chain fusée, finely pierced and engraved balance cock

White enamel dial with Turkish numerals

Circular case, the outer decorated with green and red champlevé enamel, inner case with a finely painted on enamel scene of an Ottoman shoreline landscape within a red enamel wavy-line border

46 mm. diam.

Actual Size

Edward Prior

18K gold and enamel triple case watch made for the Turkish market

Signed Edward Prior, London, movement no. 45423, case no. 41801, circa 1800

Keywound verge movement, chain fusée, finely pierced and engraved balance cock and foot

White enamel dial with Turkish numerals, gold fleur-de-lys hands

Circular triple case, the outer polychrome enamelled with flowers, glazed centre, 18K gold middle case florally decorated with polychrome enamel to complement the outer case, the centre with a fine painted on enamel scene of a ship in full sail in a calm harbour, 18K gold plain inner case

46 mm. diam.

Actual Size

Inv. 1868

Edward Prior

18K gold and painted on enamel pair case watch made for the Turkish market

Signed Edward Prior, London, no. 40767, the inner case with London hallmarks for 1813

Keywound gilt verge movement with chain fusée, balance cock pierced and engraved with foliate scrolls

White enamel dial with Turkish numerals

Circular case, the plain polished inner case stamped with maker's mark AN, the outer centered by a finely painted on enamel scene of a coastal town with ship on a calm sea and a tower and bridge in the foreground,opalescent sunset sky, bordered by opaque pink, blue, black and white champlevé enamel punctuated by gold foliage

36.5 mm. diam.

Edward Prior was the son of George Prior, and together they were among London's leading makers of watches for the Turkish and Islamic markets.

The Priors are perhaps the best known of all the English watch and clockmakers who produced wares almost exclusively for the Sultan of the Ottoman Empire and for the lucrative wider Turkish market in the late 18th and first half of the 19th centuries. Watches signed either George Prior or Edward Prior ranged from relatively modest silver cased everyday pocket watches up to superb and hugely expensive gold cased, jewelled or enamelled watches such as the present watch that would have been purchased or presented by the Sultan himself or high-ranking members of the Ottoman court.

The collection at the Dolmabahçe Palace museum displays clocks by the Priors given as gifts to Sultan Abdülhamid II. Further timepieces by George Prior are in the collection of the Topkapi Museum in Istanbul as well as the Victoria & Albert Museum in London.

The Prior watches were so popular in Turkey that even now this type of pocket watch, whoever the maker, is called a 'Prior 'Watch' in Turkey.

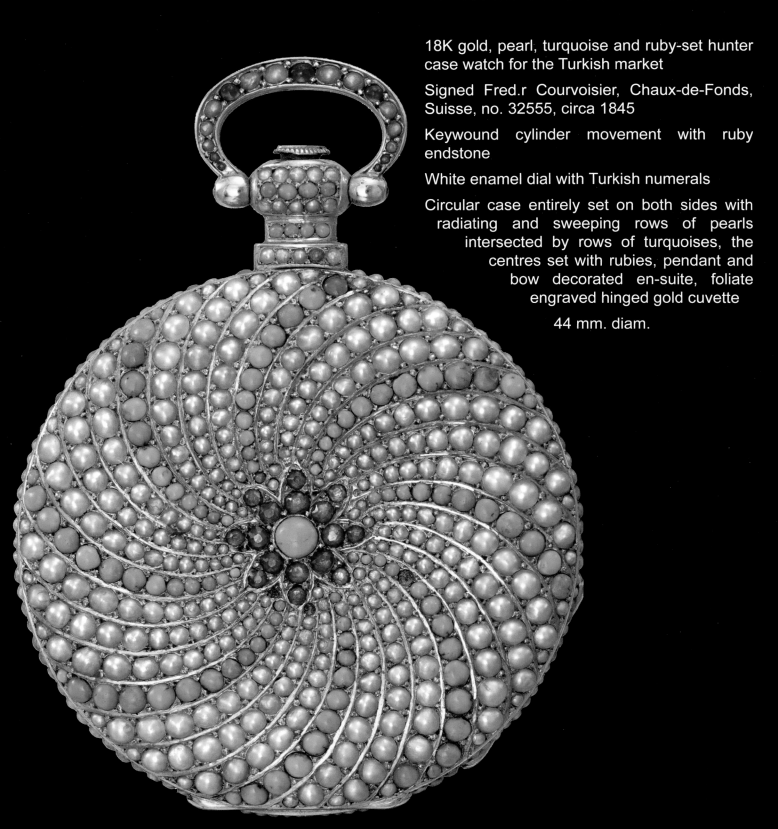

Frederick Courvoisier

18K gold, pearl, turquoise and ruby-set hunter case watch for the Turkish market

Signed Fred.r Courvoisier, Chaux-de-Fonds, Suisse, no. 32555, circa 1845

Keywound cylinder movement with ruby endstone

White enamel dial with Turkish numerals

Circular case entirely set on both sides with radiating and sweeping rows of pearls intersected by rows of turquoises, the centres set with rubies, pendant and bow decorated en-suite, foliate engraved hinged gold cuvette

44 mm. diam.

Uncommonly having a hunter case rather than the more usual open face case and entirely set with pearls and turquoises in a most pleasing swirling design, this watch is one of the most beautiful and sumptuously decorated of the genre.

Frédéric-Alexander Courvoisier, known as "Fritz" (1799–1854) was the second son of Louis (1758-1832) who founded the firm of J. Robert et Fils et Cie with Josué Robert. After several incarnations, the company became known as Courvoisier et Cie between 1811-45. According to Charles Allix, Fritz concentrated more on the commercial side of the business rather than the practical although he had attended horological school in the canton of Neuchâtel run by Henri-Louis Maillardet and Charles Frédéric Klentschi.

Frédéric-Alexander travelled extensively as a representative of the family business. He married in 1826 and after about three years had passed he became involved in serious local political troubles. Rising to the rank of Lieutenant Colonel, in 1831 he was temporarily exiled from the canton. However, after the death of his father in 1832 he and his brothers, Henri-Louis and Philippe-Auguste revived the firm of Couvoisier et Cie. After leaving the family firm in 1842, he set up his own business specializing in retailing watches.

Another watch signed Fred.r Courvoisier is in the Metropolitan Museum of Art, New York (Inv. 26.267.98).

Inv. 1150

Gift of Napoleon III

Auguste Courvoisier & Co.

18K gold and painted on enamel hunter case watch with a portrait of Napoleon III, by repute presented to Abdülaziz, Sultan of the Ottoman Empire

Signed Aug'te Courvoisier & Co., Chaux-de-Fonds, no. 45396, circa 1860

Keywound gilt lever movement

White enamel dial with Turkish numerals

Circular engraved case, the front cover with a finely painted on enamel portrait of Napoleon III within a red, white and blue champlevé

enamel border, the back cover with a painted on enamel view of the Palais de Luxembourg 50 mm. diam.

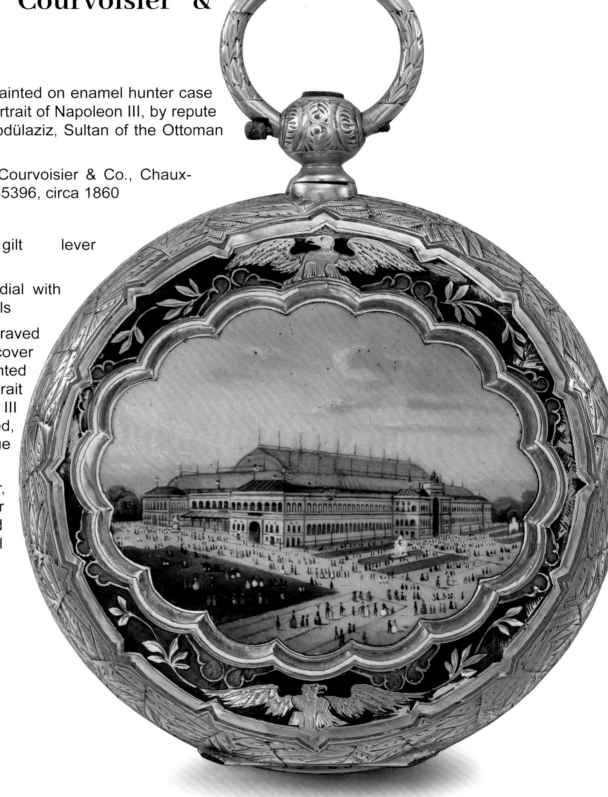

This beautifully enamelled watch is traditionally said to have been presented in Paris by Napoleon III to Abdülaziz, Sultan of the Ottoman Empire (1861-1876) during his official visit to the French capital in 1876.

Napoleon III and Empress Eugénie invited Sultan Abdülaziz to the International Paris Exhibition of 1867. It was exceptional for an Ottoman Sultan to leave his country due to security reasons and leaving the empire temporarily without a ruler. Sultan Abdülaziz's journey to Europe in 1867 was therefore a highly significant event in Ottoman history and lasted forty-seven days in all. He arrived in Paris with an entourage of fifty-six on 30 June, where he was welcomed by Emperor Napoleon III and the Empress Eugénie. Sultan Abdülaziz stayed in Paris for the next 10 days paying official visits, and attending the opening of the International Exhibition. From Paris the Sultan then travelled to England where he stayed as a guest of Queen Victoria at Buckingham Palace for eleven days.

The watchmaker Auguste Courvoisier was at times associated with Courvoisier & Co. and also with Courvoisier Frères, he also signed clocks and watches in his own name.

Swiss

Gold and painted on enamel pair case watch made for the Turkish market, accompanied by a heavy gold oval table snuff box with painted on enamel decoration matching the watch

Unsigned, case no. 15610, circa 1800

Keywound verge movement, chain fusée, engraved and pierced balance cock

Engine turned gold with scroll decoration and white enamel cartouches with Turkish numerals, outer white enamel minutes chapter ring with Turkish numerals

Circular case, the outer case with twenty lobed segments decorated in polychrome enamel with alternating flowers and fruits on the front and flowers, musical, military and love trophies to the back, finely painted central scene of a ship in full sail in a calm harbour with a translucent sky, inner case decorated with a complementary scene with scallop-edge border and surrounded by eight oval reserves decorated with flowers, translucent red ground, pink enamel and foliate chased gold band. Gold cuvette chased with stylised foliage on a blue enamel ground

Oval table snuff box with lobed segments and finely painted on enamel scenes to match the watch

52 mm. diam.

A remarkable pairing of two different yet almost identically decorated objet de luxe made for the Turkish market. Undoubtedly created in the same workshop, these pieces were designed not only to demonstrate the high art of the goldsmith and enamellist but also, by extension, the discerning taste and connoisseurship of the owner.

Inv. 1112

Sultan Abdulmejit I

Santiago James Moore French

18K gold and enamel hunter case lever chronometer watch with enamel portrait of Sultan Abdülmejid I of Turkey

Swiss, signed by the retailer J. M. French, London, "Demi-Chronometre", case no. 36629, circa 1850

Keywound lateral lever movement

White enamel dial with Turkish numerals

Circular engraved case with polychrome enamel portrait of Sultan Abdülmejid I within a green and gilt scroll swag and floral border, the back decorated with a polychrome enamel view of the historical peninsula of Istanbul, gold cuvette inscribed 'Demi-Chronometre'

49 mm. diam.

Santiago James Moore French was a fine maker and prestigious retailer who signed his watches variously: French, Santiago James Moore French, J. M. French. He is listed as working at 14-15 Sweetings Alley between 1808 and 1838 and at 18 Cornhill between 1840 and 1842. After his death in 1842 the business was taken

over by the Spanish immigrant watchmaker J.R. Losada, who had worked for French ,and married his widow. Abdülmejid I (1823–1861) was the 31st Sultan of the Ottoman Empire and succeeded his father Mahmud II on 2 July 1839. His rweign was notable for the rise of nationalist movements within the empire's territories. Abdulmejid wanted to encourage Ottomanism among the secessionist subject nations and stop the rise of nationalist movements within the empire, but failed to succeed despite trying to integrate non-Muslims and non-Turks more thoroughly into Ottoman society with new laws and reforms. He tried to forge alliances with the major powers of Western Europe, namely the United Kingdom and France, who fought alongside the Ottoman Empire in the Crimean War against Russia. In the following Congress of Paris on 30 March 1856, the Ottoman Empire was officially included among the European family of nations. Abdulmejid's biggest achievement was the announcement and application of the Tanzimat reforms which were prepared by his father and effectively started the modernisation of the Ottoman Empire in 1839. For this achievement, one of the Imperial anthems of the Ottoman Empire, the March of Abdulmejid, was named after him.

Inv. 1113

Tavannes Watch Co.

18K gold and painted on enamel watch made for the Turkish market

Signed Tavannes Watch Co., movement no. 944809, circa 1915

Keyless lever movement

Two-tone dial with Breguet numerals

Circular case, the back cover decorated with a painted on enamel view of the Golden Horn and Topkapi Palace in Istanbul, translucent Royal blue enamel border with chased rococo scrolls, coin-edge band

50 mm. diam.

The Golden Horn joins the Bosphorus Strait at the point where the strait meets the Sea of Marmara, the waters of the Golden Horn define the northern boundary of the peninsula constituting 'Old Istanbul' (ancient Byzantium and Constantinople). This inlet geographically separates the historic centre of Istanbul from the rest of the city, and forms a horn-shaped, sheltered harbour that has protected trade ships for thousands of years.

Inv.1117

Movado

18K gold and painted on enamel dress watchmade for the Turkish Market

Signed Movado, Chronomètre, case no. 5429, circa 1914

Keyless eccentric and small nickel-finished lever movement, 15 jewels

Elongated oval-shaped silvered matte dial with Roman numerals

Circular case with dial aperture to the upper half, engraved monogram to the lower half, the hinged back with a finely painted on enamel polychrome portrait of Şeyhülislam ve evkaf nazırı Ürgüplü Hayri Efendi, signed E.V. 1914

46 mm. diam.

Mustafa Hayri Efendi (1867-1922) from Urgup, was a Sheikh of Islam from 1914 to 1916.

Known as Heyri Bey, he studied at the Istanbul School of Law, later serving as the Minister of Justice and head of the State Council.

Inv. 1118

Robert Roskell

Gold and painted on enamel hunting cased noble presentation watch made for the Turkish market

Signed Robert Roskell, Liverpool, movement no. 13539, case no. 17539, circa 1850

Keywound full plate English lever movement with chain fusée, finely florally engraved cock, diamond endstone

White enamel dial with Turkish numerals, subsidiary seconds at 3 o'clock

Circular case entirely engraved, the front cover decorated with a painted on enamel portrait of a nobleman within a champlevé enamel border, the back engraved with a monogram beneath a princely crown, case maker's punch mark 'D&A'

53 mm. diam.

Robert Roskell is recorded as being active from 1798 and worked in both London and Liverpool. He is especially well-known for his watches with rack lever escapement and later for watches with Massey's lever escapements. The firm of Hunt & Roskell was founded in London in 1844.

Inv. 1616

Swiss

Gold and painted on enamel lady's hunter case nautical pendant watch made for the Turkish market

Unsigned, case maker's punch mark HL, case no. 130388, circa 1860

Keyless cylinder movement

White enamel dial with blue Turkish numerals

Anchor-shaped case formed with engraved stylised waves highlighted with black champlevé enamel, the front cover and back decorated with oval painted on enamel panels depicting a galleon at sea and a steamboat near a lighthouse, both scenes with a moonlit cloudy sky, engine turned gold cuvette

30 mm. diam.

Very few lady's watches were ever produced specifically for the Turkish market. This watch was perhaps a special commission, the nautical theme throughout with anchor and wave-shaped case and fine painted on enamel scenes of ships by moonlight are very atmospheric and unusual.

Fatio Junod

Gold and painted on enamel pair case quarter repeating watch made for the Turkish market

Signed Fatio-Junod à Genève, no. 24502, circa 1850

Keywound gilt cylinder movement quarter repeating with two hammers on two gongs

White enamel dial with Turkish numerals

Circular scallop-edged case, the inner case finely painted on enamel with a scene of a galleon in full sale in a sea port against an opalescent sky over sunray engine turning, outer case decorated with polychrome champlevé enamel around the glazed aperture

49 mm. diam.

Jacques-Alphonse Fatio-Junod was a maker of repute, he is best known for his bagnolet watches known as 'calibre Fatio-Junod'.

Fatio-Junod is recorded working in Geneva's Plainpalais quarter, Chemin Gourgas, from 1844 to 1861.

Inv. 1791

Swiss

Gold, champlevé and painted on enamel watch made for the Turkish market

Unsigned, probably Geneva, circa 1840

Keywound cylinder movement

White enamel dial with Turkish numerals, blued steel hour and minute hands pierced with cintamani and crescent star motif

Circular case engraved and decorated with green and black champlevé enamel strapwork and quatrefoil borders, central reserve painted on enamel with a view of a pavilion within a woodland, the reverse with a steamship arriving into a tropical port

46 mm. diam.

Inv. 1864

Alliez, Bachelard & TerondFils

18K gold and painted on enamel musical and quarter repeating watch made for the Turkish market

Signed Alliez, Bachelard &Terond, Genève, circa 1835

Keywound cylinder movement with music at the hours and quarter repeating on bell activated by depressing the pendant

White enamel dial with Turkish numerals

Circular case decorated with polychrome champlevé enamel and a central painted bouquet of flowers on a pale blue background, lever at 1 o'clock for melody silence

57 mm. diam.

In partnership from 1820 to around 1845, the company took the name Alliez, Bachelard et Terond Fils around 1828 and in 1829 petitioned together with others for a new observatory. Alliez, Bachelard et Terond Fils specialised in watches with Champlevé enamel, watches with enamel paintings, musical watches, repeaters and skeletonised watches, in full plate as well as Lepine caliber. They also produced watches for the Italian, French and Spanish markets.

Inv. 1792

Swiss

Gold, champlevé and painted on enamel jump hour watch made for the Turkish market

Unsigned, circa 1830

Keywound cylinder movement, gold cuvette enhanced by flowering vines in gold and opaque powder blue champlevé enamel, against a guilloché ground with translucent peach enamel

White enamel dial with Turkish numerals, aperture for jumping hours, eccentric minutes chapter ring, subsidiary seconds

Circular case with apertures displaying hours and seconds, each framed in lobed cartouches depicting bursts of spring flowers, the background with opaque blue champlevé enamel and flowering vines, the reverse with polychrome painted on enamel scene of ships anchored offshore under an opalescent sky within a scalloped frame

48 mm. diam.

Jump hour watches enjoyed a brief spell of popularity during the first half of the 19th century. Those made especially for the Turkish market are extremely rare. This watch, with its sumptuously enamelled gold case is one of the most beautiful examples known.

The jump hour system works because the usual motion work for the usual hour hand is dispensed with, the hour numerals being mounted on a ring and wheel geared directly to another wheel on the hour snail star wheel. Because the hour numeral ring is driven from it the numerals 'jump' with the star wheel to display each successive hour in the aperture.

This watch is illustrated and described in: Collectors Encyclopedia of Pendant & Pocket Watches, 1500-1950, C. Jeanenne, p. 343.

TURKISH WATCH

Inv. 1871

Bulugat

Early silver, niello and pearl-set oval pre-balance spring single-hand watch made for the Turkish market

Signed Ameli Sahibi Bulugat,

Galata, Constantinople, circa 1650

Oval gilded full plate verge movement with pearl-set pillars, three-wheel train, chain fusée, the nielloed backplate entirely and minutely engraved with scrolling foliage, steel balance wheel, pierced and engraved foliate cock with pointed foot secured by a single screw, regulation dial with Turkish numerals, Islamic inscription within a lobed cartouche

Oval nielloed dial entirely decorated with foliage and flowers, applied gilt chapter ring with pearl hour markers, engraved Turkish numerals and leaf half-hour markers, gilt single baluster hand

Oval silver case of European shape with hinged cover over the dial, entirely nielloed with stylised geometric flowers and foliage, pendant with loose ring bow

44x51 mm

Of exceptional quality, this watch, dating from the mid-17th century, before the invention of the balance spring, is one of the earliest surviving Turkish timepieces. Exquisitely decorated throughout with niello, this intriguing oval watch is constructed in the manner of a European watch of the same period yet appears to be entirely of Turkish workmanship. The European form of the case, dial and movement have been given a highly distinctive Eastern flavour in their construction and decoration, leaving no doubt that the maker must have been one of the finest native Turkish watchmakers. The close similarity of the movement of this watch to the movement of a wall clock in the Topkapi Museum by Bulugat show that it was made by the same hand.

Although clocks and watches are known to have existed in and around the Ottoman capital Constantinople as early as the 16th century, none are known to survive today. It is not widely realised that by the early 17th century, the suburb of Galata in Constantinople (Istanbul) had become an established colony of foreign goldsmiths, watchmakers and engravers. Although the Galata community was reserved for westerners, there were several Turkish clock and watchmakers who must have worked amongst the European immigrants and therefore become familiar with European styles and methods of construction. It is also probable that the European watchmakers supplied some of the basic parts which were then assembled and finished by the Turkish makers. Little is known about Turkish watchmakers biographically at this period, but some of them are known by name from the signatures found on surviving timepieces, these include: Bulugat, Sahin, Abdurrahman, Seyh Dede, Mehmed Su Liku, Terjuman Oglu and Mustafa Aksarayi.

The first western clock and watchmakers who became residents of Galata at the end of the 16th century were sent to maintain and repair clocks that had been presented as diplomatic gifts to the Sultan Murad III (1546-1595) who had a particular fascination for mechanical timekeeping. The famous diamond merchant Jean Baptiste Tavernier, who visited Istanbul in 1630, records the existence of watchmakers there working in the palace treasury.

By the mid-18th century, up to 160 people of several nationalities inhabited Galata including French, Genoese Italian, Swiss and German. They became known as 'Galatakari'. Swiss watchmakers had been trading with the Ottomans via French intermediaries since the late 16th century, one well-documented Swiss maker working in Galata was the Geneva-born watchmaker Isaac Rousseau (1672-1747), son of the master-clockmaker David Rousseau. Isaac was given the responsibility of regulating the pendulums in the Topkapi Palace, an important role, because these clocks regulated the exact time for Islamic prayers.

A Turkish wall clock by Bulugat is in the collection of the Topkapi Museum in Istanbul, (Inv. 53.86) which dates from around 1650. It has a single hand showing the hours, and the finish and decoration of the movement bears close similarity to the present watch.

Other examples of mid-17th century Turkish watches including one signed Arlo (Arlaud), Galata, are in the collection of the late Sir David Salomons, L. A. Meyer Memorial Institute for Islamic Art, Jerusalem.

A further mid-17th century oval example is in the Metropolitan Museum of Art in New York, the gift of J. Pierpont Morgan, 1917, (17.190.1560).

<u>Literature:</u>

Watches and Clocks in the Sir David Salomons Collection, George Daniels and Ohannes Markarian, 1983, p. 110.

Catalogue of Clocks and Watches in the Topkapi Sarayi Museum, Wolfgang Meyer.

European Clocks and Watches in The Metropolitan Museum of Art, Clare Vincent, Jan Hendrik Leopold, Elizabeth Sullivan.

CHAPTER 4

EROTIC

Erotic

Watchmakers in France, England and Switzerland, in particular Geneva, made examples of the rather risqué art of the erotic watch, the creation of which required the finest watchmaking and enamelling skills.

More often than not, beneath a seemingly innocent exterior, these pocket watches are the hidden stage for erotic and, in some cases musically accompanied scenes revealed by the pushing of a hidden button or a discreet slide on the case. Manufactured in very small quantities for selected customers, the sensual secrets of these watches were only to be viewed in private or with one's closest friends.

The history of erotic watches begins at the time of Louis XV when noblemen would enjoy showing such scenes to innocent young ladies to make them blush and, possibly, seduce them. Only a handful of such early erotic watches survive from the second half of the 18th century. The Masis Collection is fortunate to have two examples of these very rare pieces made by the celebrated James Cox, including a heart-shaped watch with two concealed erotic scenes.

In the construction of erotic watches, the watchmakers devised several different ways of concealing their true nature. Some erotic watches have painted enamel scenes which were hidden underneath the back cover or even a second cover that was seamless when closed. Some watches have automaton scenes that were concealed behind a sliding panel opened by a small slide on the case band. Even the grandest Geneva makers such as Henri Capt produced magnificent erotic watches, sometimes with a complicated 'innocent' automaton scene at the front; the erotic scene under the back cover was reserved for the owner's private amusement.

The decoration of a watch's case or the concealing panel sometimes alluded to what could be found within upon closer inspection. A favourite theme was the depiction of a goat. The goat was an ancient symbol used to represent lust, one of the seven deadly sins and therefore highly appropriate.

Erotic scenes were of course seen as shocking and were forbidden by the Church. As a result, the clergy regularly became the subject of the watchmaker's humour. Priests, nuns and monks featured in explicit scenarios usually within a church setting. Such subjects naturally added an extra elicit frisson for the viewer.

The Masis Collection contains one of the finest groups of erotic watches in private hands. The watches in the collection are chosen for their variety and ingenuity, pieces representing the earliest mid-18th century examples through to the late 19th century.

Swiss

18K pink gold semi-skeletonised quarter repeating openface jaquemart automaton watch with concealed erotic automaton

Unsigned, movement no. 3467, case no. 3467/9327, circa 1830

Keywound verge movement, chain fusée, quarter repeating through the pendant with two polished steel hammers on two gongs

White enamel annular chapter ring with Breguet style numerals, applied varicoloured gold standing classical automaton figures appearing to strike the hours and quarters on two bells when the repeating is activated, a panel below decorated with a cupid slides open to reveal an amorous couple on a chaise longue against a blued steel background

Circular case with reeded band, repeating locking bolt in the band and slide for opening the panel revealing the erotic automaton

55 mm. diam.

Inv. 1823

Johan Georg

Silver and Viennese painted on enamel hunter case pendant watch with concealed erotic scene

Signed Jo. Georg, Gratz, (Austria), circa 1830

Keywound gilt-finished verge movement with chain fusée, pierced and engraved balance cock

Enamel dial with Roman numerals and painted with a scene depicting two Cupids holding the Arrows of Love

Circular silver case, the interior of the front cover depicting a lady observing her reflection in a hand mirror held by Cupid possibly representing an allegory of Virtue, outer front cover depicting Apollo and the Muses of Music, Literature and Geography, the back cover painted with a love scene watched by Cupid, possibly depicting the allegory of Perfect Love, concealed erotic scene inside the back of the case under the movement

44 mm. diam.

Inv. 1124

Musy Père et Fils

18K varicoloured gold, ruby and turquoise-set quarter repeating watch with concealed painted on enamel erotic scene

Signed Musy Père et Fils, Horlogers de S.A.S., a Turin, circa 1830

Keywound movement repeating with two hammers on two gongs activated by depressing the pendant

Gold dial with Roman numerals

Circular case richly decorated with varicoloured gold flowers and set with rubies and turquoises, the back cover opening to reveal a finely painted on enamel erotic scene on the cuvette

48 mm. diam.

This lavishly decorated and exceptionally well preserved watch is an unusual example of the type in having an erotic scene concealed under the back cover. It is quite likely to have been a special order piece for a member of the Italian nobility of even the Royal family.

Musy Père et Fils were jewellers and watchmakers to the Savoy Kings and Crown Princes of Italy, established in Turin about 1707, the firm's signature and declaration "Horlogers de S.A.S." is an abbreviation of "Son Altesse sérénissime" or "Serene Highness".

Children of the Kings and Princes of Italy were entitled to the prefix Royal Highness, but more distant male descendants were Serene Highnesses by right.

Few watches are known signed by Musy Père et Fils. A signed Royal presentation jewelled gold box was sold at Christie's London, 2-3rd June, 2015, lot 252. A signed pendule d'officier clock was sold at Sotheby's Amsterdam, 21st November, 2007, lot 516.

Inv. 1154

Swiss

Very small gold and enamel watch with skeletonised movement and concealed erotic scene

Unsigned, circa 1760

Keywound cylinder movement with skeletonized plates, chain fusée

White enamel dial with Roman numerals

Circular 'Louis XV' case, the back decorated with a translucent blue champlevé enamel scene of two goats in a wooded arbour, opening to reveal the polychrome painted on enamel erotic scene, the inner back glazed to view the movement

34 mm. diam.

This small and early erotic watch is one of only a handful to survive from the second half of the 18th century. The decoration of the outer case depicting two goats alludes to the erotic nature of the watch, the goat was an ancient symbol used to represent lust, one of the seven deadly sins.

Inv. 1414

Swiss

18K gold shell-shaped quarter repeating watch with concealed erotic automaton and the original fitted leather covered shell-shaped fitted box

Unsigned, circa 1815

Keywound cylinder movement with open barrel, quarter repeating on a bell

Small white enamel dial with Arabic numerals, blue enamel background with applied silver mounts decorated with a hunting scene and flowers, the erotic automaton scene concealed behind double doors animated when the repeating is activated

Shell-shaped ribbed case with hinged ribbed glass front cover

57 mm. diam.

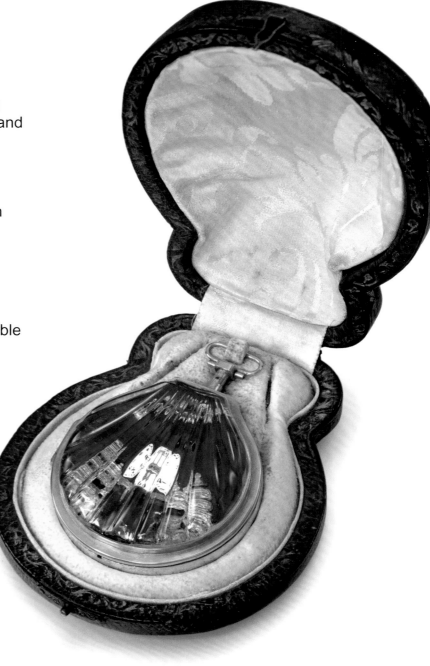

James Cox

Gilt metal heart-shaped watch with two concealed painted on enamel erotic scenes and visible balance

Signed James Cox, London, no. 402, made for the Chinese market, circa 1780

Keywound heart-shaped gilt brass full plate verge movement, chain fusée

White enamel dial with Roman numerals on the left, on the right slow/fast regulator dial, at the bottom aperture for the balance oscillating against a polished plate, all set into a blue enameled mask painted with gold scrolls

Heart-shaped case, hinged back with painted on enamel riverside landscape, the inside of the back with a scene in which a gentleman considers his options in the preliminaries to the art of love while a servant secretly looks on, on the inside dome, another painting of the couple as the scene continues, the counter-enamel with a bouquet of forget-me-nots

52 x 42 mm.

Provenance:

The collection of The Lord Sandberg (1927-2017)

Literature:

The Sandberg Collection book, p. 238-239.

Illustrated and described in 'Les Heures de l'Amour' by Roland Carrera, Editions Scriptar/Antiquorum, Geneva, 1993, p. 37.

James Cox (1723-1800) operated as a jeweller and goldsmith from his London premises at Shoe Lane, off Fleet Street. He was perhaps more in the style of a Continental marchand mercier as he also acted as agent for a number of Swiss watchmakers. His entrepreneurial nature led him to purchase the Chelsea Porcelain Factory from Nicholas Sprimont in 1769, only to sell it the following year to William Duesbury's Derby concern.

The St. James's Chronicle of 27-29 August 1772 reported that a shipment of 'English Toys' had been refused entry to China and had returned to London. This appears to have been the impetus behind Cox's opening of a Museum at Spring Gardens, Charing Cross, where the paying public could view his stock in trade. It was in the kunstkammer tradition and such private museums of curiosities were much in evidence at this period; such as Sir Ashton Lever's 'Leverian' (opened 1775) and later William Bullock's 'Egyptian Hall' (opened 1811). Cox's Museum ceased in 1775 when the contents were sold via a Public Lottery. Cox's son, John Henry, also oversaw the firm in a variety of guises operating from Canton and London but its success of the late 1760s and 1770s was its zenith with exports to China, India and Russia.

Inv. 1753

James Cox

18K gold and painted on enamel watch with three concealed erotic scenes made for the Chinese market

Signed James Cox, London, No. 1586, circa 1775

Keywound gilt brass full plate verge movement with chain fusée, single-footed gilt brass cock pierced and engraved with mask at the base, rack and pinion regulator

White enamel dial with Roman numerals,elaborate gold hands

Circular case, the back cover painted with a vase of flowers against a chiaroscuro grey-green background, the bezel decorated with green champlevé enamel leaves and engraving, the inside of the back cover with a painted enamel scene with a nude woman holding in the one hand a goblet given to her by Pan, the personification of Lust, in the other the main attribute of the Satyr. The inner dome painted with two lovers on a sofa engaged in a riding lesson, on the other side of the inner dome the same couple is depicted as the scene continues

40 mm. diam.

Vve Henri Leuba

18K gold minute repeating hunter case two-train independent jump centre seconds keyless watch with concealed erotic automaton made for the Eastern market

Signed V. H. Leuba, Chaux-de-Fonds, Suisse, no. 46464, circa 1895

Keyless lever movement, two-train independent centre seconds, tandem winding, fully jewelled, minute repeating with two hammers on two gongs

White enamel dial with outer Roman numerals and inner Turkish numerals

Circular case with repeat locking bolt in the band and five-bar hinge, hinged gold cuvette opening to reveal the polychrome painted on enamel erotic scene activated with the repeating

56 mm. diam.

Vve Henri Leuba signed variously in either Russian or French. At the 1900 Exposition Universelle they exhibited as a maker of watches with branches in Moscow and Warsaw. On display were large and small watches in gold cases as well as special designs for the Russian market.

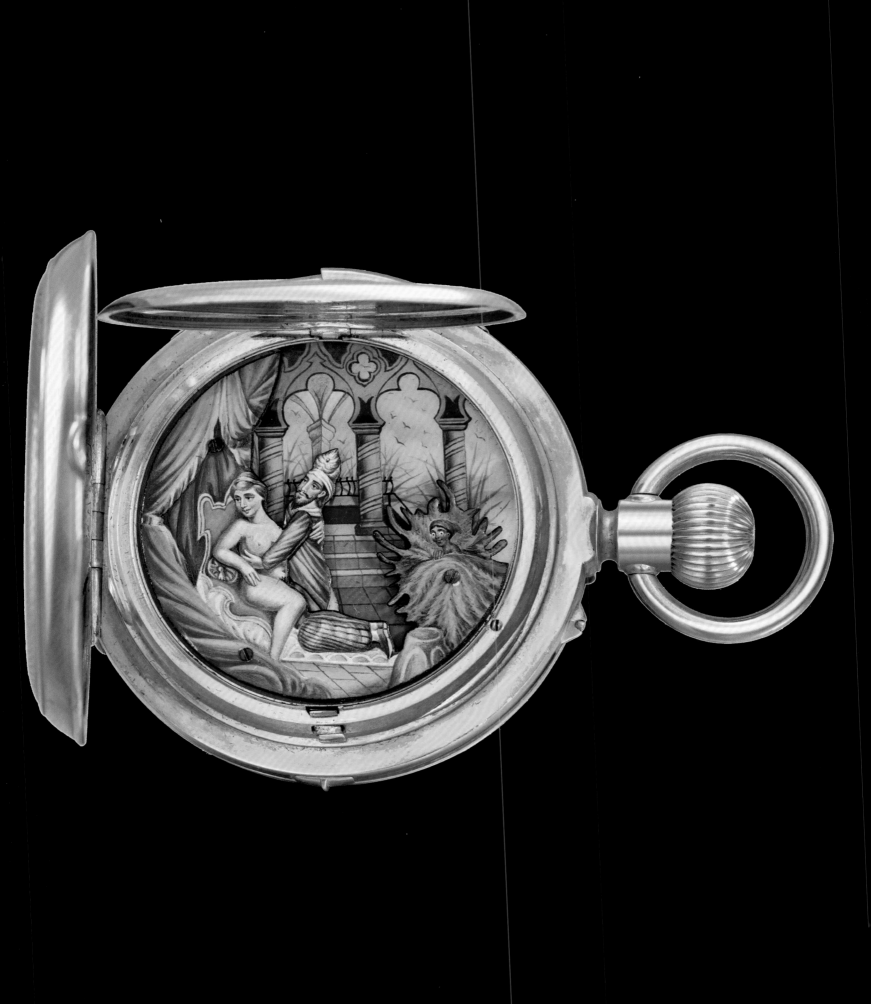

CHAPTER 5

AUTOMATON

Automaton Watches

The fascination with automata from which these incredible animated creations sprang has a long and distinguished history stretching back to ancient Greece.

It is said that King Solomon had a throne guarded by mechanical beasts that roared as he approached. The Ottomans produced automated birds that sang, immortalised in William Butler Yeats's poem Sailing to Byzantium –"But such a form as Grecian goldsmiths make, Of hammered gold and gold enamelling, To keep a drowsy Emperor awake; Or set upon a golden bough to sing".

However, it was the Swiss mechanician Pierre Jaquet Droz who, along with the Englishman James Cox and later the Geneva makers Henri Capt, John Rich, Isaac Piguet and Philippe Meylan, achieved a level of ingenuity and craftsmanship in the late 18th and early 19th centuries which enabled the realisation of extraordinary and precious automaton watches such as those found on the following pages. Production of the finest Swiss automaton watches required the skills not only of the watchmaker but also the goldsmith and enameller. Naturally, companies such as Piguet & Meylan and Henri Capt worked tirelessly to create ever more complicated and novel automaton watches, often with the addition of a miniature musical mechanism incorporated within the movement. The automaton scenes themselves are very imaginative, some of those in the Masis Collection range from domestic and bucolic workshop scenes such as Pierre Simon Gounouilhou's 'Dutch kitchen', the 'blacksmith's workshop' and the 'cooper's yard' through to Elysian and classical scenes featuring figures from Greek and Roman mythology. One of the numerous highlights of the Masis Colllection is Henri Capt's 'seesaw' watch of circa 1820 with an exceptional six automaton actions and a further concealed erotic automaton at the back.

Another strength of this collection is the so-called 'jaquemart' repeating automaton watch. The jaquemart watch usually features two or sometimes three gold automaton figures flanking the dial which, when the repeating is activated, seemingly strike bells for the hours and quarters. The group of watches with variations on this theme in the collection offer a rare and fascinating insight into the huge variety and technical differences between these automatons that are so rarely seen together for direct comparison.

To further delight the reader is a charming 'Adam & Eve' automaton watch inspired by the account of the sixth day of creation when God created Adam and Eve. The painted scene depicts Paradise with Adam and Eve and an automaton serpent revolving on the border.

Swiss

18K gold openface quarter repeating jaquemart automaton watch

Signed Berthoud a Paris, Swiss made, no. 83530, circa 1810

Keywound full plate gilt-finished verge movement, chain fusée, pierced and engraved balance cock, repeating on gongs activated by depressing the pendant

White enamel dial with Breguet numerals, deep blue enamel surround with applied varicoloured gold jacks in fashionable early 19th century dress apparently striking the hours and quarter hours on bells in unison with the repeating, a dog below

Circular case with ribbed band, gilt cuvette hinged to the movement ring

56 mm. diam.

The present watch is a high quality quarter repeating jaquemart automaton made in Switzerland at the beginning of the 19th century. In order to enhance the commercial prestige of their watches, some Swiss makers signed their watches spuriously with the names of some of the great French makers of the day, in this case Berthoud. Examples signed "Breguet" for the same reason are sometimes encountered. This practice in no way detracts from the watches themselves which are often, as with the present watch, beautifully made and highly regarded in their own right.

Inv. 1147

Attributed to Piguet & Meylan

18K pink gold musical, quarter repeating and automaton watch with four automaton actions, playing music on the hour or at will

Attributed to Piguet & Meylan, Geneva, movement and case no. 11795, circa 1820

Keywound cylinder movement with barrels for the going and musical trains, brass escape wheel and third wheel jewelled. Sur plateau musical movement with 29 tuned steel teeth playing on both sides of the pinned disc, silence/musique lever protruding from under the cuvette.

Central white enamel dial with Arabic numerals, painted on enamel scene of a classical garden with two applied multi-coloured gold cherubs resting on urns apparently striking the hours and quarters on bells, applied multi-coloured gold automaton below of a seated man playing the lyre and a cherub striking the triangle in a landscape

Circular case punched with master mark IE, reeded band, polished bezels, pendant and bow, engine turned back, the interior with engraved dedication, bolts for the music and repeat locking in the band. Hinged gilt-metal cuvette with apocryphal signature

58 mm. diam.

The master mark 'IE' punched on the inside of the caseback is that of the case maker who made many cases for Piguet & Meylan in Geneva.

This automaton is of higher specification than most, with four animations on the dial instead of the usual two.

Henri Capt, along with Isaac Piguet and Philippe Meylan, was the foremost maker of small musical automata in the late 18th and early 19th centuries. Most of his work is not signed, although he sometimes scratched his name on his movements they are rarely fully signed.

Henry-Daniel Capt was born in Chenit in 1773, he married Henriette Piguet. He specialised in the production of complicated watches, musical watches and automaton watches. Among the first in Geneva to use the musical mechanism with pinned cylinder and tuned teeth comb, he was famous for his snuffboxes with music and automaton scenes.

From Ventôse 16, An X (March 7, 1802), to 1811, he formed a partnership with Daniel Isaac Piguet, who was from the same village as he. Their signature was Piguet & Capt. In 1811, when Piguet broke off to join Meylan in a new partnership, Henry-Daniel Capt continued to work on his own until, in 1830, he went into partnership with Aubert and son, Place Bel-Air. Their signature was AUBERT & CAPT. They were among the first Genevan makers to produce watches with chronographs. In 1844 the workshop was at 108, rue Neuve in Geneva. It was then managed by Capt's son, Henry Capt Jr. After a short time it moved to 85, rue de la Fusterie, and in 1851, to 177, rue du Rhône. In 1880, the firm was bought by Gallopin and its name became H. Capt Horloger, Maison Gallopin Successeurs, a trademark registered on November 1, 1880, under the No. 44. This signature was only used for watches retailed in their own store, the watches supplied to other retailers being merely signed Henry Capt.

Inv. 1128

Courvoisier & Comp.

18K gold carillon quarter repeating skeletonized three-action jaquemart automaton watch with three hammers and three gongs

Signed Courvoisier & Comp., no. 42150, circa 1820

Keywound cylinder movement, skeletonised, repeating with three hammers on three gongs, diamond endstone

Annular white enamel dial with Arabic numerals, skeletonised centre surmounted by a varicoloured gilt scene depicting a standing gentleman striking a scythe, a monkey striking a triangle held by a hand protruding from a cloud above and a bird striking a bell, all apparently in unison with the repeating and observed by a fox, activated with the repeating

Circular case with engine turned back, casemaker's punch mark PHMI

59 mm. diam.

Jaquemart automatons with three or more figure sequences are extremely rare. This automaton is not only very attractive but particularly rare in having carillon repeating with three hammers on three gongs. Very few jaquemart watches are known with three actions, the majority having only two. The finely chased varicolored gold scene is both charming and unusual, a gentleman as the hour striking jack and a monkey striking a triangle as the first quarter jack. At the same time the bird moves its head in a pecking motion on a bell as the second quarter jack.

Inv. 1084

Swiss

18K gold openface quarter repeating jaquemart automaton watch with hidden automata scene and five actions

Unsigned, case no. 8531, circa 1810

Keywound full plate gilt-finished verge movement, chain fusée, pierced and engraved balance cock

Annular white enamel dial with Breguet numerals, blued steel Breguet hands, centred by an applied varicoloured gold classical architectural landscape, an automaton scene depicting punch fighting chronos appearing to the upper part in unison with the hour repeating, two cherubs below apparently striking the quarter hours in unison with the repeating

Circular case with ribbed band, casemaker's punch mark HC, repeating through the pendant, repeating locking bolt in the band, gilt cuvette

58 mm. diam.

"Jaquemart. figure de fer ou de fonte, représentant un homme armé, laquelle on met d'ordinaire sur le haut d'une tour pour frapper les heures avec un marteau sur la cloche de l'horloge." - *"figure made of solid or cast iron representing a man in arms, which is usually put up on top of a (clock) tower to strike the hours with a hammer onto the bell of the clock."*

Watches decorated with the miniature versions of these clock tower 'men in arms' were very popular in the early 19th century.

Comparable to several known signed examples made by Fres. Esquivillon & Deschoudens of Geneva, the present watch depicts a representation of Pulcinella combatting the passing of time represented the winged figure of chronos with his scythe. The Pulcinella figure is based on the famous 16th century personage of Italy's commedia dell'arte, he is known in many countries under different names such as 'Mr. Punch', 'Polichinelle' or 'Kasperl'.

The repertory of Pulcinella's 'descendants' corresponds broadly with that of their forebears: the protagonist fights with the beast (monstrous dog or crocodile), he has to fight to the death. He is confronted with the hangman and the gallows, but always triumphs over his opponents.

Inv. 1140

Angelica & Medoro

Achard & Fils

18K gold, painted on enamel and pearl-set openface quarter repeating jaquemart automaton watch with repeating on a bell

Signed G. Achard & Fils, Genf, no. 13646, circa 1810

Keywound full plate gilt-finished verge movement, chain fusée, pierced and engraved balance cock, repeating with two hammers on a bell

Small white enamel dial with Breguet numerals, blued steel Breguet hands, applied varicoloured gold jaquemart figures apparently striking the quarter hours in unison with the repeating, oil painted on metal landscape background,

Circular case with pearl-set bezel, finely painted on enamel scene of a young couple in classical costume entitled 'Angelica Médoro', floral and pearl-set decoration and border, repeating through the pendant

57 mm. diam.

The subject of Angelica and Medoro is derived from Ariosto's epic poem Orlando Furioso, first published in 1516.

Angelica, an Asian princess at the court of Charlemagne, was being courted by the Christian hero Orlando but fell in love with the Moorish Medoro. Together they carved their names on a tree, causing Orlando to fly into a jealous rage.

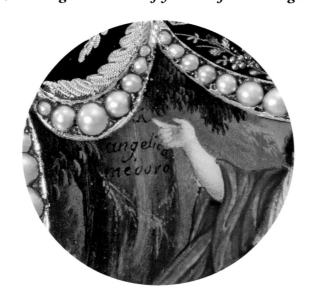

Inv. 1148

Charles Reuge

18K gold large hunter case two-train musical centre seconds pocket watch with automaton violinist, playing two tunes on a pinned cylinder at will, made for the Eastern market

Signed Charles Reuge, a Sainte Croix, no. 1297, the case with London hallmarks for 1884-1885

Keyless lever movement with double train and differential winding, musical train with pinned cylinder and 35 steel toothed comb playing two tunes at will: The Lagoon's Waltz and The Daughter of the Regiment

Two-piece white enamel dial with Roman numerals, the centre painted with a seated violinist in an interior, one arm automated holding the violin bow and activated when the music plays

Circular case with master mark JM, hinged gold cuvette with illegible engraved dedication

58 mm. diam.

Another identical watch, no. 1293, is known, the back cover decorated with a nielloed portrait of Ismail Pasha (1830-1895). It is illustrated in: Histoire de la Boite a Musique Mécanique, Alfred Chapuis, 1955, p. 256.

A similar watch by Reuge retailed by P. Orr & Sons, Madras, was sold by Christie's Geneva, 18th May 2004, lot 110.

Charles Reuge

Registered its name and the lion trademark in 1883, for the making of musical and watch movements. Only 50 of these watches were made, based on a patent registered on April 25, 1883. They were intended mostly for the Chinese and Indian markets. Reuge revived the idea of musical watches from the early 19th century but instead of using the sur plateau type mechanism favoured by Piguet&Meylan, he used a pinned cylinder similar to that found in full-size musical boxes. The cylinder type is more robust and gives a more resonant sound, but requires a thicker case to house it. It also allows for more than one tune to be played from the same cylinder.

The Lagoon Waltz is a beautiful song from the operetta EineNacht in Venedig, composed by Johann Strauss II and first performed in 1883. It was therefore a brand new tune at the time this watch was made. The Daughter of the Regiment or 'La Fille du Régiment' is an opera comique in two acts by Gaetano Donizetti. Written while the composer was living in Paris, the French libretto is by Georges Henri Vernoy de Saint-Georges and Jean-Bayard.

Swiss

18K gold carillon quarter repeating three-action jaquemart automaton watch with three hammers on three gongs

Unsigned, case no. 13561, circa 1820

Keywound verge movement, repeating with three hammers on three gongs

White enamel dial with Arabic numerals, gilt scene depicting two standing figures in period costume apparently striking bells in unison with the repeating

Circular case with gilt dust cover

59 mm. diam.

Jaquemart automatons with three or more figure sequences are extremely rare. This automaton is not only very attractive but particularly rare in having carillon repeating with three hammers and three gongs. Very few jaquemart watches are known with three actions, the majority having only two

Inv. 1704

Swiss

18K pink gold skeletonised openface musical and quarter repeating jaquemart automaton watch with additional automaton, playing music on the hour or at will

Unsigned, circa 1820

Keywound full plate cylinder movement

Skeletonized dial centred by a small white enamel annular chapter ring with Arabic numerals, skeletonized surround surmounted by a varicoloured gilt scene depicting two clasically dressed standing figures holding cornucopia appearing to strike the bells, below the dial a further rotating automaton scene depicting farming activities, all activated in unison with the repeating, sur plateau musical movement activated on the hour or at will

Circular engine-turned case with engraved musical score, gilt metal cuvette

58 mm. diam.

Inv. 1171

Adam & Eve

Swiss

18K gold openface Adam & Eve watch with automaton serpent

Unsigned, circa 1810

Keywound full plate gilt-finished verge movement, chain fusée, engraved and pierced balance cock

Enamel dial with painted polychrome scene depicting various animals in the Garden of Eden, eccentric hour dial with Breguet numerals, glazed circular aperture to the upper half displaying a moving metal serpent to indicate the seconds meandering around a painted enamel scene depicting Eve offering the apple to Adam

Circular polished case

53 mm. diam.

In the account of the Creation, on the sixth day God created Adam and Eve, together with the plants and the animals, Book of Genesis 1:24-31. According to Genesis 2:21-2, Eve was fashioned from one of Adam's ribs while he slept. Adam and Eve lived in the Garden of Eden, or terrestrial paradise. God had warned Adam not to eat the fruit of "the tree of the knowledge of good and evil" but the serpent convinced Eve that she should try one of those fruit (usually represented as an apple or a fig) so that she could become like a god with the knowledge of good and evil. Eve ate the fruit which she shared with Adam. "Then the eyes of both of them were opened and they discovered that they were naked; so they stitched fig-leaves together and made themselves loincloths", (from The Temptation, Gen. 3:1-7). Adam and Eve were expelled from the Garden of Eden, clothed in skins, having lost their immortality (see The Expulsion, Gen. 3:8-24).

'Adam and Eve' automaton watches usually feature the scene depicting the Paradise painted on the enamel dial, Adam and Eve on a small panel over the visible balance, the serpent revolving on the border.

A similar watch from the Stanley Burton Collection was sold by Sotheby's London, 4th June 1992, lot 103.

Inv. 1183

Swiss

18K gold and enamel automaton watch depicting a working forge with three actions

Unsigned, probably Geneva, no. 34738, circa 1800

Keywound two train verge movement, chain fusée

White enamel dial, Roman numerals, glazed back with a painted polychrome enamel landscape surmounted by a vari-coloured gold automaton scene depicting a blacksmith's workshop, one blacksmith fanning the flames, one forging iron on an anvil while a stream of water is running out of the fountain, activated by depressing the pendant

Circular polished case

54 mm. diam.

This watch is a very fine example of an automaton watch made in Geneva around 1800, it can perhaps be attributed to the firm of Humbert & Mairet when compared to a near-identical signed watch sold by Christie's Geneva on 10th November, 2014, lot 378.

Featuring three automatons: a blacksmith fanning the flames, one forging iron, while simultaneously a stream of water is realistically flowing out of the fountain.

The vari-coloured gold scene is of wonderful quality and impresses by the finely chased details, enhanced by the painted enamel landscape to the background, demonstrating the celebrated art of enamel miniatures originating from Geneva in the early 19th century.

Inv. 1784

Swiss

18K pink gold openface quarter repeating jaquemart automaton watch with three actions

Unsigned, circa 1820

Keywound full plate verge movement

Small white enamel dial with Breguet numerals, gold surround engraved with stripes and a foliate border, surmounted by varicoloured gold standing figures appearing to strike the bells, below the dial a further winged putto strikes a   further bell, all activated in unison with the repeating

Circular polished case with reeded band, case maker's initial 'H&I'

56 mm. diam.

Jaquemart automatons with three or more figure sequences are extremely rare, the majority having only two.

This watch is unusual in having a polished and engraved gold dial plate and jaquemart figures dressed in the contemporary fashions of the 1820s rather than figures inspired by classical antiquity.

Attributed to Chevalier & Cochet

18K gold quarter repeating watch with bell striking jaquemart automaton figures

Attributed to Chevalier & Cochet, Geneva, circa 1810

Keywound verge movement, fusée and chain, continental cock, repeating on visible bells activated by depressing the pendant

Small eccentric white enamel dial with Breguet numerals, translucent blue enamel background decorated with gold paillone border, applied varicoloured gold jaquemart figures of Chronos and a lady striking recessed bells during repeating

Circular polished Empire-type case with engraved band

61 mm. diam.

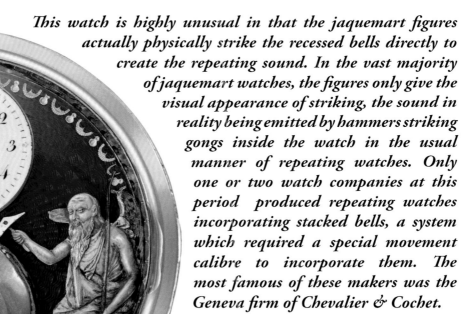

This watch is highly unusual in that the jaquemart figures actually physically strike the recessed bells directly to create the repeating sound. In the vast majority of jaquemart watches, the figures only give the visual appearance of striking, the sound in reality being emitted by hammers striking gongs inside the watch in the usual manner of repeating watches. Only one or two watch companies at this period produced repeating watches incorporating stacked bells, a system which required a special movement calibre to incorporate them. The most famous of these makers was the Geneva firm of Chevalier & Cochet.

Inv. 1206

Commedia dell' Arte

Bouvier Frères

18K gold and enamel double dialled automaton watch

Signed Bouvier Frères, no. 6412, circa 1800

Keywound gilt brass full plate verge movement, cylindrical pillars, fusée and chain, plain brass balance

White enamel with off set dial, Arabic numerals, sector for fast/slow adjustment

Circular case with blue champlevé enamel decoration, vases standing on plinths, trophy in the centre with doves and a quiver, a fan-shaped aperture at the top displaying six automaton figures from the commedia dell' arte passing over a painted landscape background, rotating once every minute

50.5 mm. diam.

Provenance: Marouf Collection III, Auktionen Antiker Uhren, March 27th, 1971, lot 102.

Bouvier Frères was well known for high quality automaton watches made for the English and French markets, the firm is recorded in: Dictionnaire des Horlogers Genevois, Geneva, 1999, p.118.

Inv. 1184

Attributed to Henri Capt

18K gold, enamel and pearl-set musical and seesaw automaton watch with six actions and further concealed erotic automaton scene

Unsigned, circa 1820

Keywound full plate double train movement with cylindrical pillars, going barrel and cylinder escapement, plain gilt three-arm balance, repeating on gongs activated by depressing the pendant, regulator arm protruding from under the cuvette with engraved scale at the edge. Musical train with pin-barrel and six stacked steel blades

Small white enamel dial with Arabic numerals, very finely painted on enamel garden landscape scene applied with finely chased varicoloured gold seesaw automaton with standing putto holding a garland, seated swinging figure of Apollo holding a lyre, dancing dog and a winged putto playing the kettle drum with both arms. Beneath the back cover the polychrome enamel concealed erotic scene a couple in a sumptuous boudoir while another gentleman peers round the door

Circular case with pearl-set bezel and border, the back cover set with a polychrome painted on enamel scene of a calm harbour after Jean-Louis Richter (1766-1841)

59 mm. diam.

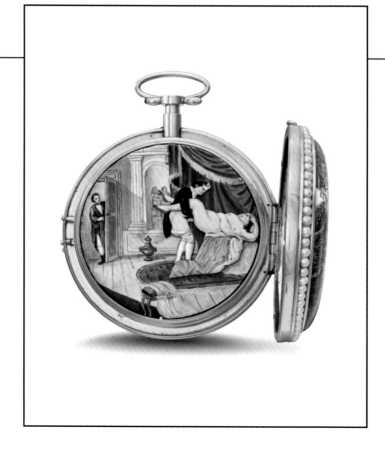

This superb seesaw automaton watch is almost certainly the work of the exceptional Genevan watchmaker Heny Capt, and can be compared directly to other examples signed by him. Capt is considered as one of the foremost makers of small musical automata of the late 18th and early 19th centuries. Watches with seesaw automaton are amongst the rarest of the genre. The present watch is particularly unusual in having a scene inspired by classical mythology rather than the more usual bucolic subjects.

With concealed erotic automaton in addition to the dial automaton, it is one of very few known examples with two complex automaton scenes in the same watch. It is also of higher specification than most, with six animations on the dial instead of the usual two or three. The seesaw rocks up and down and the putto standing on its left arm moves up and down with the seesaw's action, the seated figure of Apollo moves up and down and also rocks back and forth, the dog jumps up and down and the putto plays the kettle drum with both arms. The enamel erotic scene concealed beneath the back cover, a type which features in several of Capt's surviving watches, is traditionally said to depict Napoleon.

A watch with almost identical erotic automaton was sold by Antiquorum, Hong Kong, 17th June 1994, lot 274.

A further example was sold by Antiquorum Geneva, 27th March 2011, lot 187.

Henry-Daniel Capt (born 1773)

Henry-Daniel or Henri Capt, together with Isaac Piguet and Philippe Meylan, was one of the leading manufacturers of musical automata at the end of the 18th and beginning of the 19th century. He specialised in the production of complicated watches, musical and automaton timepieces, and was amongst the first manufacturers in Geneva to use a mechanical mechanism with pinned cylinder and tuned-tooth comb. Around 1789, Capt settled in Geneva and worked for several renowned companies such as Jaquet-Droz, Godet, Leschot and his brother-in-law Isaac Daniel Piguet.

When Piguet left to enter a partnership with Philippe-Samuel Meylan in 1811, Henry Capt continued to work first on his own, later with his son Charles Henry, until around 1830, when he joined forces with Aubert and son, Place Bel-Air in Geneva.

The Blacksmiths

Attributed to Henri Barbezat-Bôle

18K gold hunter case 'repetition àutomates' watch with blacksmith jaquemarts automaton made for the Hispanic market

Attributed to Henri Barbezat-Bôle, Locle, retailed by Heiniger y Bachmann, Medellin, no. 2063, circa 1900

Keyless lever movement with 23 jewels, quarter repeating with two hammers on two gongs

Annular white enamel dial with Roman numerals, blued steel centre with animated blacksmiths forging at the anvil during the repeating creating the illusion that the sound is made by striking the anvil, subsidiary seconds

Circular polished case with repeating slide in the band, hinged gold cuvette

50 mm. diam.

The 'forgerons' or blacksmith automaton watches are rare, only a few examples are known.

Henri Barbezat-Bôle (1851-1921) was a maker of complicated ebauches. After his death the company was run by his son, around 1930 they took over the Paul Buhre Company.

The retailer Heiniger y Bachmann were based in Medellin, the second largest city in Colombia, South America.

The Knife Grinder

Attributed to Frères Esquivillon & Deschoudens

18K gold skeletonised openface quarter repeating watch with varicoloured gold jaquemarts automaton with four actions

Attributed to Frères Esquivillon & Deschoudens, Geneva, bearing the signature 'Breguet&Fils', No. 119, circa 1820

Keywound full plate gilt-finished cylinder movement, quarter repeating on two gongs

White enamel annular dial with Breguet numerals, skeletonized centre surmounted by a varicoloured gold scene depicting the interior of a knife grinder's workshop, the knife grinder grinding a knife while his assistant is driving the wheel, above two putti apparently striking the bells in unison with the repeating activated by depressing the pendant

Circular case, engine-turned hinged back, gilt-metal cuvette

45 mm. diam.

Called 'Le Rémouleur' or 'The Knife Grinder', this watch can be compared to a similar example signed by Frères Esquivillon & Dechoudens, Geneva, formerly in the F. Conty Collection, Geneva. This watch is illustrated in: Le Monde des Automates, Alfred Chapuis and Edouard Gélis, vol. 2, p. 35, ill. 297.

In order to enhance the commercial prestige of their watches, some Swiss makers signed their watches spuriously with the names of some of the great French makers of the day, in this case Breguet.

Frères Esquivillon & Dechoudens were master watchmakers working in the last quarter of the 18th century and in the early 19th century. In 1774, Gédéon-François Esquivillon became associated with his brother, Joseph Esquivillon, and Jaques Dechoudens.

Inv. 1594

Philipe Terrot

Gold, painted on enamel, varicoloured gold and pearl-set quarter repeating automaton watch

Signed Philipe Terrot, Genève,circa 1780

Keywound full plate verge movement

Small central white enamel dial with Arabic numerals, surrounded by a polychrome painted on enamel garden scene depicting a lady strumming a lute and a pair of dancing children, the background with an architectural setting depicting a palace and its gardens, the hours and quarters apparently struck by a flying winged putto on bell above while another holding a garland looks on

Circular case, the back centered by a polychrome painted on enamel portrait of a lady holding a harp, framed within swag borders decorated with translucent red and blue enamel and partly set with seed pearls

54 mm. diam.

This watch is an extremely beautiful example of an automaton combined with a delicate detailed enamel scene and a fine enamelled case.Terrot was a maker of great repute who specialized in very high quality enamel watches, making some of the most exquisite enamelled Genevan timepieces of the period. His automaton watches are quite distinctive in combining particularly detailed and finely painted on enamel background scenes with unusually elegant and well-proportioned varicoloured gold figures. The overall effect is very well balanced and pleasing to the eye. In the present watch, the winged putti appear to fly in the sky above the painted figures lending the watch an air of sophisticated grandeur.

Philippe Terrot (1696-1781), a French refugee, arrived in Geneva and obtained Swiss naturalization in 1732. He formed a partnership with Jean-Pierre Thuillier between 1735 and 1750.

Inv. 1596

Swiss

Gold and enamel automaton watch with chatelaine

Bearing the signature 'Breguet à Paris', circa 1800

Keywound full plate verge movement

White enamel dial with eccentric meantime, sector for regulator

Circular case decorated with translucent red guilloche enamel with a scene of a mother dove feeding her nesting young, flanked by flowering vines over midnight blue enamel, fan-shaped aperture revealing six Commedia dell' arte automaton figures passing over a painted landscape background, bezels and band with champlevé enamel in blue and white. Gilt metal chatelaine set with blue hardstone roundels terminating in decorative tassels and key

50 mm. diam.

Commedia dell'arte

In Italian 'comedy of the profession', is an Italian theatrical form that flourished throughout Europe from the 16th until the end of the 18th century. Outside Italy, the form had its greatest success in France, where it became the Comédie-Italienne. In England, elements from it were incorporated into the harlequinade in pantomime and in the Punch and Judy show, a puppet play involving the commedia dell'arte character Punch. The comical Hanswurst, of German folklore, was also a commedia dell'arte character.

Inv. 1824

Jean-Antoine Lépine

Gold quarter repeating semi-skeletonized watch with jaquemart automaton and virgule escapement

Signed Lépine à Paris, circa 1815

Keywound gilt brass movement with virgule escapement, steel escape wheel, repeating on gongs activated by depressing the pendant

White enamel annular chapter ring with Breguet numerals, transparent centre with a multi-colored chased gold scene with a rampant lion and a monkey, striking the hours and quarters on scythe and triangle held by Father Time

Circular case, transparent cuvette

62 mm. diam.

Jean-Antoine Lépine (1720-1814)

Now regarded as one of the greatest and most innovative French watchmakers, the son of Jean "The King's Mechanical Expert", he was born at Challex, a village a few kilometers north of Geneva. He arrived in Paris in 1774 and became a workman for André Charles Caron, the King's clockmaker. He married Caron's daughter in 1756 and was himself appointed King's clockmaker around 1765. In 1763 Lépine had invented a new repeating mechanism for watches which was published in 1766. His new caliber invented around 1770 was a revolutionary concept replacing the back plate by bridges. Known as the 'Lépine caliber', its purpose was that the individual parts of the movement could be separately removed for repair and maintenance.

Lépine was also responsible for a number of other inventions, notably the virgule escapement, a simplified version of the double virgule invented by his father-in-law. The virgule was intended to compete with the English cylinder escapement but due to its delicacy and the difficulty of manufacture, it did not generally achieve wider success.

Lépine's other innovations included wolf's tooth wheels intended to reduce friction and a method of keyless winding operated by pumping the pendant. In addition, he also developed a new form of case with hidden hinges and fixed bezel so that the watch was only accessible from the back therefore protecting it from dust and preventing damage to the dial and hands.

Lépine was active in the company until his death at the great age of 93 on 31st May, 1814.

Dutch Kitchen

Inv. 1790

Swiss, Attributed to Pierre Simon Gounouilhou

Gold and painted on enamel watch with an automaton kitchen scene with five actions

Unsigned, the automaton movement attributed to Pierre Simon Gounouilhou, Geneva, circa 1815

Keywound gilt brass full plate cylinder movement, chain fusée, automaton driven by an independent movement with going barrel and five-wheel train, eccentrically mounted and adjustable pinion as the governor, driving the automata by means of cams and levers, activated by depressing the pendant

White enamel dial with Breguet numerals, varicolored gold automaton scene applied over a finely painted ground depicting a kitchen: a lady using a pestle and mortar sitting by a fire over which meat is being roasted, to the right, a dog running in a rotating cage turns the spit

Circular polished case with glazed back

57 mm. diam.

'The Kitchen'

This form of automaton watch appears to have been produced only by Pierre Simon Gounouilou and Dubo is & Fils. Those made by Gounouilhou employ fusée and chain, rarely found in Swiss watches, whereas Dubois used a going barrel, and his kitchen was run from the repeating mechanism. The automaton mechanism controls: the lady's hand; the spit's rotation; the fire's flames; the dog's running; the wheel turning.

Pierre Simon Gounouilhou (1779-1847) was born in 1779, settled in Geneva in 1799. A maker of great repute, he produced automata and musical objects and watches.

Gounouilhou left very interesting shop notes with an abundance of information about the habits and customs of early 19th century Geneva watchmakers.

Swiss

18K gold openface quarter repeating jaquemart automaton watch with a figural gold key

Unsigned, case no. 12961, circa 1820

Keywoundfull plate gilt-finished verge movement, chain fusée, pierced and engraved balance cock

Small white enamel dial with Breguet numerals, blued steel Breguethands, translucent royal blue enamel surround with applied varicoloured gold male and female rustic figures seated on scroll brackets appearing to strike bells in unison with the repeating, flower basket below

Circular polished case with ribbed band, casemaker's punch mark OQ, repeating through the pendant, repeating locking bolt in the band, gilt cuvette

58 mm. diam.

Swiss

18K pink gold quarter repeating and musical automaton watch

Unsigned, case no. 7334, circa 1815

Keywound full plate gilt-finished movement, repeating with two hammers on two gongs, pin barrel musical movement

White enamel annular dial withBreguet numerals, pierced and engraved varicoloured gilt scene over black enamel background depicting a lady playing a lyre beneath a tree, a fountain with realistically flowing water to the right, all in unison with the music

Circular polished case, music and automaton activated by a sliding lever in the ribbed band, repeating through the pendant, gilt cuvette, case stamped with casemaker's initials FLB and numbered 733

59 mm. diam.

Swiss

18K gold quarter repeating jaquemart automaton watch with additional swimming swan automaton, made for the Turkish market

Unsigned, circa 1820

Keywound full-plate cylinder movement with fusee and chain, repeating on gongs activated by depressing the pendant

White enamel annular chapter ring with Turkish numerals, multicolored gold chased automaton scene applied on a blued steel plate and driven by the repeating train, two figures in classical costume strike the hours and quarters, in an aperture below the dial a swan swims in unison with the repeating

Circular case with reeded band, case maker's punch mark QPD, possibly for Quartier, Paris

55 mm. diam.

Roman Bordier & Cie

118K gold and painted on enamel large two-train quarter repeating musical automaton watch

Signed Roman Bordier& Cie., attributed to Henry Capt, no. 20'935, circa 1815

Keywound two-train gilt-brass Lépine calibre cylinder movement with free standing going barrels, quarter repeating on two hammers, musical pin barrel with 6 vibrating steel blades, a steel cam fixed on top of the pin barrel driving the three automatons, music and automaton activated by depressing a button in the band,

Eccentric engine-turned gold dial, Breguet numerals, finely painted polychrome enamel classical landscape view, applied varicoloured gold automaton scene depicting a couple playing lyres while a lady to the right weaves a floral crown, all automated in unison with the music

Circular case, ribbed band, an engraved pastoral scene to the back

60 mm. diam.

The present timepiece is a fine example of an automaton watch made in Geneva around 1815-20, featuring a repeating mechanism, a musical pin barrel and a scene with three automatons: a couple playing lyres while a seated lady is waving a crown of flowers. The varicoloured gold scene is enhanced by the contrasting finely painted enamel background landscape view, a delightful example of the art of the Geneva enamellists in the early 19th century.

Although signed Roman Bordier & Cie., the movement can be attributed to Henry Capt, one of Geneva's most celebrated makers and renowned for his high quality musical watches and automata. It illustrates the ultimate development of Capt's work and his use of a Lépine-style movement with free standing barrel while maintaining the use of the musical pin-drum at a time when most of the other Geneva makers were using the pin-disc or the pin-cylinder type movement.

Swiss

18K pink gold and painted on enamel openface two-train automaton watch with three actions, made for the Chinese market

Unsigned, circa 1810

Keywound two-train cylinder movement with going barrel, independent train for the automaton mechanism

Eccentric white enamel dial with Arabic numerals, polychrome painted on enamel scene depicting a rural river landscape, surmounted by a four-coloured gold automaton scene depicting a cooper's yard, one cooper sanding and one hammering while a fountain is running, activated at will by a sliding lever in the band

Circular case with geometrically decorated engraved bezel and rim

56mm. diam.

It is possible that this watch and another very similar example were made by the famous maker and retailer John Rich who worked in London and Geneva from the end of the 18th century to circa 1825. He specialised in automaton watches, singing bird boxes and scent bottles, often made for the Chinese market.

CHAPTER 6

FORM
WATCHES

Form Watches

The concept of the form watch, that is, a watch made in the image of another object originates in the late 16th and early 17th centuries. In common with most western art of the period, early form watches were often of an ecclesiastical nature or had their shapes inspired by natural forms. The crucifix-form watch and twelve-lobed flower-form watches being the most recognisable shapes. Such timepieces, some crafted from carved rock crystal,some set with precious gems or enamel, were not only awe-inspiring to behold but extremely expensive, instantly conveying the high status of the owner to contemporary observers.

The 17th century preoccupation with the brevity of life inspired one of the most enduringly popular themes for the form watch, the skull-form or 'memento mori' watch in which the movement and dial are concealed within an often realistically made silver or enamelled skull-shaped case.

The years between 1790 and 1820 were the heyday of the form watch. The Swiss city of Geneva became the centre for the making of what were known at the time as 'toys', with the 'surprise' watch and its mechanism concealed inside.These enchanting miniaturised watches made in precious metals, jewelled or pearl-set were very often exquisitely enamelled – a craft at which the craftsmen of Geneva excelled. The shapes of form watches took their inspiration from a range of subjects, including flowers such as tulips, pansies, roses and floral baskets. Others took the shape of fruit or animals: strawberries, cherries, peaches and apples, shells, birds, beetles, fantastical fish or exotic butterflies. Some were even in the form of everyday objects such as shoes and purses, watches were even miniaturised to the point of being able to be fitted into finger rings.

The Masis Collection of form watches is fortunate to have at its core the almost complete collection of form watches assembled by the fabled connoisseur Gustav Blochin Vienna in the early years of the 20th century. Watches in the form of musical instruments are particularly strongly represented here and include harps, mandolins, cello and lyres. The musical instrument theme was popularised by the importance of music in the arts in the early 19th century.

Inv. 1845

Joseph Weichberger

Gold champlevé and painted on enamel diamond-set, musical harp-form desk watch

Joseph Weichberger, Vienna, movement no. 2716, circa 1890

Keywound verge movement

White enamel dial

Harp-form case, the sound box painted en plein with trophies and figures, below a hinged compartment, the base drum pierced and containing a musical movement, on four scroll supports, decorated overall in polychrome champlevé enamels with leaves, spirals and lozenge motifs, each gold string topped by a rose diamond pin

95 mm. overall height.

Josef, son of Josef Weichberger Senior (1845-1881) and his wife Maria Lixl, is recorded as active between 1883 and 1899. As 'Pretiosen-Schätzmeister', he is described in 1889 with a studio specialising in gold and enamel objects of vertu. At that date he was working at 6b Kaunitzgasse, Vienna VI (MAK, Wiener Gold- und Silberschmiede, 2005).

A very similar Viennese enamel harp was in the Bloch-Bauer collection, see: Elisabeth Sturm-Bednarczyk, Phantasie-Uhren, Vienna, 2002, no. 62.

Memento Mori

Swiss.

18K gold and enamel diamond-set skull-form pendant watch with visible balance

Signed Romillyà Paris, circa 1800

Keywoundverge movement, pierced and engraved balance cock, chain fusée

White enamel dial with Roman numerals

Skull-form case overlaid with opaque cream enamel, rose-cut diamond-set eyes and teeth, the lower jaw hinged, the base of the skull with glazed aperture to view the movement, spring hinged covers opening to reveal the dial

40mm. high.

Watches and clocks with memento mori, latin for "reminder of death", motifs were amongst the standard subject matter of 17th century vanitas still lifes which included objects with an underlying moral message: such as the combination of a skull and a watch, both reminders of the passage of time.

Particularly en vogue again during the 19th century, it was common practice amongst watchmakers of the period to reproduce such watches.

Jean Romilly 1714-1796 was an eminent French watchmaker, he originally came from Geneva and settled in Paris. He became Master in 1752, the Technical Director of the Royal Clock Manufactory from 1789-90, perfected the double virgule escapement and in 1758 presented to the Academy a year-going watch. He was an associate member of the Salon de la Correspondence, and as a friend of Jean-Jacques Rousseau was in contact with the Parisian intelligentsia.

Inv. 1279

Frères Veigneur et Petiet

18K gold and enamel pearl-set shield-form pendant watch with visible diamond-set balance

Signed Frères Veigneur et Petiet, movement no. 14514, circa 1800

Keywound cylinder movement

Small white enamel dial with Arabic numerals, surrounded by shield- shaped enamel decoration of an urn and laurel leaves, rose-cut, diamond-set visible balance

Shield-shaped case with engraved gold and champlevé enamel border, both borders set with split pearls, case back with translucent red guilloché enamel heightened with gold depicting a landscape scene with a well, love birds and a swan

51 mm. overall length

Inv. 1314

Swiss

Pink gold, enamel and pearl-set navette-shaped ring watch

Unsigned, circa 1810

Keywound calibre 6 ¾''' hinged full plate verge movement with cylindrical pillars, three arm brass balance, chain fusée, micrometer adjustment, pierced and engraved foliate cock

White enamel dial with Breguet numerals

Navette-shaped case, pearl-set bezel, decorated with black champlevé

enamel and a dove and quiver, engraved shoulders

21 x 36 mm. dim.

Exquisitely made, gold, enamelled and jewelled ring watches such as this were sold in Geneva as novel and intriguing 'toys' for the very rich and members of the aristocracy. What today would be considered a feminine object would also have been perfectly acceptable for a man to wear during the period it was made. In the early 19th century, a ring watch would have been hugely expensive and regarded as a mechanical marvel in miniature.

Swiss

Pink gold and pearl-set oval ring watch with visible balance

Unsigned, circa 1820

Keywound cylinder movement with going barrel

White enamel dial with Arabic numerals in the lower half, visible balance above

Oval case with pearl-set bezel, the back with sliding gold panel over the winding and setting squares with engraved instructions

35 mm. overall length

Since their first appearance in the 16th century, ring watches have always been the object of great fascination, perhaps because of their decorative aspect, perhaps the horological tour de force needed to construct a perfectly functioning movement of, for the period, such small size to be set into a piece of jewellery. Production of these extraordinary pieces required exceptional skill and was therefore exclusively executed by the best watchmakers, jewellers and enamellers of the time.

Particularly fashionable between the late 18th and mid-19th centuries, ring watches represented an alternative to traditional jewellery. Their shapes varied from round and oval to rectangular and navette, the bezels of the most luxurious examples were decorated with pearls or diamonds, some, such as the present example, have off-centred dials allowing space for a visible balance.

Inv. 1637

Christian Moricand

Gold and painted on enamel ball-form pendant watch with concealed dial, the enamel in the manner of Jean-Louis Richter

Signed Ch.t Moricandà Genève, no. 36418, circa 1790, later Viennese hallmark for 1806/7

Keywound verge movement with chain fusée

White enamel dial with Arabic numerals

Ball-form gold case hinged in two halves and decorated with a continuous band of very finely painted on enamel children in a landscape and under a deep blue sky, one boy playing the tambourine to lead the dance, enclosed by engraved gold zig-zag borders against black champlevé enamel, the upper half of the sphere with a dove and the lower with a lyre

25 mm. diam.

The extremely beautiful and charming enamel scene painted on this watch is in the style of the celebrated Genevan enamellist Jean-Louis Richter (1766-1841).Made after English genre works painted by artists specialising in scenes of romantic English rural life, such as William Hamilton, Francis Wheatley and William Redmore Bigg. These paintings enjoyed enormous popularity at the time and were often used by Genevan enamellers as a template to embellish their masterpieces.

Christian Moricand (1715-1791) I recorded as a watchmaker who from 1752 to 1755 was associated with his brother Benjamin and the watchmaker François Colladon.

A very similar watch also by Moricandis in the collection of the Patek Philippe Museum in Geneva(Inv. S-86).

Provenance:

The collection of Dr. Gustav Bloch, Vienna.

By descent to Therese Bloch-Bauer

The present owner

Exhibited:

Austrian Museum of Art and Industry, Vienna, 1917

Literature:

The Collection of Form Watches of Gustav Bloch in Vienna, Edmund Wilhelm Braun-Troppau, 1917, p.22, III. 21.

Phantasie-Uhren, Treasures from the Collection of Therese Bloch-Bauer, Elisabeth Sturm-Bednarczyk, 2002, no. 42.

Inv. 1120

Bordier

18K gold and enamel mandolin form watch with concealed dial

Signed Bordier à Genève, circa 1830

Keywound verge movement, chain fusée, engraved and pierced balance cock

White enamel dial with Arabic numerals

Mandolin-form case with polychrome blue, black and white champlevé enamel decorated panels, chased gold foliage, soundboard with painted on enamel scene of three courting couples in a landscape, gold tuning pegs over blue enamel head, gold strings, short length of gold chain attached to the case and head

62 mm. overall length

The frères Bordier were working from 1787. In 1815 they are recorded at the Place Grand Mézel in Geneva. They are particularly known for repeating watches, form watches, and watches decorated with precious stones and enamel with classic fusée and verge escapement movements.

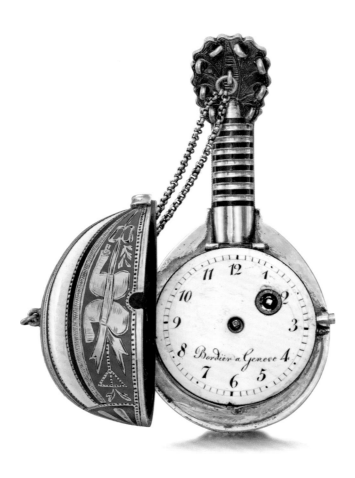

Nouzou

18K gold and enamel cello-form watch with concealed dial

Signed Nouzou à Paris, movement no. 272, circa 1810

Keywound verge movement, chain fusée, engraved and pierced balance cock

White enamel dial with Roman numerals

Cello-form case overlaid with translucent red enamel, chased gold foliage and a white enamel musical score, gold tuning pegs, gold strings, concealed compartment with stopper

76 mm. overall length

The cello-form case is one of the scarcest amongst the various musical instrument form watches which include the violin, mandolin and harp.

Inv. 1205

Swiss

18K gold, enamel and diamond-set folding lorgnette with concealed watch

Unsigned, circa 1850

Keywound cylinder movement

White enamel dial with Roman numerals, gold surround engraved with the technical details of the movement

Shaped case engraved with foliate scrolls, spring-loaded lorgnette, spring-loaded cover over the dial decorated with translucent royal blue guilloche enamel, and with a rose-cut diamond-set flower spray

86 mm. overall length

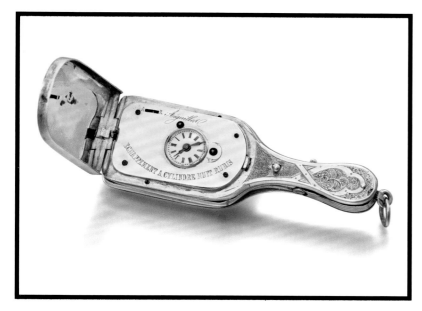

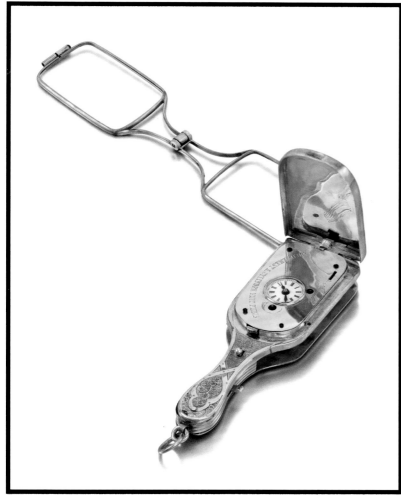

Inv. 1628

Swiss

18K yellow and pink gold and champlevé enamel nanga-form watch made for the Islamic Market

Unsigned, circa 1820

Keywound verge movement with chain fusée

White enamel dial with Roman numerals

Nanga-form case decorated with translucent green, white and red champlevé enamel, back enamelled over a bark-finished background, centred by a gold stylised flower, the panels decorated with trophies of music, bark-finish decorated yellow gold sound board pierced with the star and crescent symbols, curved neck with white, green and red geometrical decoration, nine gold strings, snake's head finial, gold tuning pegs

73 mm. overall length.

The present watch is in the shape of a nanga, an early form of the ancient harp popular in Egypt, at the time part of the Ottoman Empire.

Inv. 1534

Swiss

Gold and enamel and pearl-set, mandolin-form pendant watch

Unsigned, circa 1810

Keywound verge movement with chain fusée

White enamel dial with Roman numerals

Mandolin-form case with circular resonator, the front overlaid with translucent blue enamel over an engraved ground, the back overlaid with translucent royal blue enamel over an engraved ground, engraved gold branch and a white enamel sheet of music, six gold wire strings

30 mm. wide, 65 mm. overall length.

A very similar Viennese enamel mandolin watch is illustrated in:

The Collection of Form Watches of Gustav Bloch in Vienna, Edmund Wilhelm Braun-Troppau, 1917, p. 23, III. 26.

Phantasie-Uhren, Treasures from the Collection of Therese Bloch-Bauer, Elisabeth Sturm-Bednarczyk, 2002, no. 65.

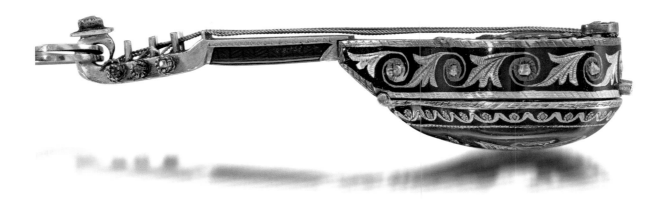

Inv. 1640

Joseph Ranna

Gold, two-colour enamel and pearl-set, harp-form pendant watch with visible balance

Signed Joseph Ranna in Wein, no. 573, circa 1830

Keywound verge movement with chain fusée

White enamel dial with Arabic numerals

Harp-form case with round resonator an S-shaped neck, the front overlaid with translucent red enamel over an engraved ground, gold engraved foliage with white champlevé enamel flowers, the balance visible through the glazed pearl-bordered sound hole, the back overlaid with translucent royal blue enamel over an engraved ground, engraved gold foliage with green opaque enamel leaves and a white enamel sheet of music, gold wire strings with five pegs

29 mm. wide, 60 mm. overall length.

An almost identical watch, the movement signed Bartholomäus Hanhart, is in the collection of the Patek Philippe Museum in Geneva (Inv. S-55).

Provenance:

The collection of Dr. Gustav Bloch, Vienna.

By descent to Therese Bloch-Bauer

The present owner

Exhibited:

The Austrian Museum of Art and Industry, Vienna, 1917.

Literature:

The Collection of Form Watches of Gustav Bloch in Vienna, Edmund Wilhelm Braun-Troppau, 1917, p. 23, III. 23.

Phantasie-Uhren, Treasures from the Collection of Therese Bloch-Bauer, Elisabeth Sturm-Bednarczyk, 2002, no. 59.

The maker Joseph Ranna is recorded in: Meister der Uhrmacherkunst, JurgenAbeler, 1977, p.501.

Inv. 1641

Mallet

Gold, two-colour enamel and pearl-set lyre-form pendant watch with visible balance

Signed Mallet à Paris, no. 288, the Austrian case with maker's mark 'JW' for Josef Weichbergersen., circa 1830, later Austrian hallmark for 1867-1872

Keywound verge movement with chain fusée

White enamel dial with Arabic numerals

Lyre-form case with heart-shaped resonator, the front overlaid with translucent red enamel over an engraved ground, gold engraved flowers with white champlevé enamel flowers and green leaves, the balance visible through the glazed pearl-bordered sound hole, the back overlaid with translucent royal blue enamel over an engraved ground, engraved gold branch and a white enamel sheet of music, four gold wire strings with pearl-set attachments

30 mm. wide, 50 mm. overall length.

Provenance:

The collection of Dr. Gustav Bloch, Vienna.

By descent to Therese Bloch-Bauer

The present owner

Exhibited:

Austrian Museum of Art and Industry, Vienna, 1917

Literature:

The Collection of Form Watches of Gustav Bloch in Vienna, Edmund Wilhelm Braun-Troppau, 1917, p. 23, III. 26.

Phantasie-Uhren, Treasures from the Collection of Therese Bloch-Bauer, Elisabeth Sturm-Bednarczyk, 2002, no. 65.

Inv. 1422

Memento Mori

Elisabeth Petronin

Silver-gilt and painted on enamel skull-form pendant watch with concealed dial

Signed Elisabeth Petronin in Vienna, mid-19th century

Keywound verge movement with chain fusée, finely pierced and engraved balance cock

Painted on enamel dial with white annular chapter ring with Roman numerals, the centre decorated with the figure of Chronos

Silver-gilt skull-form case overlaid with realistically painted enamel, the jaw and lower part hinged and opening to reveal the dial, trefoil pendant decorated with translucent red enamel and white dots

52 x 53 x 35mm.

Marking the passage of time, watches and clocks were quite naturally adapted to objectify memento mori, latin for "remember you must die". Skull-form watches were produced from the 17th century onwards and their message is an artistic or symbolic reminder of the inevitability of death, closely related to vanitas still life paintings of the same period often depicting a skull, hour glass, guttering candle etc.

Memento moriskull-form watches gained in popularity again during the 19th century and to satisfy demand, European watchmakers made examples mainly in silver, occasionally gold and more rarely realistically painted enamelled pieces such as the present watch.

Inv. 1632

Esquivillon et Dechoudens

Gold filigree, enamel and pearl-set lyre-form pendant watch with visible balance

Signed Esquivillon et Dechoudens, movement no. 78478, circa 1820

Keywound verge movement with chain fusée

White enamel dial with Arabic numerals

Gold filigree and pearl-set lyre-form case decorated with black, blue, red and green champlevé enamel with engraved gold flowers and leaves, visible balance through the glazed pearl-bordered sound holes, suspended from four gold chains with star-shaped terminal

45 mm. wide, 55 mm. overall length.

Frères Esquivillon&Dechoudenswere master watchmakers working in the last quarter of the 18th century and in the early 19th century. In 1774, Gédéon-François Esquivillon became associated with his brother, Joseph Esquivillon, and JaquesDechoudens.

Provenance:

The collection of Dr. Gustav Bloch, Vienna.

By descent to Therese Bloch-Bauer

The present owner

Exhibited:

Austrian Museum of Art and Industry, Vienna, 1917

Literature:

The Collection of Form Watches of Gustav Bloch in Vienna, Edmund Wilhelm Braun-Troppau, 1917, p. 21, no. 19.

Phantasie-Uhren, Treasures from the Collection of Therese Bloch-Bauer, Elisabeth Sturm-Bednarczyk, 2002, no. 30.

Inv. 1639

Jacques Patron

Four-colour gold and enamel rose cut diamond-set, lyre-form lorgnette with integral watch

Signed Js. Patron à Genève, movement no. 22644, last quarter of the 18th century

Keywound verge movement with chain fusée

White enamel dial with Arabic numerals

Gold lorgnette decorated on both sides with applied four-colour gold flowers, leaves and symbols emblematic of musical and theatre, border of stylized leaves enamelled in green, the lorgnette with flower-shaped hinges set with diamonds, the lorgnette released by a diamond-set lever, lyre-shaped lower section lavishly decorated with flowers, the lyre frame with a winged putto on each side overlaid with translucent enamel, the handle set with a watch with ribbon and bead bezel, the back decorated with four-colour gold sacrificial scene, royal blue enamel border

28 mm. wide, 150 mm. overall length.

A masterpiece of the goldsmith's art, this spectacular multi-coloured gold lorgnette was quite probably a special order piece for an aristocratic lover of the arts. The maker Jacques Patron is recorded working in Geneva in the last quarter of the 18th century.

The author G. H. Baillie in his book 'Watchmakers and Clockmakers of the World' mentions a 'four-colour gold watch in lorgnette' by Jacques Patron, this is quite likely to be the present piece.

Provenance:

The collection of Dr. Gustav Bloch, Vienna.

By descent to Therese Bloch-Bauer

The present owner

Exhibited:

Austrian Museum of Art and Industry, Vienna, 1917

Literature:

The Collection of Form Watches of Gustav Bloch in Vienna, Edmund Wilhelm Braun-Troppau, 1917, p.28, III. 46.

Phantasie-Uhren, Treasures from the Collection of Therese Bloch-Bauer, Elisabeth Sturm-Bednarczyk, 2002, no. 40.

Swiss

18K gold, enamel and diamond-set scarab beetle-form pendant watch

Unsigned, circa 1890

Keyless cylinder movement

White enamel dial with blue Arabic numerals

Case in the form of a beetle with hinged wings concealing the dial, the wings overlaid with translucent blue enamel over engine-turning and set with rose-cut diamonds, the head of the beetle further enhanced by opaque black enamel, rose-cut diamonds and ruby-set eyes, the underside realistically chased as the body

20 mm. wide, 50 mm. overall length.

The scarab beetle dates back to Ancient Egypt as a symbol of rebirth, the form was often immortalised as jewellery or as amulets to be carried for good luck and to ward off evil spirits.

The tradition continues to this day and reached a pinnacle of inventiveness and design during the mid to late 19th century when the scarab form was adapted to a pendant watch case, often finely chased and enamelled as seen with the present watch.

Inv. 1636

Swiss

Gold and champlevé enamel ruby-set whale-form pendant watch with original whale-form key

Unsigned, circa 1800

Keywound verge movement with chainfusée

White enamel dial with Breguet numerals

Whale-form gold case minutely engraved with scales and inlaid with translucent blue and opaque black champlevé enamel, the nose and mouth in red translucent enamel on an engraved ground, ruby-set eyes, suspended from four gold chains from a ring.

Original gold key in the shape of a small whale, finely engraved and enamelled

27 mm. wide, 47 mm. overall length.

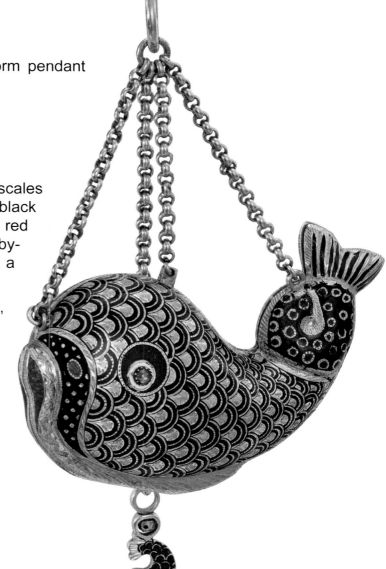

An almost identical watch is in the collection of the Patek Philippe Museum in Geneva(Inv. S-676).

Provenance:

The collection of Dr. Gustav Bloch, Vienna.

By descent to Therese Bloch-Bauer

The present owner

Exhibited: Austrian Museum of Art and Industry, Vienna, 1917

Literature:

The Collection of Form Watches of Gustav Bloch in Vienna, Edmund Wilhelm Braun-Troppau, 1917, p.19, III. 11.

Phantasie-Uhren, Treasures from the Collection of Therese Bloch-Bauer, Elisabeth Sturm-Bednarczyk, 2002, no. 45.

Inv. 1638

Swiss

Gold and champlevé enamel pendant watch in the form of a pair of billing doves

Unsigned, circa 1810

Keywound verge movement with chain fusée

White enamel dial with Arabic numerals

Case in the form of a pair of billing doves, engraved feathers overlaid with translucent red, blue, black and white enamel, suspended from three gold chains

42 mm. wide, 40 mm. high.

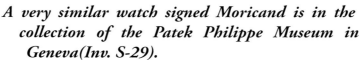

A very similar watch signed Moricand is in the collection of the Patek Philippe Museum in Geneva(Inv. S-29).

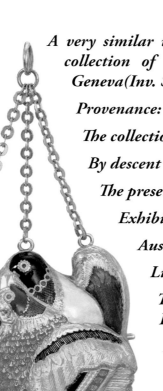

    Provenance:

      The collection of Dr. Gustav Bloch, Vienna.

       By descent to Therese Bloch-Bauer

        The present owner

      Exhibited:

        Austrian Museum of Art and Industry, Vienna, 1917

       Literature:

        The Collection of Form Watches of Gustav Bloch in Vienna, Edmund Wilhelm Braun-Troppau, 1917.

        Phantasie-Uhren, Treasures from the Collection of Therese Bloch-Bauer, Elisabeth Sturm-Bednarczyk, 2002.

Inv. 1635

Viennese

Gold and enamel bird's nest-form pendant watch with concealed watch

Unsigned, circa 1830

Keywound verge movement with chain fusée

White enamel dial with Arabic numerals

Gold bird's nest case with gold wire spiral edge, a polychrome champlevé enamelled gold bird with engraved feathers sits on a clutch of speckled eggs, suspended from four gold chains from an enamelled terminal, the hinged base opening to reveal the dial

33 mm. wide, 40 mm. high.

Provenance:

The collection of Dr. Gustav Bloch, Vienna.

By descent to Therese Bloch-Bauer

The present owner

Exhibited:

Austrian Museum of Art and Industry, Vienna, 1917

Literature:

The Collection of Form Watches of Gustav Bloch in Vienna, Edmund Wilhelm Braun-Troppau, 1917, p.17, no. 8.

Phantasie-Uhren, Treasures from the Collection of Therese Bloch-Bauer, Elisabeth Sturm-Bednarczyk, 2002, no. 44.

Inv. 1633

Swiss

Gold, champlevé and painted on enamel pearl-set double eagle-headed perfume flask and concealed watch with visible diamond-set balance made for the Chinese market

Unsigned, circa 1800

Keywound cylinder movement with visible diamond-set balance

White enamel annular dial with Arabic numerals below the balance and with white enamel annular seconds dial above, chased navette-shaped surround with engraved gold leaves

Lyre-shaped flask with two realistically modelled chased gold eagle's head stoppers, the body with chased gold flowers and foliage and a musical trophy, inlaid with translucent and opaque red, blue and green champlevé enamels and set with graduated split-pearls, the back with a sprung and hinged concealed panel decorated with two finely painted on enamel oval medallions of statues in wall niches opening to reveal the winding and setting apertures, opened by depressing a button in the band

30 mm. wide, 72 mm. overall length.

This exquisite and magnificent objet de luxe is of the highest quality, undoubtedly made by the finest Geneva goldsmiths and enamellers of the period it would have been intended for a client of very high status. It is related to two other known flasks of almost identical form but with different decoration which were once in the collection of King Farouk of Egypt, see: Sotheby & Co., The Palace Collections of Egypt, Koubbeh Palace, Cairo, March 10th-17th, 1954, lots 529 and 530.

Provenance:

The collection of Dr. Gustav Bloch, Vienna

By descent to Therese Bloch-Bauer

The present owner

Exhibited:

Austrian Museum of Art and Industry, Vienna, 1917.

Literature:

The Collection of Form Watches of Gustav Bloch in Vienna, Edmund Wilhelm Braun-Troppau, 1917, p. 21, III. 18.

Phantasie-Uhren, Treasures from the Collection of Therese Bloch-Bauer, Elisabeth Sturm-Bednarczyk, 2002.

Inv. 1634

Swiss

Gold and painted on enamel pearl-set flower basket-form pendant watch

Unsigned, circa 1810

Keywound verge movement with chain fusée

White enamel dial with Roman numerals

Flower basket-form case overlaid on both sides with royal blue translucent guilloche enamel with split pearl-set edges, the front cover decorated with a finely painted reclining Cherub amongst flowers, the back with garden flowers

37 mm. wide, 32 mm. high.

A very similar watch is in the collection of the Patek Philippe Museum in Geneva(Inv. S-52).

Provenance:

The collection of Dr. Gustav Bloch, Vienna.

By descent to Therese Bloch-Bauer

The present owner

Exhibited:

Austrian Museum of Art and Industry, Vienna, 1917

Literature:

The Collection of Form Watches of Gustav Bloch in Vienna, Edmund Wilhelm Braun-Troppau, 1917.

Phantasie-Uhren, Treasures from the Collection of Therese Bloch-Bauer, Elisabeth Sturm-Bednarczyk, 2002.

Inv. 1794

A. Frankfeld

Gold and painted on enamel book-form watch with miniature prayer inside

Signed A. Frankfeld, Genève, circa 1880

Keyless heart shaped cylinder movement

White enamel dial with Roman numerals

Book-form case decorated with a polychrome painted on enamel figure of the Madonna flanked by putti, the back with aperture for the dial framed by painted on enamel floral swags, the interior with printed prayer, hinged rectangular cuvette

28mm. wide, 32 mm. high.

A.Frankfeld was a maker of repute, the firm was one of the exhibitors at the Philadelphia World's Fair Exhibition in 1876.

Swiss

18K gold, silver, enamel and diamond-set strawberry-form watch with concealed dial

Unsigned, circa 1880

Keyless gilt-finished jewelled cylinder movement

White enamel dial with red and blue Arabic numerals

Hinged strawberry-form case with lozenge-shaped gold accents to the red guilloche enamel ground, engraved band, with diamond-set silver calyx to the top and gold suspension hoop, enlarged reeded and beaded bezel which winds the watch when rotated

41 mm. high including suspension hoop

Two similar strawberry-form watches of slightly earlier date are in the collection of the Patek Philippe Museum in Geneva (Inv. S-42 & Inv. S-968).

Swiss

Gold and painted on enamel watch in the form of a vase

Unsigned, probably Geneva, circa 1795

Keywound verge movement with chain fusée

White enamel dial with Arabic numerals

Vase-form case decorated in the Sévres-style with translucent blue enamel over an engine-turned ground, highlighted by opaque white enamel and gold paillons, the back centred by a painted enamel scene of a courting couple in 18th century costume with their dog in landscape

80 mm. high.

An almost identical vase-form watch is in the collection of the Patek Philippe Museum in Geneva (Inv. S-329).

Swiss

Gold and painted on enamel watch in the form of
a shell with concealed dial

Unsigned, circa 1810

Keywound verge movement with chain fusée

White enamel dial with Roman numerals

Shell-form case, the front and back both with
opaque white and black enamel decoration,
surrounding painted polychrome enamel scenes
on each side of cherubim frolicking within a floral
landscape,suspended by a gold chain attached
on either side

33 mm. high.

Inv. 1795

Paul Flato

14K gold and enamel envelope-form watch with concealed dial

Signed Flato, circa 1938

Keyless lever movement

Pink dial with baton and Arabic numerals

Rectangular case designed as an envelope, engraved with address and painted on enamel postage stamp, opening to reveal a rectangular watch, the reverse of the inner case with an engraved love note

43 mm. wide,32 mm. high.

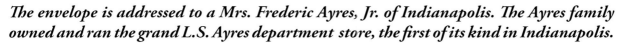

The envelope is addressed to a Mrs. Frederic Ayres, Jr. of Indianapolis. The Ayres family owned and ran the grand L.S. Ayres department store, the first of its kind in Indianapolis.

Paul Flato launched his career in 1920s New York, where he gained fame creating ingenious designs for well-heeled clients such the Rockefellers, the Vanderbilts, and tobacco heiress Doris Duke. He prided himself on producing 'conversation pieces' which, as touted in a self-penned advertisement for his 57th Street store, were 'sometimes wicked, always sophisticated [and] invariably smart.'

Gide & Blond et Fils

Gold and enamel camellia flower-form pendant watch with concealed dial

Signed Gide & Blondet Fils, Genève,the case probably Viennese, circa 1850

Keywound gilt full plate verge movement with chain fusée and pierced and engraved balance cock

White enamel dial with Arabic numerals

Camelia flower-form case overlaid with translucent red enamel over an engraved ground, gold stem and green enamel calyx, the petals decorated with champlevé enamel small flowers, opening to reveal the dial

36mm. diam.

Two almost identical watches with Austrian-made cases are in the collection of the Patek Philippe Museum in Geneva (Inv. S-19 & Inv. S-393).

Another example of the same design is illustrated in: Montres de Fantasie, Patrizzi and Sturm, Geneva, 1979, fig. 77.

Inv. 1856

Swiss

Gold painted on enamel and pearl-set watch in the form of a tulip with concealed dial

Unsigned, the case probably Viennese, circa 1820

Keywound verge movement with chain fusée

White enamel dial with Breguet numerals

Polychrome and champlevé enamel tulip-form case, gold and painted on polychrome enamel hinged petals, pearl-set gold stamens, twisted gold stalk-shaped pendant above a champlevé green enamel foliate and engraved decoration, scarlet enamel over engine-turned ground, four gold small chain suspensions

40 mm. overall height including stalk-pendant

Two almost identical tulip-form watches with Austrian-made cases are in the collection of the Patek Philippe Museum in Geneva (Inv. S-21& Inv. S-357).

Inv. 1890

Attributed to Piguet&Capt

Gold and painted on enamel perfume flask with concealed watch showing seconds, made for the Chinese market

Unsigned, circa 1810

Keywound fire-gilded full-plate cylinder movement,the seconds driven by an additional wheel geared to the escape wheel pinion

White enamel dial with Breguet numerals, separate white enamel dial for small seconds

Case in the shape of an oblong flask with flat sides and canted corners, the front with two finely decorated panels, the upper part with painted on enamel basket of fruit, the lower part with floral engraving and overlaid with translucent red and blue enamel, a hinged and spring-loaded panel opens to reveal the dials when a small push-piece in the side is depressed, the back decorated with a painted on enamel vase of flowers and decorated to match the front, the border in alternating azure and white enamels in a geometrical pattern, the sides classically decorated with translucent red, blue, and green enamel, screwed enamelled cap fitted with a small spatula for perfume application

29mm. wide. 87 mm. overall length.

Attributable stylistically to Piguet and Capt who are considered amongst the most important makers of small objects that incorporated music, automata and watches working in Geneva at the end of the 18th and beginning of the 19th centuries, this exquisite gold and enamel perfume flask is a great rarity in having a miniature watch concealed within. It is also particularly unusual in having a separate small seconds indication, a feature seldom seen on form watches. It is exactly the type of precious object that would have been bought or acquired by the Chinese Emperor. Indeed, similar pieces are recorded as being looted from the Imperial Summer Palace by French and British forces during the second opium war in 1860.

Isaac Daniel Piguet (1775-1841) and Henri Capt (1773-1837) were partners from 1802 until 1811 in the firm bearing their name, Piguet& Capt.

Inv. 1789

Marqués de España

Swiss

Unique gold and painted on enamel, pearl and gem-set shield shaped armorial pendant watch with solid gold sculptural movement and concealed champlevé enamel zodiac numeral dial, with original matching gold gauntlet-form winding key and a hardstone-set key, made for a Spanish noble family

Unsigned, circa 1850

Keywound with gold plates entirely engraved and deeply foliate chased sculptural cylinder movement, the third and fourth wheel bridge in the form of a lion, the centre wheel bridge formed as a snake, the barrel bridge as an eagle holding a banner engraved with the motto "Veritas Vincit" (Truth Conquers), jewelled to the centre, balance bridge modelled as the figure of Chronos holding his scythe which is engraved with the regulation scale

Translucent green, red and dark blue champlevé enamel dial with painted gold zodiac symbols as numerals, blue and white striped gothic border decorated with painted gold stylized foliage, serpentine gold hands

Shield shaped case with pierced and engraved gold scrollwork frame, pearl and gem-set coronet above, the front cover decorated with a translucent and painted on enamel coat of arms, the back cover with a finely painted on enamel military trophy flanked by Spanish flags, suspended from two chains and a gauntleted hand

55 x 72 mm.

This magnificent and highly individual pendant watch must certainly have been made as a unique special commission for its first owner to proudly display his aristocratic lineage. Every element of its construction has a heraldic symbolism coming together as a whole to convey a powerful message to the observer. The workmanship of the movement, dial and case is exceptional and its mediaevalist design has been conceived as a complete entity with every element carefully considered. Although it has not been possible to fully identify the coat of arms, the separate elements confirm that it was made for a Spanish nobleman and the pearl and gem-set coronet is that of a Marqués (Marquess in English).

The movement is a horological and artistic masterpiece, made of solid gold in a shield-shape to match the case, it is entirely hand-engraved with fronds of foliage. Its most remarkable feature is however the design and construction of the wheel bridges which are of two dimensional animal and figural design. The barrel bridge is in the form of an eagle holding a banner in its beak which is engraved with the family motto, the centre wheel bridge is a coiled serpent and the bridge for the second and third wheels is in the form of a lion. For the balance bridge, the figure of Chronos holds his scythe, the blade of which is engraved with the regulation scale.

Also of completely unique design, the dial and case are triumphs of the Swiss enameller's art. Made using the champlevé technique, the dial has the unusual feature of the twelve signs of the zodiac in place of traditional numerals. The case is crafted in gold in the shape of an armorial shield with a three-dimensional scroll border surmounted by the coronet, the chains suspending the watch are held by a clasped gauntleted hand to continue the chivalrous theme. The covers are exquisitely enamelled, the front with the full coat of arms of the Marqués done in the champlevé technique, the back with a very finely painted on enamel military trophy with armour and weapons flanked by the flags of Spain.

CHAPTER 7

EUROPEAN WATCHES

18TH CENTURY ONWARDS

European Watches, 18th Century Onwards

This chapter encompasses a period of enormous progression in both the decorative and technical development of the mechanical timepiece. The Masis Collection includes watches made right up to the Art Nouveau period in the early 20th century. However, for the watches that are illustrated in the following pages its strength lies in the timepieces made from the mid-18th century in France and England and the golden age of Swiss enamel-decorated watches from about 1780 to 1820.

The ancient metalworking technique of repoussé enjoyed a revival during the second and third quarters of the 18th century and was particularly successful for the decoration of watch cases at a time when the rococo style was at its height. Hammered out from behind and then chased, the designs of repoussé watch cases very often depicted scenes from either the Old Testament or classical antiquity and mythology. The Masis collection brings together several superb gold repoussé watches showcasing both English and continental workmanship.

Case decoration in the second half of the 18th century and early 19th century demonstrates how important the goldsmiths, lapidaries and enamellers were in the production of watches as functional works of art. The collection includes carved hardstone, German porcelain and of course painted on enamel cases which preserve for posterity the work of exceptional artists many of whose names are unknown today. Often the scenes were copied directly from engravings of famous paintings which where readily available at the time. The Masis Collection has several such watches including an exquisite scene depicting 'The Rape of Europa' after Luca Giordano and "pensent-ils au raisin" after François Boucher's painting of 1747.

Watches incorporating complicated and rare mechanical functions or novel ways of displaying the hours and minutes show the sheer ingenuity of their makers. The collection has examples of watches with 'wandering hours', sunrise and sunset indications .

Watches made for Royal presentation and depicting images of famous persons feature in this chapter, including pieces given by King George III of England, Prince Frederik of the Netherlands and a watch by Courvoisier presented by Napoleon III to the Ottoman Sultan Abdülaziz during his visit to Paris in 1876. Of American interest is the specially commissioned watch decorated with a portrait of George Washington taken from Gilbert Stuart's famous painting of the President.

Inv. 1783

Chevalier et Compe

18K gold and painted on enamel quarter repeating watch

Signed Chevalier et Compe, circa 1790

Keywound verge movement with chain fusée, quarter repeating on a gong activated by depressing the pendant

White enamel dial with Roman numerals

Circular case, the back painted with a scene of a classically dressed lady on a translucent blue enamel background over sunray engine turning, gold pailloné decorated border and bezel

52 mm. diam.

Listed working in Geneva at the end of the 18th and beginning of the 19th centuries, Chevalier et Compe specialised in gold watches with either enamel or pearl decoration.

Julien Le Roy

Gold and bloodstone quarter repeating á toc watch

Signed Julien Le Roy, Paris, circa 1760

Keywound verge movement, chain fusée, pierced and engraved balance bridge, baluster pillars

White enamel dial with Roman numerals and Arabic outer highlighted by applied diamonds, polychrome painted garland of flowers to the centre

Circular gold-mounted bloodstone case, the bloodstone bezel highlighted with gold swags and diamonds, diamond-set pendant and thumb piece

42 mm. diam.

Julien Le Roy

Gold and painted on enamel watch

Signed J Le Roy, circa 1750

Keywound full plate verge movement, chain fusée, pierced and engraved balance bridge

White enamel dial with Roman numerals, winding through dial

Circular case with finely polychrome painted on enamel scene of Mars and Venus within a cloudy landscape, bezel similarly painted with a continuous landscape, inside case back painted with two putti

49 mm. diam.

Julien Le Roy was one of the most celebrated French watchmakers of his time. Born in Tours in 1686 into a family of five generations of watch and clockmakers, he had already made his first clock by the age of 13. In 1699, he moved to Paris for further training. Together with his brothers, he founded one of the most important clock and watch workshops of the time. Le Roy's reputation was based on his mechanical discoveries, including a special repeating mechanism that improved the precision of watches and clocks. In 1713 he became "maître horloger", then 'juré' of his guild. Further appointments followed, including the Directorship of the 'Société des Arts', but the pinnacle of his achievements was being appointed clockmaker (Horloger Ordinaire du Roi) to King Louis XV in 1739.

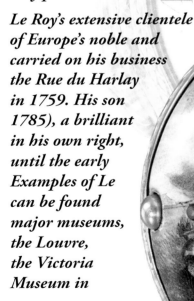

Le Roy's workshop also produced a large number of ordinary clocks and watches to satisfy wide public demand. During his life he is known to have made or supervised over 3,500 watches, amounting to an average of one hundred movements a year, or one every three days. In contrast, other workshops only produced between thirty and fifty pieces per year.

Le Roy's extensive clientele included many members of Europe's noble and royal families. He carried on his business from premises in the Rue du Harlay until his death in 1759. His son Pierre (1717-1785), a brilliant clockmaker in his own right, continued until the early 1780s. Examples of Le Roy's work can be found in many major museums, notably the Louvre, Paris, and the Victoria and Albert Museum in London.

William Grantham

Gold repoussé pair case watch with gilt-metal and shagreen outer protective case, made for the Dutch market

Signed Grantham, London, no. 9353, London hallmarks for 1765

Keywound full plate verge movement with chain fusée, square baluster pillars and pierced and engraved balance cock

White enamel dial with Roman numerals, arcaded minute ring with Arabic minutes numerals, marcasite-set hands

Circular cases, the plain gold inner case with winding aperture, the top of the pendant with decorative boss, maker's mark JF beneath a star incuse, pierced repoussé outer case in very high-relief with a scene depicting Joseph being sold to into slavery surrounded by chased and engraved shell and scroll work, the bezel similarly decorated, gilt-metal glazed outer protective case with shagreen bezels secured with gilt-metal pin work

45 mm. diam.

This watch is notable for the wonderful high-relief and pierced background of the gold repoussé work, which gives an added impression of depth to the scene. William Grantham appears to have specialised in making gold repoussé watches for the Dutch market. He is recorded working in London in the mid-18th century.

A similar high-relief gold repoussé watch signed William Grantham was formerly in the collection of The Lord Sandberg CBE.

Uhlmann & Branchu Fils

18K gold and painted on enamel hunting cased quarter repeating watch

Signed Uhlmann & Branchu Fils, circa 1850

Keyless cylinder movement, repeating with two polished steel hammers on coiled gongs

White enamel dial with Roman numerals

Circular case, the front cover decorated with a very finely painted on enamel portrait of a young girl, the rear cover with a Swiss alpine lake and mountain scene, both with pale blue champlevé enamel borders with engraved gold flowers, repeating slide in the band, gold cuvette

42 mm. diam.

Exquisitely enamelled, this watch must have been a bespoke commission perhaps from the parents of the young girl. The portrait is sensitively and tenderly rendered and is evidently by one of the great Geneva enamellists of the period. The bucolic Swiss lake scene with the distant Alps in the background is almost certainly a view from the shores of Lac Léman(Lake Geneva) near the Château de Chillon.

The firm of Uhlmann&Branchu Fils is recorded as working in Geneva in 1857.

Inv. 1663

Wooden Watch

Turned and carved boxwood watch with wooden movement and matching key

Unsigned, European, circa 1780

Wood full plate verge movement with turned baluster pillars, chain fusée, pierced continental balance cock

Wooden dial with carved and painted Roman numerals, wooden arrow hands

Circular boxwood case with turned details

53 mm. diam.

This watch is of a type made in Western Europe during the second half of the 18th century, predominantly in bone, ivory, or boxwood, and always with full-plate movements. Almost a century later, the Bronnikov family of watchmakers working in Vjatka, Russia, made quite distinctive watches whose movements are also usually made of wood or bone. In contrast to Bronnikov's watches, the dial of the present watch is made as a separate piece.

Inv. 1614

German

Small Gold and porcelain watch

Unsigned, possibly Berlin, circa 1770

Keywound full plate verge movement, chain fusée, pierced and engraved balance bridge

White enamel dial with Arabic numerals

Circular gold case, porcelain back painted with Watteauesque figures in a landscape, porcelain bezel decorated to match with fête galante scenes

33 mm. diam.

This unusually small and charming 18th century porcelain watch is thought to be Berlin porcelain. Although the porcelain parts of such watch cases were rarely signed by their makers due to space restrictions, they were often in fact made by the great German and French porcelain factories of the day.

Inv. 1732

Balsiger & Fils

18K gold and pearl-set pendant watch

Signed Balsiger & Fils à Genève, circa 1830

Keywoundgilt full-plate verge movement with chain fusée, pierced and chased continental balance cock

Gold dial with applied Roman numerals, varicolored gold foliate border, engine-turned centre

Circular case with hinged sprung bezel set with pearls and seed pearls, the back set with radiating graduated pearls

44 mm. diam.

Balsiger & Filswere active in Geneva from around 1820 to 1840. The firm specialized in the production of watches embellished with engravings, enamelled motifs, pearl and precious stone settings.

The present watch is a wonderful example of such a watch, distinguished by the lavish pearl decoration, a tour-de-force of the jeweller's art.

A watch signed Balsiger&Fils is in the collection of the Rijksmuseum (object no. BK-VBR-350-A)

Portrait of George Washington

Swiss

18K gold and painted on enamel hunter cased watch

Signed by the retailer James E. Spear, Charleston, S. C., circa 1850

Keywound gilt bar movement with lateral lever escapement

White enamel dial with Roman numerals

Circular case entirely foliate engraved and decorated with champlevé enamel leaves and flowers, the front cover with a finely painted on enamel portrait of George Washington after Gilbert Stuart, the back with a painted on enamel portrait thought to be Senator Daniel Webster, hinged gold cuvette engraved with flowers and with engine turned border

48 mm. diam.

This very rare watch, evidently a specially commissioned piece, is decorated with an image of George Washington taken from Gilbert Stuart's celebrated "Athenaeum" painting of the first President. The portrait on the back of the watch almost certainly depicts U.S. Secretary of State, Senator Daniel Webster. Made in Switzerland, the watch was retailed by the silversmith, jeweller and watchmaker, James Emmons Spear of Charleston, South Carolina. Born in 1817, his premises were located at 235, King Street, Charleston where he is recorded working between 1846 and 1871. He died in 1871.

George Washington (1732–1799) was the first President of the United States of America from 1789 until 1797. Washington was a military general, statesman, and Founding Father who led Patriot forces to victory in the War of Independence. Washington has been called the 'father of his country' for his leadership in the early days of the new American nation.

The artist Gilbert Stuart (1755-1828) created the most famous and popular portrait of Washington which has played a large part in establishing him as a cultural icon.

Daniel Webster (1782-1852) was a United States Senator and Secretary of State. Famed for his ability as an orator, Webster was one of the most important figures in the Second Party System from the 1820s to the 1850s.

Among Webster's most often quoted sayings is: "God grants liberty only to those who love it, and are always ready to guard and defend it".

Inv. 1082

Apollo

Jonathan Cater

18K gold repoussé pair case watch with gilt and shagreen outer protecting case

Signed Jonathan Cater, London, movement no. 6817, circa 1750

Keywound verge movement, chain fusée, pierced scroll pillars, finely chased, engraved and pierced scroll decorated balance cock

White enamel dial with Roman numerals and arcaded minute track

Circular case, plain gold inner case, the outer case pierced and decorated in repoussé with a scene of hunters paying homage to Apollo, scroll border

57 mm. diam.

This watch exhibits the rare type of repoussé work whereby the decoration in high relief is partially pierced to give the impression of extra depth to the scene.

Evidently working in London during the middle of the 18th century, few watches signed Jonathan Cater are known and scant biographical details are recorded. Another watch signed Jonathan Cater, no. 5930, also features a gold repoussé case, although of typical form unlike the dramatic high-relief decoration of the present watch.

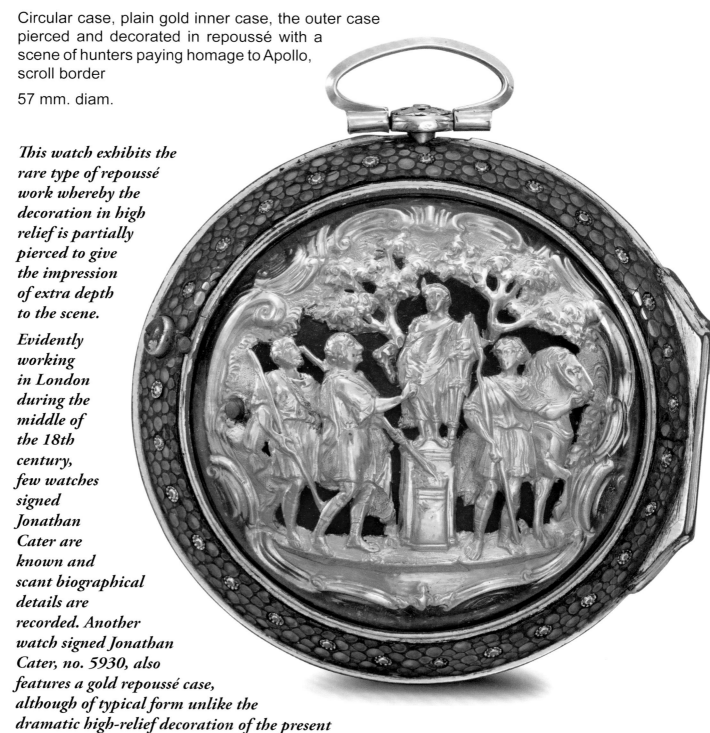

Inv. 1199

Swiss

18K pink gold skeletonised watch, the movement in the shape of a vase

Unsigned, circa 1820

Keywound skeletonized vase-shaped movement, verge escapement, chain fusée, visible balance

White enamel dial with Arabic numerals

Circular case glazed on both sides, reeded band

46 mm. diam.

Legend has it that once, when leaving Holland, Napoleon's coach got stuck in the mud. A passer-by helped to get the coach moving again and for his help was given a "gold watch with vase-shaped movement" as a token of his gratitude.

A similar watch was in the Stanley Burton Collection, sold by Sotheby's London, 4th June 1992, lot 109.

Inv. 1092

Swiss

18K gold and painted on enamel pearl-set watch

Unsigned, circa 1800

Keywound verge movement, chain fusée, continental balance cock

White enamel dial with Breguet numerals, pierced gold urn hands

Circular case 'Directoire' style, the bezel decorated with white and blue champlevé enamel in a geometric pattern, polished band, the back decorated with a finely painted polychrome enamel scene of a young couple in a formal garden, he seated holding a guitar, split-pearl-set border, the surround decorated with engraved gold drape, red and blue translucent enamel, flowers and a pair of doves above

50 mm. diam.

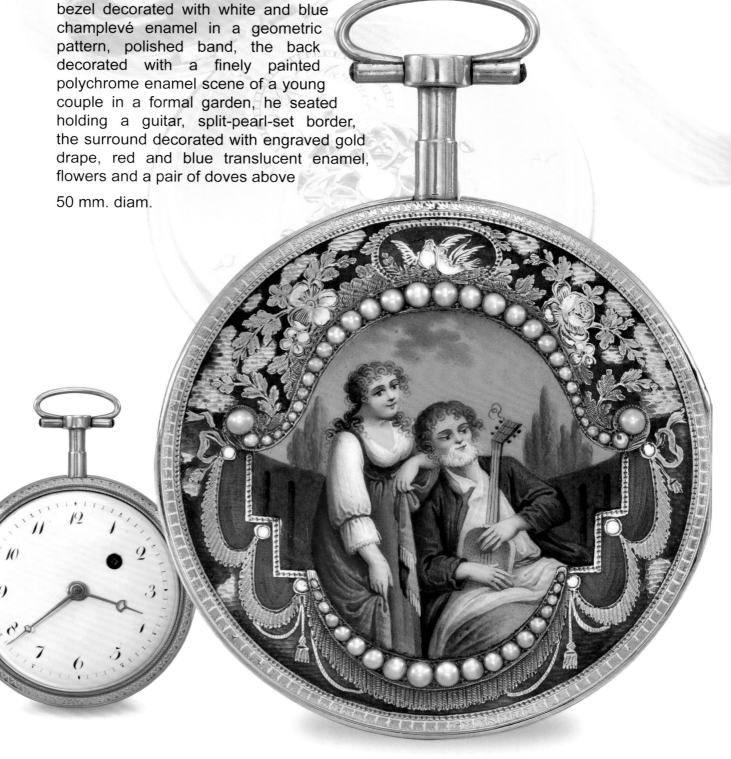

Inv. 1204

Elizer & Rebecca

French

Louis XV gold repoussé and enamel watch

Unsigned, circa 1760

Keywound verge movement, pentagonal baluster pillars, chain fusée, pierced and engraved balance cock

White enamel dial with Roman numerals and outer Arabic five-minute numerals, green enamel and gold repoussé centre

Circular case overlaid with blue enamel imitating hardstone and gold repoussé scene representing Elizer and Rebecca, a camel to the right and well to the left, the bezel decorated with foliate motifs

46 mm. diam.

The enamel of the case of this watch can be attributed to Bouvier and a similar example is in the Cognacq Jay Museum in Paris, A further example was in the Bloch-Pimentel Collection, Hotel Drouot, Paris, 1961.

Inv. 1368

Gregson

18K gold, painted on enamel and pearl-set openface watch

Signed Gregson à Paris, movement no. 7104, circa 1810

Keywound gilt full-plate verge movement, chain fusée, pierced and engraved continental cock

White enamel dial with Arabic numerals, pierced filigree gold hands

Circular case with half pearl-set bezel and border, the back with a finely painted on enamel portrait of a young bride wearing roses in her hair

53 mm. diam.

Jean-Pierre Gregson originally came from England. In 1776 he was appointed watchmaker to the King in Paris. He was one of the first watchmakers of his time to use the Lépine calibre.

Inv. 1207

Dubois & Fils

18K gold wandering hour and quarter repeating watch

Signed Dubois & Fils, no. 7328, circa 1820

Keywound cylinder movement, unusual balance bridge, gilt scrolls on the barrel, repeating with two hammers on two gongs

White enamel dial, segment division for minutes, Arabic numerals, central gold panel engraved with figure of Chronos, wandering enamel cartouche for hour indication pointing to the precise minute indication

Circular Empire-style case, the back engine turned with a small cartouche with engraved initials, gilt and gold spring loaded cuvette, inside case back stamped with case maker's mark 'PHPI'

57.5 mm. diam.

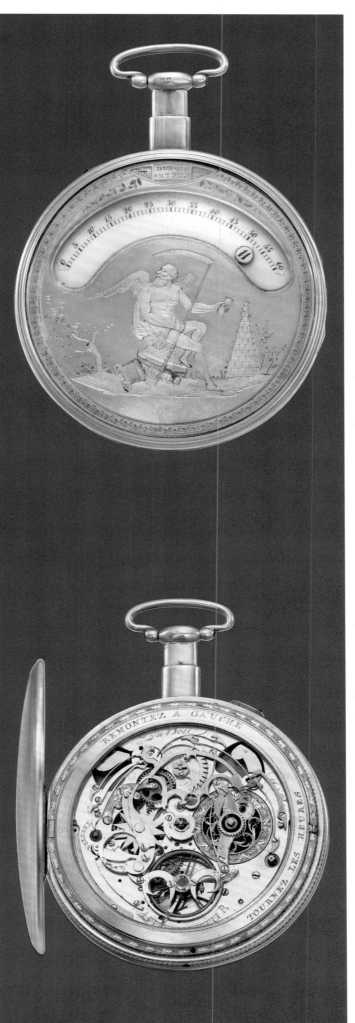

Watches with a wandering hour dial first appeared in the 17th century and have enjoyed intermittent revivals ever since. More recently, the idea was introduced into the wristwatch.

Interestingly, Aimé Janneret-Dubois is known to have made watches which were sold under the Breguet name, an example by him and retailed by Breguet in 1824 was sold by Antiquorum, Geneva, May 15, 2005, lot 191.

A similar watch was formerly in the Sandberg Collection, sold by Antiquorum Geneva, October 16, 2005, lot 51. Another signed Dubois & Fils, was sold by Christie's Hong Kong, 31st May 2005, lot 2054 and another example from the Stanley Burton Collection was sold by Sotheby's London, 4th June 1992, lot 108.

It would appear that most of the wandering hour watches from this period were made or finished in the same workshop and bear the same case mark 'PHPI' as the present watch.

Dubois & Fils watchmakers are recorded in: Dictionnaire des Horlogers Genevois, La 'fabrique' et les arts annexes du XVIe siècle à nos jours, Genève, p. 166.

François Louis Chavanne

Small gold and painted on enamel hunter case pendant watch

Signed F. L. Chavanne in Wien, movement no. 1367, circa 1810

Keywound verge movement, chain fusée, engraved and pierced balance bridge

White enamel dial with Roman numerals, the centre painted with a scene of a classically dressed young couple

Circular case, entirely painted on enamel with scenes depicting Venus and Mars with cupid, the inside cover and back painted with classical ruins and figures strolling amongst ruins in a landscape

28 mm. diam.

François Louis Chavanne originally came from Geneva, he died in 1823. He is recorded in: Viennese Clockmakers, F.H. van Weijdom Claterbos, Schiedam, 1979, p.152.

Inv. 1364

Lhoest

18K three-colour gold granulation decorated and gem-set openface quarter repeater watch

Signed Lhoest à Paris, circa 1830

Keywound full plate verge movement, chain fusée, pierced and engraved continental cock, quarter repeating with two hammers on two gongs activated by depressing the pendant

Engine turned gold dial decoratively engraved between the champlevé Roman numerals

Circular case with applied three-colour gold foliate decoration and set with coloured semi-precious stones, hinged gold cuvette

40 mm. diam.

Granulation, a technique using tiny beads of gold, was employed, and probably invented, by the ancient Etruscans. The present lot employs real granulation, which is rare. Most of the watches from the period using this method employed a technique in which ready-to-apply gold beads wires were soldered onto the surface, thereby forming the desired pattern.

The maker Lhoest is recorded by Tardy as working in Paris around 1820 at rue du Fg St-Honoré.

Inv. 1400

Johann Friedrich Stalpp

Pink gold and carved bloodstone watch

Signed Stalpp, Dresden, circa 1780

Keywound verge movement, chain fusée, pierced and engraved balance bridge, baluster pillars

White enamel dial with Roman numerals and Arabic outer

Circular gold-mounted bloodstone case, the back decorated with putti flanking a fountain carved in relief, bloodstone bezel carved with flowers also in relief

45 mm. diam.

Johann Friedrich Stalpp is recorded working in Dresden and became Master in 1767, he died in 1789.

Another carved bloodstone watch by Stalpp is in the collection of the Mathematisch-Physikalischer Salon in Dresden.

Bloodstone, or heliotrope, is a variety of jasper; particularly the green form with inclusions of red hematite, supposedly resembling spots of blood; hence the name 'bloodstone'. It features as an invisibility stone in Boccaccio's Decameron, and is sometimes used in carved signet rings and is the traditional birthstone for March.

Inv. 1396

The Rape of Europa

Attributed to Augustin Heckel

Gold and painted on enamel watch, the enamel painted after Simon Vouet (1590-1649)

Signed Henkeels, circa 1760

Keywound full plate gilt verge movement with chain fusée

White enamel dial with Roman numerals and outer Arabic five-minute numerals

Circular case with engraved and chased gold bezel and band, the back decorated with a very finely painted on enamel scene of ,'The Rape of Europa' after Simon Vouet

40 mm. diam.

The case is very finely enamelled and extremely beautiful. Evidently painted by the hand of a highly skilled, almost certainly Geneva based artist, it conveys a real depth, strength and richness of colour which is comparable to Simon Vouet's original painting "The Rape of Europa", circa 1640, now in the Museo Nacional Thyssen-Bornemisza, Madrid, Inv. no. 428 (1966.4). The general aura of the enamel scene faithfully recaptures the style of the late 17th century, being almost Huaud-esque in technique. In the traditional way, the enamellist would have copied the image first from an engraving of the subject, the finished enamel scene therefore being in reverse to Vouet's original picture.

The watchmaker signing 'Henkeels' is obscure. It is possible that the maker was Augustin Heckel (1690-1770), working in London but originally from an Augsburg family of goldsmiths. However, this is conjecture and remains unsubstantiated. Equally, the signature may simply be apocryphal.

An earlier watch circa 1645, with later movment signed Lambertus Vrythoff, decorated with the same subject is in the collection of the Metropolitan Museum of Art in New York, the Gift of J. Pierpont Morgan, 1917, (Inv.17.190.1413).

Philipe Miège à Genève

Gold and painted on enamel watch

Signed PhilipeMiège à Genève,circa 1770

Keywoundgilt verge movement, chain fusée,balance bridge pierced and engraved with foliate scrolls, quadrangular pillars

White enamel dial

Circular case with polychrome painted on enamel still life of fruit and flowers on a ledge, within an engraved gold border, the bezel decorated with enamel flower sprays

45 mm. diam.

Philipe Miège of Geneva was born in 1702 and died in 1785.

Philipe Miège à Genève

The Family

H.R. Ekegren

18K gold hunter case minute-repeating split-second chronograph watch with date and unique enamel family portrait by John Graff, circa 1885

Signed H. R. Ekegren, the enamel signed J. Graff

Keyless damascened nickel lever movement, swan-neck regulator

White enamel dial, two vertical subsidiary dials for date and seconds, painted enamel portraits of George Ehret and his wife Anna

Circular case, the front and back covers with vari-coloured gold monogram and date, concealed cover with painted polychrome enamel portrait of the Ehret family, signed J. Graff

51 mm. diam.

This watch was especially customized for George Ehret, one of the leading American beer brewers of the 19th century. Born in Germany in 1835, Ehret's father, Anselm had emigrated to New York City in 1852. George became widely known and greatly respected and was noted for his scientific attention to detail and high quality product. His Hell Gate Brewery in Yorkville on the Upper East Side of Manhattan made him a millionaire after he became one of the first brewers to introduce lager beer to the American market.

This watch was given to Ehret on his 50th birthday by his wife Anna and nine living children. The exquisite portrait of all the family members by J. Graff, as well as the portraits of Ehret and his wife on the dial show the wealth and high character of the family.

John Graff (1836-1902) created portraits in enamel of such high quality and resemblance to their subject that his work was world-renowned around the globe. He received commissions from Indian maharajas, European nobility and American industrialists, among others. Because of his mastery in the field, John Graff's signature on watches and snuff boxes became highly sought-after during his lifetime and continues to attract the connoisseur of enamel works today.

J. Graff's enamel portraits are illustrated in: Technique and History of the Swiss Watch, E. Jaquet & A. Chapuis, pl. 133, for a discussion of his work, see p. 100 of the same text.

The firm of H.R. Ekegren was founded in 1856 by Henri-Robert Ekegren (1823-1896). The company became the official watchmaker to the King of Denmark. The son of Daniel Ekegrén, a Swedish watchmaker, Henri-Robert worked for Jules Jürgensen in in Le Locle, Winnerl in Paris, and Henri Golay in Geneva, where he had moved in 1847. At the 1867 Paris Exhibition, Ekegren displayed thirty-six watches, winning a gold medal.

In 1891, Edward Koehn, a director of Patek Philippe bought the company and from that date the watches were signed Ed. Koehn, Successors to H. R. Ekegren.

Elkington & Co.

18K gold and pearl-set openface watch with part-visible movement

Signed Elkington & Co., Regent Street, London, movement no. 20443, circa 1850

Keywound full plate movement with English lever escapement, chain fusée

White enamel dial with Arabic numerals

Circular case glazed on both sides, pierced and engraved gold monogram over the movement, bezels set with split-pearls

48 mm. diam.

ELKINGTON & CO.

From relatively small beginnings as manufacturers of gilt-toys, spectacle cases and silver-mounted scent bottles, the firm of Elkington rose to prominence when its founder George Richards Elkington perfected and patented in 1840 the technique of electroplating. The invention revolutionised the silver-plate industry, particularly as Elkington allowed other manufactures under licence, including Christofle et Cie. of Paris, to use the process. The huge demand transformed Elkington and Christofle into manufacturers on an industrial scale. Elkington continued, however, to show artistic commitment by producing exact copies in electrotype, with silver, gold or bronze finishes, of some of the greatest historical vases and vessels of ancient and medieval art. They thus responded to that peculiarly Victorian brand of historic kleptomania, and the desire of the bourgeois to own objects which convey lineage and connoisseurship.

Bolstering their credentials as the archetypal manufacture of 'industrial art' and to ensure their output reflected the latest fashions, Elkington employed the finest artists of the day to produce unique designs, including Benjamin Schlick, Pierre-Emile Jeannest, Leonard Morel-Ladeuil, Auguste Adolphe Willms and Edward Welby Pugin, G. Halliday and Christopher Dresser. Therefore, although Elkington produced a vast output of all types of silver and electroplate, the huge revenues this generated allowed them to commission artists to craft 'haute couture' objets d'art for display and so demonstrate the supreme capabilities of their workshops.

Inv. 1377

Bordier

Pink gold, painted on enamel and split pearl-set quarter repeating watch

Signed Frères Bordier à Genève, circa 1815

Gilt full plate verge movement, chain fusée, pierced and engraved balance bridge, repeating on a bell

White enamel dial with Arabic numerals

Circular case, the back decorated with a polychrome painted on enamel scene of a young couple at the altar of love, both bezels set with a double row of pearls, gilt metal outer protecting case with glazed back

56.5 mm. diam.

The frères Bordier were working from 1787. In 1815 they are recorded at the Place Grand Mézel in Geneva. They are particularly known for repeating watches, form watches, and watches decorated with precious stones and enamel with classic chain fusée and verge escapement movements.

Inv. 1809

Louis Duchêne & Fils

18K gold and painted on enamel pearl-set quarter repeating watch

Signed Ls. Duchêne & Fils, circa 1795

Keywound verge movement with chain fusée, engraved and pierced balance cock, repeating with two hammers on a bell activated by depressing the pendant

White enamel dial with Arabic numerals

Circular case with pearl-set bezels, the back decorated with a finely painted on enamel scene of two lovers from classical antiquity in a landscape with winged Cupid looking on and two dogs at their feet, blue and white paillonné border

50 mm. diam.

The master watchmaker Louis Duchêne (1730-1804) of Geneva was renowned for his repeating and automata watches. From 1791 his son was taken into partnership and the firm became "Louis Duchêne & Fils". The company excelled in the manufacture of finely enamelled form watches and watches with all conceivable complications.

Several watches signed Ls. Duchêne & Fils are illustrated in:Technique and History of the Swiss Watch, Eugène Jaquet and Alfred Chapuis,

pl. 74, 87, 102 and 110.

Inv. 1842

Guex

18K gold, painted on enamel and pearl-set watch

Signed Guex, no. 13787, circa 1790

Keywound gilt verge movement with chain fusée, pierced and engraved balance cock

White enamel dial with Arabic numerals

Circular case, the back decorated with a polychrome painted on enamel scene of a lady in classical costume and a putto holding a mirror, translucent royal blue enamel ground over engine turning, painted and gold Pailloné border, both bezels set with spilt-pearls

48 mm. diam.

The Paris watchmaker Guex is recorded working around 1790, specialising in enamelled and pearl-set watches. Other watches signed Guex were in the Ilbert and Feill collections and an example in the form of a lyre is in the collection of the Mathematisch-Physikalischen Salon, Dresden.

Klett A Sühl

Steel and varicoloured gold watch with chinoiserie decorated case

Signed Klett A Sühl, circa 1760

Gilt full plate verge movement, baluster pillars, pierced and engraved balance bridge, chain fusée

White enamel dial with Roman numerals and outer Arabic five-minute numerals, rose-cut diamond-set hands

Steel case with applied three-colour gold decoration, the bezelinlaid and applied with chased gold geometric patterns, the back inlaid with a chased gold scene of Chinese inspiration, the border decoration matching that of the bezel

44mm. diam.

This steel watch inlaid with multicoloured gold is a fascinating and rare example of a watch case made by the famous Klett family, shotgun and rifle makers since 1578 in the German town of Sühl, 130 miles north of Nuremberg. Until the late 19th century, Sühlwas the centre of Germany's arms production. Iron had already been produced in the southern valleys of the Thuringian Forest since the 13th Century, by the 16th century, the town, beside the river Hasel, developed into a centre of weaponry makers, establishing the worldwide reputation of German gunsmiths.

On occasion, gunsmiths such as Klett used their metalworking skills to create refined precious objects. This watch is one of the very few surviving examples of its type. The chinoiserie decoration of the case was the height of fashion in mid-18th century Europe, its design may well have been inspired by the chinoiserie porcelain being produced by the Meissen factory near Dresden at the same period.

Inv. 1811

Mikhail Semyonovitch Bronnikov

Small watch entirely made of boxwood with original wooden box and remnants of chain

Signed Bronnikov, Vjatka, (Russia), circa 186

Keywound movment entirely made of wood with pinned bridges, going barrel with steel mainspring, cylinder escapement, plain wood balance

Wooden with Arabic numerals on white cartouches and subsidiary seconds

Circular wooden case with hinged back cover, polished, bezels with turned ribs at the edges

35.5 mm. diam.

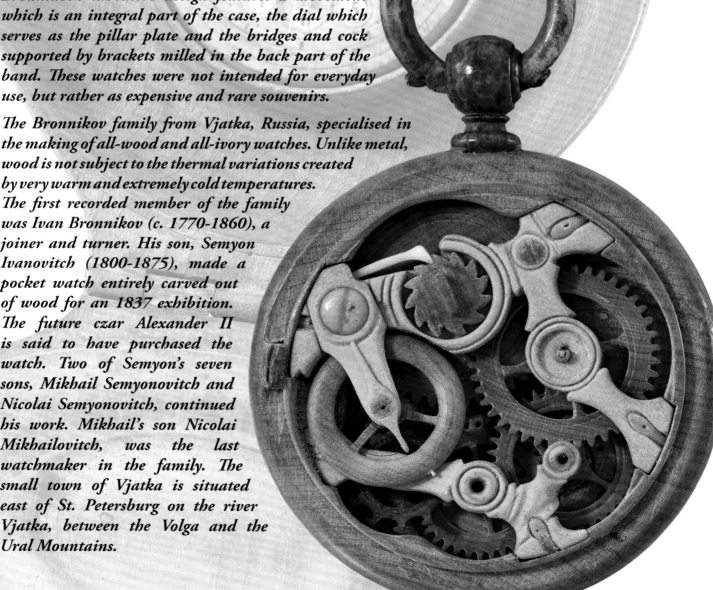

Bronnikov's inventive design features a movement which is an integral part of the case, the dial which serves as the pillar plate and the bridges and cock supported by brackets milled in the back part of the band. These watches were not intended for everyday use, but rather as expensive and rare souvenirs.

The Bronnikov family from Vjatka, Russia, specialised in the making of all-wood and all-ivory watches. Unlike metal, wood is not subject to the thermal variations created by very warm and extremely cold temperatures. The first recorded member of the family was Ivan Bronnikov (c. 1770-1860), a joiner and turner. His son, Semyon Ivanovitch (1800-1875), made a pocket watch entirely carved out of wood for an 1837 exhibition. The future czar Alexander II is said to have purchased the watch. Two of Semyon's seven sons, Mikhail Semyonovitch and Nicolai Semyonovitch, continued his work. Mikhail's son Nicolai Mikhailovitch, was the last watchmaker in the family. The small town of Vjatka is situated east of St. Petersburg on the river Vjatka, between the Volga and the Ural Mountains.

Inv. 1879

Mikhail Semyonovitch Bronnikov

A pocket watch entirely made of bone with original carved bone chain, key and hook

Signed Bronnikov, Vjatka, (Russia), circa 1865

Keywound movment entirely made of bone with pinned bridges, going barrel with steel mainspring, cylinder escapement, plain bone three-arm balance

The dial is made of bone with Arabic numerals on white cartouches and subsidiary seconds

Circular bone case with hinged back cover engraved with Cyrillic initials below the mitre of a Russian orthodox bishop, polished, bezels with turned ribs at the edges

41 mm. diam.

Traditionally thought to be made of mammoth bone, Bronnikov's all-bone watches are the rarest type with only one or two other examples known. Entirely hand-made, each Bronnikov watch is actually a unique piece.

Bronnikov's wooden and bone watches were more expensive than a gold watch at the time and although less reliable and accurate, they were highly prized in Russia and often used as expensive unique gifts. They were also awarded numerous Russian and international prizes.

Jean-François Poncet

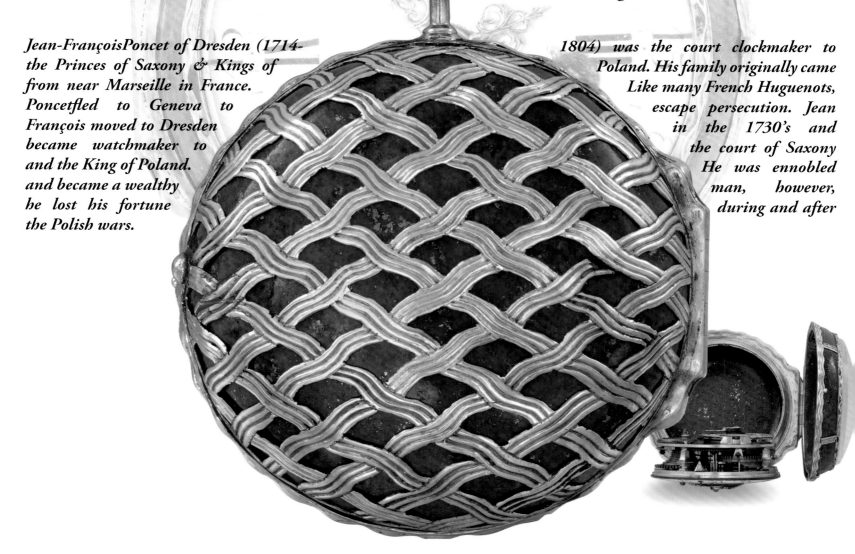

Gold and lapis lazuli watch

Signed Poncet A Dresde, circa 1775

Gilt full plateverge movement, pierced and engraved balance bridge, chainfusée

White enamel dial with Roman numerals, Arabic five-minute numerals, pierced gold hands

Circular lapis lazulimounted case with chased gold wavy-line basket-weave mounts, the bezel set with four curved panels of lapis lazuli

44mm. diam.

This very beautiful watch is one of only a handful of known examples with a lapis lazuli case. In the second half of the 18th century, Dresden was famous for the production of incredibly fine precious objects combining the art of the lapidary and the goldsmith. Exemplified by the work of Johann Christian Neuber (1736-1809), court goldsmith in Dresden, his father-in-law Heinrich Taddel and Christian Gottlieb Stiehl (1708-1792) who made hardstone-set watch cases inspired directly by enamelled gold watchcases made in Paris. Stiehl held appointments to Augustus the Strong, King of Poland and Elector of Saxony (1670-1733), and his successor, Augustus III (1696-1763).

Jean-FrançoisPoncet of Dresden (1714-1804) was the court clockmaker to the Princes of Saxony & Kings of Poland. His family originally came from near Marseille in France. Like many French Huguenots, Poncetfled to Geneva to escape persecution. Jean François moved to Dresden in the 1730's and became watchmaker to the court of Saxony and the King of Poland. He was ennobled and became a wealthy man, however, he lost his fortune during and after the Polish wars.

J. F. Bautte & Cie

Gold and painted on enamel watch

Signed J. F. Bautte à Paris, no. 49690, circa 1835

Keywound Lépine calibre cylinder movement

Silvered engine turned dial with Roman numerals

Circular case with twelve segments painted on enamel with alternating flowers, musical, military and love trophies, hinged gold cuvette

42 mm. diam.

The firm J.F. Bautte & Cie. in Geneva was founded by the celebrated Swiss watchmaker Jean-François Bautte (1772-1837). He established the most complete factory at the time and employed around 300 workers for the production of movements, watchcases, dials, jewellery and automatons. The firm counted many European Royal Families among their clientele and supplied watches also to Turkey, India and China.

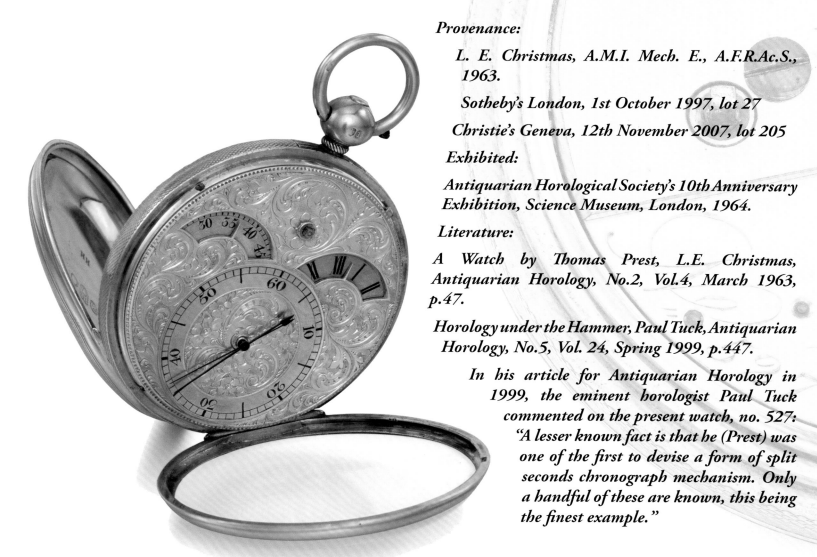

Inv. 1891

Thomas Prest

18K gold splittable seconds openface timing watch with sector apertures for hours and minutes with a gold and lapis lazuli chain and key

Signed Thomas Prest, Chigwell, no. 527, the case with London hallmarks for 1840

Keywoundgilded full plate lever movement with chain fusée,seconds splitting mechanism visible under the dial with recessed barrel pivoted around the fourth wheel pivot, spiral spring surmounted by the split-seconds hand

Gold dial plate with engraved scroll and foliate decoration, large eccentric seconds ring with Arabic ten second divisions with two blued steel seconds hands, two sectors for Roman hours and Arabic minutes, hand setting square above 60

Circular engine turned case, button in the pendant for stopping one seconds hand, movement stop slide beneath the bezel for stopping both hands, back and cuvette punched with casemaker's mark HH inc use (possibly Henry Hardy),plain polished gold cuvette

51.5mm. diam.

Provenance:

> *L. E. Christmas, A.M.I. Mech. E., A.F.R.Ac.S., 1963.*
>
> *Sotheby's London, 1st October 1997, lot 27*
>
> *Christie's Geneva, 12th November 2007, lot 205*

Exhibited:

Antiquarian Horological Society's 10th Anniversary Exhibition, Science Museum, London, 1964.

Literature:

A Watch by Thomas Prest, L.E. Christmas, Antiquarian Horology, No.2, Vol.4, March 1963, p.47.

Horology under the Hammer, Paul Tuck, Antiquarian Horology, No.5, Vol. 24, Spring 1999, p.447.

> *In his article for Antiquarian Horology in 1999, the eminent horologist Paul Tuck commented on the present watch, no. 527: "A lesser known fact is that he (Prest) was one of the first to devise a form of split seconds chronograph mechanism. Only a handful of these are known, this being the finest example."*

Thomas Prest was apprenticed to John Roger Arnold in January 1784 and became his foreman before establishing his own business in Chigwell, Essex, about 1820. Today, Prest is remembered largely for his patent no.4501 of 20th October, 1820, for akeyless winding system, the first such mechanism to be commercially viable, pre-dating Adrien Philippe's keyless system of 1845. It has been suggested that early in his working life, Thomas Prest may perhaps have worked for the great Abraham-Louis Breguet in Paris.

Certainly this exceptional and very rare predecessor of the split-seconds chronograph is the product of a highly skilled watchmaker with an original and inventive horological mind.

The split-seconds chronograph mechanism as we know it today appeared in the last quarter of the 19th century. Its primary function is to time different events that begin but do not end together. The present watch, dating from 1840 and therefore of a much earlier date, can be used for this purpose too, for very short periods. It is extremely interesting both in its quality and as one of the earliest ancestors of the true split-seconds chronograph. Furthermore, it also predates the first standard chronograph with a reset function patented in England by Adolphe Nicole in 1844 under number 10348 (registered again in Paris by Henri-Feréol Piguet of Nicole et Capt in Solliat in 1862). However, unlike the Adolphe Nicole patent, the hands of the present watch cannot be reset to zero nor can both hands be stopped without stopping the main train.

By depressing the button in the pendant, one of the seconds hands is stopped and 'splits' from its twin, the other hand continues to run. When the button is released, the second hand that was halted flies back to join the running hand. A period of 25 seconds elapses before an arm on which one end of the spring to which the seconds hand is attached engages a pin to the underside of the plate to prevent the spring from being overwound.

Inv. 1075

Patek Philippe

18K gold, enamel and diamond-set openface pendant watch with brooch and original box

Signed Patek Philippe & Cie., Genève, movement no. 104'854, case no. 217'316, manufactured in 1895

Cal. 10''' keyless lever movement, 18 jewels, bimetallic compensation balance, wolf's tooth winding, 18K gold-rimmed glazed dust cover

Translucent scarlet enamel dial on guilloché sunburst design background, gilt Breguet numerals, gold Louis XV hands

Circular outer case with translucent scarlet champlevé enamel on guilloché background and diamond-set floral and foliage decorated bezel and rim, the reverse centred by an asymmetrical painted polychrome enamel miniature depicting a nymph holding a cornucopia, surrounded by a diamond-set border, together with a matching 18K gold and translucent scarlet enamel wing-shaped brooch enhanced with diamond-set Ottoman motifs

27 mm. diam., 73 mm. overall length

Accompanied by the Patek Philippe Extract from the Archives confirming production of the present watch with red enamel dial and dauphine hour markers, 'Amour' surrounded with rose-cut diamonds and red enamel to the 18K yellow gold inner case in 1895 and its subsequent sale on 25 September 1899. With Patek Philippe original fitted leather presentation box numbered 104'854 containing a spare crystal.

The Extract from the Archives also confirms an outer case in 18K pink gold with 'Hercule' in repoussé work which does not exist anymore. However, given the fact that the presentation box of this watch was originally fitted to house it with a brooch, the outer case might have been used for the manufacture of the brooch shortly after the purchase of the watch in 1899.

Similarly decorated pendant watches are on permanent exhibition at the Patek Philippe Museum in Geneva.

Inv. 1835

Patek Philippe

18K gold and painted on enamel diamond-set hunter case lady's pendant watch

Signed Patek Philippe & Co., Genève, no. 38'755, sold on 17th November 1871

Keyless lever movement, the balance with gold adjustment screws

White enamel dial

Circular case entirely engraved, the front cover painted on enamel with two putti and a flower garland around a black central oval cartouche set with old-cut diamonds, the back cover decorated with painted on enamel flower garland around a black oval cartouche with engraved gold centre, both covers with black champlevé enamel borders

37 mm. diam.

Patek Philippe for Tiffany & Co. New York

18K gold, enamel and diamond-set Art Nouveau pendant watch with matching brooch

Signed Patek Philippe & Cie, Genève delivered to Tiffany & Co., New York, movement no. 124'917, case no. 235'142, manufactured in 1904

Keyless movement with compensation balance

White enamel dial with Breguet numerals

Circular case with a moulded and chased profile of a young girl in high Art Nouveau style, her face overlaid with opalescent enamel, her jewellery set with diamonds, the background in translucent green enamel. 18K gold brooch with almost identical matching decoration

28 mm. diam.

According to the Patek Philippe Extract from the Archives, this watch was made in 1904 and sold on August 30th, 1904.

This exquisite watch and its matching brooch is a full expression of Art Nouveau gold and enamel work of the finest workmanship and made by Switzerland's greatest manufacturer, Patek Philippe. The Art Nouveau style when applied to watches was beloved in particular by the American market, this example is no exception and was made especially for Tiffany & Co., the celebrated New York-based jeweller and retailer of exclusive luxury items whose products have adorned many of the leading socialites and stars of the past one and a half centuries.

Tiffany & Co.

Originally founded as Tiffany & Young by Charles Lewis Tiffany and John B. Young in 1837, the firm has grown from its first outlet in New York's Manhattan district to one of the world's foremost jewellers.

Few jewellers have captured the public imagination to such an extent as Tiffany & Co. The firm's diamonds, rings and necklaces have been worn by members of some of the wealthiest nineteenth and twentieth centuries families of the new world, including the Astors and the Vanderbilts. Another faithful and most notable patron of Tiffany & Co. was the prominent banker Henry Graves Junior, owner of the to date most valuable Patek Philippe "grand complication" watch ever sold at auction.

The house's fame was further immortalised by the 1961 movie 'Breakfast at Tiffany's' starring Audrey Hepburn, and the song 'Diamonds Are a Girl's Best Friend' sung by Marilyn Monroe in 1953s 'Gentlemen Prefer Blondes'.

Tiffany & Co.'s strong links to the world of horology span almost 160 years, starting with the collaboration between Patek Philippe & Co. dating back to 1849. The agreement heralded one of the most famous relationships in the world of horology and in 1851, Tiffany & Co. began to officially retail Patek Philippe watches at its New York store, thus becoming Patek Philippe's oldest retailer and, importantly, providing the celebrated manufacturer with a gateway to the new world. By the 1940s, the United States of America had become Patek Philippe's largest and most important market.

A formal agreement covering the import and sale of Patek Philippe watches was signed by the two companies in 1854 and the ties deepened further in 1878 when Tiffany & Co. decided to sell its Geneva factory to Patek Philippe. Thereafter, Patek Philippe supplied the jeweller with both movements for Tiffany-branded watches from the Geneva plant and also their own timepieces for sale in the U.S.

Such was Tiffany's importance that Patek Philippe double signed the wristwatches it sold at the New York store with a Tiffany & Co. signature, a process reserved for only a handful of the firm's selected retailers.

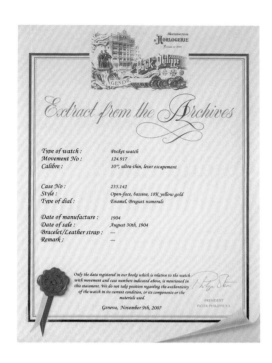

HORLOGERIE

Extract from the Archives

Type of watch :	Pocket watch
Movement No :	124.917
Calibre :	10''', ultra-thin, lever escapement
Case No :	235.142
Style :	Open-face, bassine, 18K yellow gold
Type of dial :	Enamel, Breguet numerals
Date of manufacture :	1904
Date of sale :	August 30th, 1904
Bracelet/Leather strap :	—
Remark :	—

Only the data registered in our books which is relative to the watch
with movement and case numbers indicated above, is mentioned in
this statement. We do not take position regarding the authenticity
of the watch in its current condition, or its components or the
materials used.

Geneva, November 9th, 2007

PRESIDENT
PATEK PHILIPPE S.A.

Inv. 1894

Marcinhes

Gold double-dialled watch with mock pendulum and slow-beat frictional rest escapement with pirouette

Signed Marcinhes à Paris, circa 1780

Gilt brassfull plate movement with conical pillars, going barrel, frictional rest escapement, the escape-wheel with "C" shaped teeth, steel balance staff mounted with the counterpoised mock pendulum arm, inverted three-arm balance wheel mounted between the dial and frontplate with toothed rim geared to the three-arm brass pirouette wheel, blued steel flat balance spring, index regulator lever in the dial-plate

Mean time dial: white enamel with Roman numerals, outer Arabic five minute numerals, winding aperture at 12, secured by a screw, gold "beetle and poker" hands. Reverse dial: small, eccentric, white enamel with Roman numerals, outer Arabic five minute numerals, border of finely chased varicoloured gold leaf-swags above four pillars and a vase of flowers, engraved gold, mirror-polished and blued steel background, aperture for the mock pendulum below

Circular "Louis XV" case with engraved bezels, both sides glazed.

43 mm. Diam.

Both highly decorative and technically sophisticated, this fine and important double dialled watch appears to be the only surviving example of its type to be signed by the little-known Paris maker Marcinhes. It is probable that Marcinhes was related to the accomplished Genevan miniaturist Pierre-François Marcinhès (1739-1778).

Its concept and construction would have required considerable mathematical and practical ability, which suggests that its creator may well have trained in the workshops of one of the great Paris makers such as Le Roy or Lépine. The slow-beating frictional rest escapement is a variation of the cylinder escapement. Its purpose in this watch is presumably to allow the mock pendulum to display an elegant slower swing so as to be more pleasing to the eye. In theory the watch could be used to show two different times if required. However, it was made long before the concept of time-zones existed, therefore, itwould have been made as an exquisite and expensive novelty for a rich customer. One side of the watch has a standard white enamel dial, the other side a miniature clock. The illusion of the 'swinging pendulum' would have mesmerised and fascinated the observer at the time who would not have comprehended how such a 'pendulum' could be seemingly working in a pocket watch.

Courvoisier & Compagnie

18K gold large quarter repeating watch with sunrise and sunset indications, date and months calendar

Signed Courvoisier et Comp., case no. 2134, circa 1820

Keywound full plate cylinder movement with steel escape wheel, going barrel, balance and escape wheel jewelled, skeletonized steel cock, repeating work on the back plate

Annular white enamel dial with Breguet numerals, gold centre with engraved foliate decoration, day and night aperture at 12, date at 4 and months at 8

Circular Empire type case with engine turned back, reeded band, glazed cuvette hinged to the movement ring

60 mm. diam.

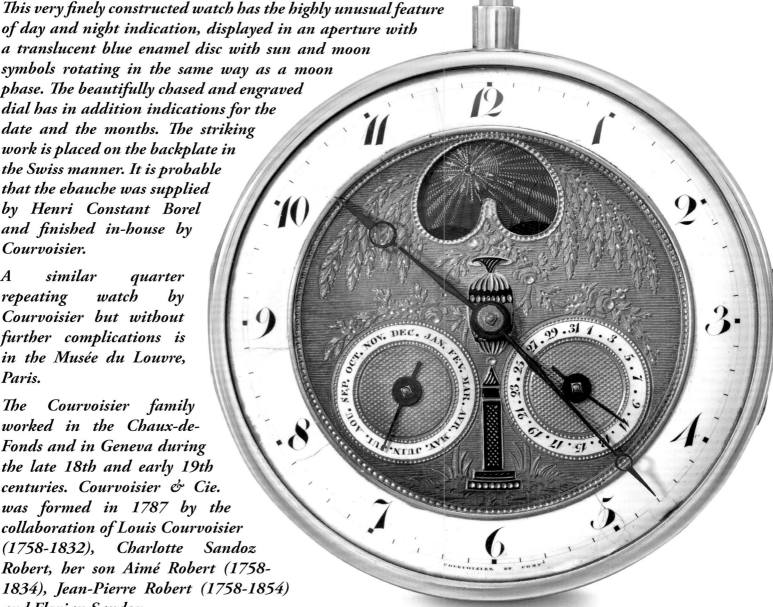

This very finely constructed watch has the highly unusual feature of day and night indication, displayed in an aperture with a translucent blue enamel disc with sun and moon symbols rotating in the same way as a moon phase. The beautifully chased and engraved dial has in addition indications for the date and the months. The striking work is placed on the backplate in the Swiss manner. It is probable that the ebauche was supplied by Henri Constant Borel and finished in-house by Courvoisier.

A similar quarter repeating watch by Courvoisier but without further complications is in the Musée du Louvre, Paris.

The Courvoisier family worked in the Chaux-de-Fonds and in Geneva during the late 18th and early 19th centuries. Courvoisier & Cie. was formed in 1787 by the collaboration of Louis Courvoisier (1758-1832), Charlotte Sandoz Robert, her son Aimé Robert (1758-1834), Jean-Pierre Robert (1758-1854) and Florian Sandoz.

Lépine

18K pink gold and enamel watch with digital jump-hours

Signed Lépine à Paris, case no. 32, circa 1810

Keywound Lépine calibre cylinder movement with standing barrel

Silver engine-turned dial with eccentric minute ring, at the top the aperture for the jumping hours, subsidiary seconds, blued steel hand

Circular case with engraved gold and champlevé black enamel bezels, the back decorated with a finely engraved map of Southern Italy with black detailing, overlaid with translucent blue enamel, hinged silver cuvette

54 mm. diam.

Jean-Antoine Lépine (1720-1814)

was born in Challex, near Geneva and moved to Paris in 1744. He first worked for the King's Clockmaker André Charles Caron, whose daughter he married in 1756. Lépine was received Master in 1765 and at around the same time he became King's Clockmaker. In 1766 he succeeded Caron. Lépine's workshops were located in 1772 in the Place Dauphine, in 1778- 1779, Quai de l'Horloge du Palais, then in the rue des Fossés Saint Germain l'Auxerrois near the Louvre in 1781, and finally at 12 Place des Victoires from 1789.

Moricand & Degrange

18K gold and enamel watch with jump hours

Signed Moricand & Degrange, circa 1830

Keywound Lepine calibre cylinder movement with standing barrel

Silver engine-turned dial with eccentric minute ring and aperture for the jump hours

Circular gold case decorated with the map of Northern Italy in black and turquoise champleve enamel

49 mm. diam

The Geneva firm of Moricand&Degrange are recorded working between 1828 and 1835. A noted naturalist, Moïse-Etienne Moricand (1779-185?) was involved in founding the Musée d'Histoire Naturelle de Genève in addition to being the proprietor of the watchmaker and jewellers, Moricand & Degrange.

"Early Perpetuelle"

Swiss

Gold early self-winding "perpetuelle"centre seconds watch with polychrome painted on enamel dial

Unsigned, attributed to Moyse Gevril Fils, Le Locle, circa 1785

Keywoundfull plate cylinder movement with oscillating winding weight mounted on the backplate, banking springs on each side, standing barrel, gilt dust ring

Polychrome painted on enamel dial depicting a young gentleman and a lady in a landscape setting, the man playing a lute, the lady holding a musical score, regulation sector above, eccentric white enamel dial beneath for hours and minutes with Roman numerals, outer annular white enamel ring with large Arabic numerals for the centre seconds

Circular polished case with ribbed bezel edges

52mm. diam.

This watch is a rare survival from the earliest period in the development of the self-winding watch, it is particularly notable for its beautifully conceived painted on enamel dial.

In the third quarter of the 18th century, several watchmakers in France and Switzerland including Abraham-Louis Breguet and Louis Recordon were experimenting with the idea of the keyless or 'self-winding' watch. These makers realised that the invention of a successfully working self-winding watch could bring fame and fortune.

The present watch can reasonably be attributed to the Swiss watchmaker Moyse Gevril of Le Locle. Close similarities can be seen when compared to a related example signed on the barrel 'Moyse Gevril, fils', with the mainspring dated January 1781. That watch is illustrated in Alfred Chapuis and Eugène Jaquet's 'The History of the Self-Winding Watch'. The dial of the present watch both in the execution of its painted on enamel scene and the layout of its eccentric dial and regulation arc are very similar to the signed MoyseGevril example. In addition, the backplate of the movement, the winding weight and its fixing also correspond to the documented Gevril watch.

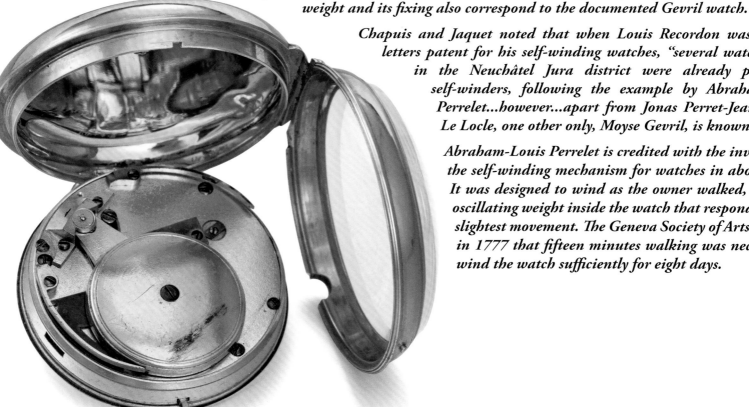

Chapuis and Jaquet noted that when Louis Recordon was granted letters patent for his self-winding watches, "several watchmakers in the Neuchâtel Jura district were already producing self-winders, following the example by Abraham-Louis Perrelet...however...apart from Jonas Perret-Jeanneret of Le Locle, one other only, Moyse Gevril, is known so far".

Abraham-Louis Perrelet is credited with the invention of the self-winding mechanism for watches in about 1777. It was designed to wind as the owner walked, using an oscillating weight inside the watch that responded to the slightest movement. The Geneva Society of Arts reported in 1777 that fifteen minutes walking was necessary to wind the watch sufficiently for eight days.

Perrelet sold some of his self-winding watches to Breguet who developed the idea and perfected it – something which no other watchmaker achieved at the time. Breguet stated that by 1780 both the Ducd'Orleans and Marie Antoinette were already in possession of his perpetuelle watches.

Literature:

The History of the Self-winding Watch, Alfred Chapuis and EugèneJaquet (revised English edition, 1956, pp.189-190)

Moyse Gevril

Moyse Gevril and his brother Daniel established their reputations with watchmaking innovation and fine decorative enamelling. Interestingly, their father Jacques Gevrilhad accompanied the genius watchmaker Pierre Jaquet-Droz on a trip to Madrid in 1758 to present some.

Inv. 1066

Attributed to Longines

18K gold, enamel and diamond-set openface keyless watch made for the Indian market, signed enamel by Pierre-Amédée Champod

Unsigned, attributed to Longines, St. Imier, movement no. 1307054, circa 1900

Keyless lever movement, 21 jewels, bimetallic compensation balance, patented micrometer regulator

White enamel dial with Arabic numerals, gold Louis XV hands

Circular translucent Royal blue enamel decorated case, diamond-set bezel, the reverse centred by a painted polychrome enamel scene depicting a horse race signed A.C for Pierre-Amédée Champod, surrounded by a diamond-set border, diamond-set floral decoration and a diamond-set horseshoe

51 mm. diam.

The enamel scene on the present watch is signed AC for Pierre-Amédée Champod (1834-1913), one of Geneva's most celebrated enamel and miniature painters of the late 19th and early 20th centuries. He studied with the artists Huguenin, Sauerländer and Charles Glardon who had the strongest impact on his style.

Champod excelled in his lifelike hunting scenes but was also renowned for his beautiful landscape and floral motifs which decorated the finest timepieces destined for the Indian and Chinese markets. His enamel miniatures can be found on watches of celebrated manufacturers such as Bovet, Vaucher, Vrard, Courvoisier Frères, Maurice Ditisheim and others.

For Champod's autobiography and description and illustrations of his work see: La Montre Chinois by Alfred Chapuis, pp. 192-194, plates pp. 152, 192 and 212.

The movement of the present watch is fitted with a micrometer regulator as patented by Ernest Francillon, founder of Longines Watch Co. (Swiss patent No. 3884, registered on 31 August 1891).

King George III Royal Presentation Watch

Hugh Gordon

18K gold, enamel and diamond-set Royal presentation watch with the cipher of King George III of England (reigned 1760-1820)

Signed Hugh Gordon, Fort St. George, Madras, movement no. 3596, circa 1800

Keywound full plate cylinder movement, chain fusée, florally engraved, pierced balance cock engraved with a grotesque mask and mythical creature, diamond endstone

White enamel with Roman numerals

Circular case overlaid with translucent Royal blue guilloche enamel and applied with the diamond-set monogram 'GR' of King George III beneath a crown, the bezel and border decorated with chased gold stylised leaves and light blue champlevé enamel, casemaker's punch mark 'PD'

52 mm. diam.

Hugh Gordon was apprentice to Patrick Gill, watchmaker. After some time in the service of the East India Company he joined his brother Robert, who was a watchmaker in Madras. He appears in a list of inhabitants residing in the Black Town and environs of Fort St. George (the former name of Madras) in 1799 (New Oriental Register 1800). In 1808 he bought the Scottish estate of Woodhill near Inverurie. It had previously been called Badifurrow but renamed it Mannar after the straits of that name which lie between Ceylon (Sri-Lanka) and the south east of India.

Jean-Jacques-Baptiste Verdier

Gold and painted on enamel watch with fine enamel scene attributed to Hamelin and double virgule escapement

Signed Verdier, circa 1775

Keywound full plate double virgule movement with chain fusée, pierced and engraved balance bridge

White enamel dial with large Arabic numerals

Circular case chased with scrolls, the back centered with a polychrome painted on enamel still life in the Dutch style attributed to Hamelin, blue enamel band

41.5 mm. diam.

Although it is not signed, the high quality enamel on this watch can be compared with the work of the best French enamellers of the period, such as Hamelin and Duhamel. Though little is known about Hamelin, he is considered to be one of the finest 18th century French painters in enamel.

Jean-Jacques-Baptiste Verdier worked in Paris and became a Master in 1737. He is recorded as being established in 1739 in the Rue des Marais, and in 1773 became a Juré.

The double virgule escapement was the subject of one of the biggest horological scandals of 18th century France. In 1753, horloger du Roi, Jean-Andre Le Paute published a description of a new escapement for watches derived from the pin-wheel escapement which had been used with great success in clocks. The new escapement, the details of which were given in Le Paute's book, was called the 'double virgule' escapement. However, the 21-year old Pierre-Augustin Caron, son of another horloger du Roi, Andre-Charles Caron, wrote in an open letter to the Mercure de France that in July 1753 he had shown Le Paute the escapement, of his own invention, and that Le Paute had copied it and claimed it for his own. The affair caused such a stir that the matter was referred to the Academie Royale des Sciences and on March 4, 1754 they ruled in favor of Caron as the inventor. In December 1754, watchmaker Jean Romilly presented another version of the double virgule to the Academy, which that institution decided had been invented independently of Caron. Therefore both watchmakers were credited with its invention.

Although the double virgule produced good results it was very rarely used, probably because of the difficulty of making it and its extreme fragility. Today, watches with this escapement are extremely rare.

Inv. 1398

The Rape of Europa

Pierre Michau

Gold and painted on enamel watch

Signed Michau, circa 1760

Keywound full plate cylinder movement with chain fusée, pierced and engraved balance bridge

White enamel dial with Roman numerals

Circular case decorated with a polychrome painted on enamel scene depicting 'the Rape of Europa' after Luca Giordano (1634-1705)

46 mm. diam.

The scene of 'The Rape of Europa' on the back of the case is copied in miniature derived from Luca Giordano's painting of the same subject.

The watchmaker Pierre Michau is likely to be the same maker who signed his watches variously: Michau or Michaux or Michaud. He was originally from Orléans, and became a master in Geneva in 1771. Michau seems to have had an earlier career in Paris, as this watch would indicate, but there are no traces of him in the records of the time. He is likely to have been a Protestant and therefore his religion would have prevented him becoming a master watchmaker in Paris.

Inv. 1378

French or Swiss

Gold and painted on enamel watch, the enamel scene after François Boucher's 'pensent-ils au raisin'

Unsigned, circa 1765

Keywound full plate verge movement with chain fusée, pierced and engraved balance bridge

White enamel dial with Roman numerals, winding through the dial

Circular case, the back decorated with a finely painted polychrome enamel scene after François Boucher's 'pensent-ils au raisin', the bezel decorated with a continuous landscape, the interior with a painted on enamel basket of flowers, amethyst-set thumb piece

49 mm. diam.

François Boucher's famous painting of 1747 entitled 'pensent-ils au raisin' or 'are they thinking about the grape' was a relatively new work of art when this watch was made in the 1760's. Paintings by famous artists of the day were available to a wider audience via the medium of engravings or prints. Which were very popular and widely distributed. The enameller of the present watch almost certainly copied his design from such an engraving in which the image is in reverse to Boucher's original painting, now in the Art Institute of Chicago. The decoration of the present watch closely resembles an 18th-century engraving produced in Paris by Jacques Philippe Le Bas (1707-1783)

Inv. 1849

Philippe Terrot

Gold and painted on enamel pearl-set quarter repeating watch

Signed Phe. Terrot, movement no. 12012, circa 1780

Keywound full-plate verge movement with chain fusée, pierced and engraved balance cock, repeating with two hammers on a bell activated by depressing the pendant

White enamel dial with Arabic numerals

Circular case with split pearl-set bezel, the back with a finely painted on enamel and pearl-set scene depicting a female huntress gazing into a rocky pool in a landscape, a finely painted portrait of a mother and child in an oval vignette above

49 mm. diam.

Philippe Terrot is recorded working in Geneva from 1767 to 1780. He specialised in making highly decorative watches, often for the French and Spanish markets.

Farine & Racle

Gold and porcelain watch

Signed Farine & Racle, Paris, circa 1770

Keywound full plate verge movement, chain fusée, pierced and engraved balance bridge

White enamel dial with Roman numerals

Circular gold case, porcelain back painted with Watteauesque figures in a landscape surrounded by scrollwork, bezel decorated to match

50 mm. diam.

Watches dating from the 18th century with porcelain cases are rare, few having survived until the present day due to their inherently fragile nature. Although the porcelain parts of watch cases were rarely signed by their maker due to space restrictions, they were often in fact made by the great porcelain factories of the day.

A similar porcelain watch was in the Time Museum, Rockford, Illinois, sold by Sotheby's, Masterpieces from the Time Museum Part Two, 19th June 2002, lot 37.

Little is known about the makers Farine & Racle. However, Jean Baptiste Farine is recorded working in Paris and died in 1777.

Badollet

Gold painted on enamel and pearl-set quarter repeating watch

Signed J. J. Badollet, circa 1790

Keywound full plate pin-pallet lever movement quarter repeating on a gong activated by depressing the pendant

White enamel dial with Roman numerals

Circular case with pearl-set bezel and border, the back decorated with a painted on enamel scene allegorical of love with a young couple in a classical landscape with a perfume burner and a pair of white doves

51 mm. diam.

The Badollet watchmaking family made fine watches for around 235 years. Jean Badollet, became the first watchmaker in the family, his father having moved from the Haute-Savoie in France to Geneva in 1535. He was succeeded by Jean II, who published the treatise 'L'Excellence de L'Horlogerie' in 1689. His five sons followed him as watchmakers. Jean-Jacques I, the maker of the present watch, was so highly regarded that he supplied ébauches and finished watches to Abraham-Louis Breguet in Paris. The company ceased trading in 1872.

George Achard & Fils

18K gold and painted on enamel pearl-set open face watch

Signed G. Achard & Fils, Genève, no. 12946, circa 1795

Keywound full plate gilt-finished verge movement, chain fusée, pierced and engraved balance cock

White enamel dial with Arabic numerals

Circular case with a very finely painted on enamel scene of children playing in a landscape, black champlevé enamel and pearl-set border

50 mm. diam.

Georges and Jean-François Achard were a father and son partnership working in Geneva in the late 18th century, their association ended in 1796.

CHAPTER 8

CHINESE MARKET

Chinese Market Watches

The Chinese Emperors had an avid interest in horological and scientific instruments. The first western watches to be made for the Chinese were reputed to have been made by Jesuit missionaries during the Ming Dynasty in the late 16th century. However, it was the period between the last quarter of the 18th century and the mid-19th century that the production of watches in Switzerland and London for the Chinese Market reached its apogee.

To satisfy the demand for watches from China, master goldsmiths, enamellers and technicians combined their skills and artistry to manufacture increasingly lavish and whimsical timepieces and objects of fantasy. European objects destined for the export to China were not, as maybe supposed, made strictly in the Chinese style but were designed in the Louis XV, Louis XVI, Directoire and Empire styles which were favoured by the Chinese. These timepieces, snuff boxes, fans and other objects were of distinctive design, distinguished by their unsurpassed quality and splendid decoration. Decoration and forms were inspired by nature and everyday items, such as sealing wax cases, fruits, animals, musical instruments, cherubs, classical paintings, mirrors, sewing necessaries, singing bird boxes, automatons, telescopes, form watches and many others, the spectacular cases ornamented with precious and semi-precious stones, pearls and enamel miniatures, genuine works of art created by the most famed artists of the time.

The tribute system was at the centre of the Chinese world order, the giving of gifts and the ritual of a foreign prince or his envoy kowtowing in front of the Chinese Emperor were part of a hierarchy that placed the Emperor at the centre of the civilised world. By the end of the 18th century, Chinese dignitaries and members of the Imperial Court expected to be offered only the finest watches, featuring complicated movements such as repeating, music or automatons. The watchmakers rose to satisfy this desire and produced watches created for their exceptional mechanical cunning and aesthetics, the cases were highly enamelled and sometimes in the shape of exotic flowers, absolutely no expense or effort was spared in their manufacture.

It is also interesting to contemplate the route undertaken by these objects during their journey from Geneva to Canton. Once completed in Geneva and the Neuchâtel Jura, the watches were carried over land to Mediterranean ports such as Genoa and Marseille from where they would travel by sea to the Port of Macau, and finally on a Chinese river junk on the Pearl River to the Port of Canton - a long and perilous undertaking prone to a large number of calamities.

By the middle of the 19th century, the trade in Chinese market watches had expanded to such a degree that several of the Swiss manufacturers including Bovet moved themselves and their families to China.

Inv. 1203

Bovet

18K gold, painted on enamel and pearl-set jump centre seconds watch made for the Chinese market

Signed Bovet Fleurier, no. 699, circa 1840

Keywound duplex movement, mirror polished, 8 jewels, standing barrel

White enamel dial with Roman numerals

Circular case with engraved and champlevé enamel band, pendant and bow, the back with a finely painted on enamel panel of two white doves amongst summer flowers on a pale blue ground, pearl-set bezels, pendant and bow

56 mm. diam.

Inv. 1091

Bovet

18K gold and painted on enamel jump centre seconds watch made for the Chinese market

Signed Bovet a Fleurier, case no. 969, circa 1840

Keywound duplex movement, engraved gilt plates, standing barrel

White enamel dial with Roman numerals

Circular case with foliate engraved and champlevé enamel band, pendant and bow, the back with a finely painted on enamel panel of two white doves amongst summer flowers on a pale blue ground

58 mm. diam.

Bovet Fleurier

The history of the celebrated Chinese market watches signed Bovet Fleurier began with the Swiss master watchmaker Edouard Bovet (1797-1849). Born in Fleurier, the 21 year old Edouard arrived in Canton in 1818 and almost immediately sold four watches for 10,000 Francs, over one million US dollars today. He consequently decided to stay in Canton where he established in 1822 a trading company in partnership with his brothers, the firm founded by charter in London the same year.

Very soon, the name 'Bo Wei' or 'Bo-vay' became synonymous for "watch" and in the turmoil of late Manchu China, Bovet watches spread throughout the country as a medium of exchange. In the meantime, their hometown Fleurier in the Val-de-Travers had become the European centre for the manufacture of Chinese watches, with several brands dedicated only to that flourishing market.

Bovet's production of high quality watches made in Switzerland for the Imperial Chinese market was a resounding success. 'Chinese watches' as they were soon called were elaborately decorated pocket watches, generally sold in symmetrically opposed pairs. Their gold cases often featured enamel miniatures painted by the most celebrated artists of the time, cloisonné and champlevé decorations and pearl-set borders. Bovet further specialised in the art of engraving and skeletonising movements, hence enhancing the appeal of his high-end Chinese watches with its Mandarin customers.

Inv. 1818

Mandarin Duck

Bovet

18K gold, painted on enamel and pearl-set pocket watch with centre seconds, made for the Chinese market

Signed Bovet Fleurier, circa 1835

Blued mirror-polished steel duplex movement with standing barrel

White enamel dial with Roman numerals

Circular case, the back decorated with a very finely painted polychrome enamel mandarin duck within a rocky mountain landscape, champlevé enamel border and bezel set with graduated half-pearls, pendant and bow set with graduated half-pearls, hinged and glazed cuvette

57mm diam.

This highly colourful and very rare Chinese market watch is one of a small series by Bovet made in the first half of the 19th century featuring the Mandarin Duck as the subject for the enamel painting. Beautifully rendered, it is thought that less than a dozen similar pieces were made. Each known watch is unique and shows the duck in different although related landscape settings. All known examples appear to be painted by the same Swiss enamellist.

Two other watches are known that feature the mandarin duck as the subject. One of these watches is today a highlight in the private collection of the House of Bovet.

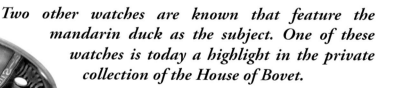

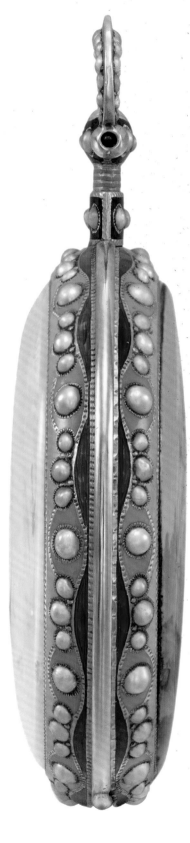

Inv. 1133

Swiss

18K gold, painted on enamel and pearl-set minute repeating openface keyless chronograph watch with triple strike quarters, made for the Chinese market

Unsigned, no. 3391, circa 1900

Keyless lever movement, minute repeating with two hammers on two gongs, the quarters with triple hammer strike, repeating activated by a slide in the band

White enamel dial with Roman numerals

Circular case with seed pearl-set bezels, engraved decorative band, the back with a delicately painted on enamel scene of a young gentleman courting an elegant damsel, both in period costume within a tranquil country setting, blue guilloche enamel border

53 mm. diam.

The triple strike of the quarters is a somewhat unusual setup in the construction of striking mechanisms in repeating watches. It concerns the quarter repeating pattern where the quarter-hour sounds not as the standard 'ding-dong' but has an additional strike of the hammer to create a more tuneful 'ding-dong-ding' chime. This is achieved by three extra teeth which enable the first striking hammer to strike the additional 'ding'.

Inv. 1372

William Pybus.

Gilt metal and paste-set double dial dual time watch with sweep centre seconds, date and lunar calendar, made for the Chinese market

Signed William Pybus, London, circa 1790

Gilt-finished verge movement, chain fusée

White enamel dial with four subsidiary dials indicating the time with Roman numerals, date, lunar calendar and regulator, on the reverse white enamel dial indicating the second time zone with Roman numerals

Large circular case, paste-set, chased and engraved floral and foliate decorated bezels

62 mm. diam.

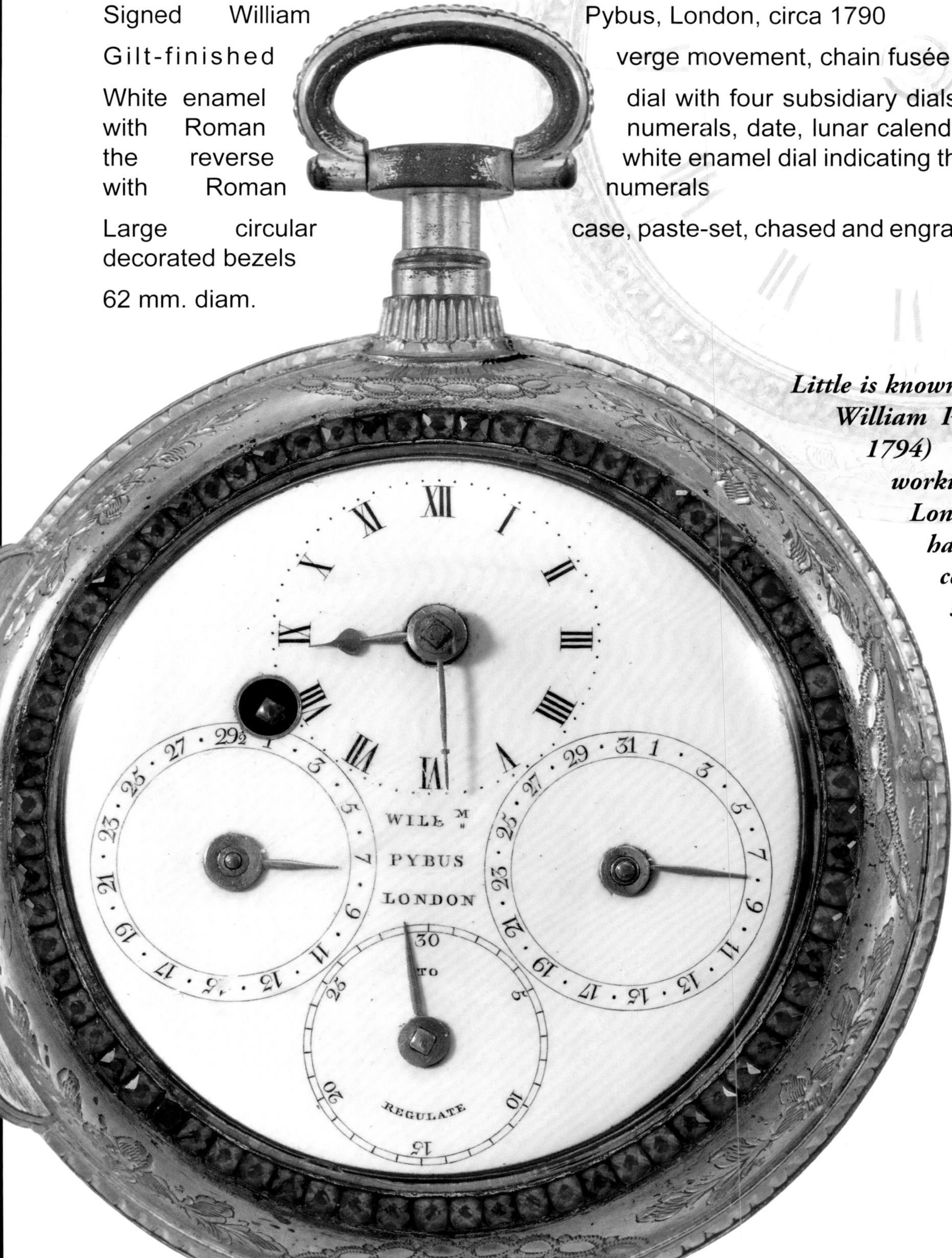

Little is known of the watchmaker William Pybus (active 1788-1794) who is recorded working in Geneva and London in the second half of the 18th century. He evidently specialised in large complicated and decorative watches for export to China, the present watch is a fine and representative example of the watches made by him.

363

Inv. 1354

Edouard Juvet

18K gold and painted on enamel centre seconds watch, made for the Chinese Market

Signed Edouard Juvet, Fleurier in Chinese characters, no. 20X, circa 1860

Keywound finely engraved and chased gilt-finished lever movement, standing barrel, three-arm steel balance with winged weights

White enamel dial with Roman numerals

Circular case with translucent polychrome guilloché and champlevé enamel stylised floral decorated bezel, rim, pendant and bow, the reverse centred by a finely painted polychrome enamel scene depicting Titus and Berenice in a courtyard with translucent scarlet guilloché enamel background, gilt-metal cuvette hinged to the movement ring

56 mm. diam.

Another similar watch by Edouard Juvet decorated with a version of the same scene, was sold by Christie's Geneva, 16th May, 2001, lot 199.

Edouard Juvet (1820-1883) was one of the most eminent makers working for the Chinese Market. He opened his workshop in Buttes in 1842 and moved to Fleurier in 1844.

Edouard's sons Ami-Louis and Léo worked in the family's firm in Shanghai where they were only rivalled by the Bovets. The firm opened branches in Tien-tsin and Saigon and prospered to such an extent that Léo wrote 'Our watches sell like salt'.

In 1873, Edouard Juvet registered a trademark in Chinese characters which was used for all their products. After his death in 1883, Léo took over the management of the company.

The present watch features a fine enamel scene depicting Titus and Berenice. Titus and Berenice were the tragic lovers featured in the play of 1670 by Jean Racine. Their story was first told by the Roman historian Suetonius. Berenice, daughter of King Herod Agrippa I, belonged to the Herodian Dynasty, which ruled the Roman province of Judaea from around 39 B.C. to 92 A.D. She had several marriages, one of which made her become the queen of Chalcis. Around 68 AD., she began a love affair with Titus Flavius Vespasianus, who would become the Roman emperor after the first Jewish-Roman War. Berenice, also bearing the Roman name Julia, was disliked by the Roman people, so Titus dismissed her when he became emperor.

The enamel scene pictured on the present watch is likely depicting the turning point of the relationship between Titus and Berenice, when he rejects her upon his ascension to emperor in 79 AD. It is not known if Titus intended to send for Berenice after regaining approval from the people, and he died suddenly in 81 AD. Given her ascent to becoming a potential empress of Rome, her story became well known and is written about in the New Testament Book of Acts.

Inv. 1816

William Ilbery

Gold, dendritic agate and carnelian, enamel and pearl-set centre seconds watch made for the Chinese market

Signed Ilbery, London, No.6116, circa 1800

Keylwound chased and engraved gilt duplex movement with standing going barrel, five arm flat-rim steel balance with diamond endstone

White enamel dial with Roman numerals

Octagonal case with polished frame, inset with 32 panels of carnelian and moss agate, the back centered with a further large panel of moss agate within a split-pearl set border, scarlet white and blue champlevé enamelled pendant, bow and button finial.

65 mm. wide. 108 mm. overall length.

The present watch is one of the extremely rare, unusually shaped watches set with chalcedony made by Ilbery for the Chinese market. It is a magnificent example of the combined talents of the watchmaker, jeweller and lapidary. Dendritic agate, more commonly known as 'moss agate', is chalcedony containing visible impurities in the form of dendrite shapes that resemble organic forms.

William Ilbery or Ilbury (c.1760-1851) was a celebrated watchmaker from London, renowned for his exceptional timepieces made for the Chinese market. In 1836 Ilbery settled in Fleurier, left for Macao in 1839 and then to Canton, China. There he was known to have become friendly with Bovet and they met regularly, even though they were rivals.

Ilbery's movements show the influence of the free standing barrels of the Lépine caliber as used in Jaquet Droz's Swiss production signed in London and that of William Anthony, who worked in London. William Anthony (1764-1844), another celebrated watchmaker of his day, was sixteen years senior to Ilbery. He influenced greatly the latter's work and contributed substantially to the development of Chinese watches, however it is still William Ilbery who is known as the 'father' of the Chinese watch.

The duplex escapement, as seen on the present watch, is often found in English watches from the late 18th century until around 1860. It was probably invented by Pierre Le Roy and was patented in 1782 by Thomas Tyrer. The duplex movement was featured in finer quality pocket watches. A duplex escapement wheel has a double set of teeth, or has two superimposed escape wheels.

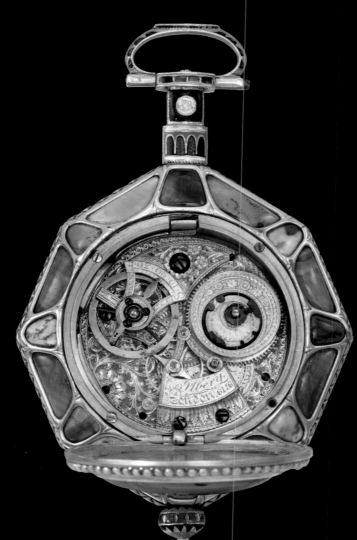

Ilbery

18K gold and painted on enamel watch with early ruby duplex escapement, made for the Chinese Market

Signed Ilbery, London, no. 5936, the enamel in the manner of Jean-Louis Richter, circa 1810

Keywound full plate, chain fusée, duplex escapement with ruby insert in the staff, three-arm balance, gilt dust cap

White enamel with Roman numerals and subsidiary seconds

Circular case, the bezels with red and blue champleve enamel decoration, the back enamel panel painted with a very fine lakeside landscape after Vernet, outer translucent blue champlevé enamel decoration, the back cover opening 180 degrees, gold engine-turned fixed cuvette

60 mm. diam.

Ilbery's early watches, such as the present watch, were very much in the English style, fitted with full plate movements and duplex escapements. His later movements showed the influence of the freestanding barrels of the Lepine caliber as used in Jaquet Droz's Swiss production signed in London and that of William Anthony, who worked in London. William Anthony (1764-1844), another celebrated watchmaker of his day, was sixteen years senior to Ilbery. He influenced greatly the latter's work and contributed substantially to the development of Chinese watches, however it is still William Ilbery who is known as the 'father' of the Chinese watch.

The duplex escapement, as seen on the present watch, is often found in English watches from the late 18th century until around 1860. It was probably invented by Pierre Le Roy and was patented in 1782 by Thomas Tyrer. The duplex movement was featured in finer quality pocket watches. A duplex escapement wheel has a double set of teeth, or has two superimposed escape wheels.

Inv. 1415

William Ilbery

18K gold and painted on enamel pearl-set sweep centre seconds watch with enamel attributed to Jean-Louis Richter (1766-1841), made for the Chinese market

Signed Ilbery, London, no. 6.704, circa 1810

Keywound finely chased and engraved floral and scroll decorated gilt-finished duplex movement, standing barrel, diamond endstone

White enamel dial with Roman numerals and outer Arabic numerals, sweep centre seconds with half-second beat

Circular case, polychrome champlevé enamel decorated bezel, rim, pendant and bow, the back cover decorated with a finely painted polychrome enamel scene of a dismounted young huntsman with his horse and two spaniels in a landscape, split pearl-set frame and translucent blue enamel border. Hinged gold cuvette no. 872

59 mm. diam.

This exceptional timepiece made for the Chinese market impressively combines a high quality movement by William Ilbery of London with a lavishly decorated gold case distinguished by the finely painted enamel miniature attributed to the Genevan enamellist Jean-Louis Richter (1766-1841).

The cases Ilbery used for his timepieces were always of the highest quality, lavishly decorated by the best Genevan enamellists of the time, notably Jean-Louis Richter and Jean-François-Victor Dupont. Both artists decorated watches and boxes for the Chinese market and worked frequently with Ilbery, Piguet & Meylan, Rochat Frères and others. Examples of their work can be found in renowned museums, including the Patek Philippe Museum in Geneva.

The charming painted enamel scene decorating the present watch derives from English genre paintings by artists from the Royal Academy, such as Joshua Reynolds (1723-1792), Francis Wheatley (1747-1801), William Hamilton (1751-1801), William Redmore Bigg (1755-1828), and others, who specialised in images of romanticised English rural life in the last quarter of the 18th century. Their paintings were engraved and sold as prints, which were enormously popular and were used as models for the Genevan enamellers, including Jean-Louis Richter.

Bovet and Ilbery were both courting Anna Vaucher, daughter of Charles-Henry Vaucher of Fleurier, one of Bovet's competitors in Canton. Ilbery was in fact engaged to Anna Vaucher and even though he was constantly on his travels Anna remained faithful to him and resisted the proposals of Bovet who hoped one day to win her over. Sadly no marriage ever took place, since Anna became ill and died in 1845.

The duplex escapement was only featured in high quality pocket watches. A duplex escape wheel has a double set of teeth, or has two superimposed escape wheels. The action of the duplex escapement is without recoil and therefore similar to a chronometer which made it an ideal escapement to provide 'jump' centre seconds, a feature which was so prized in the Chinese market.

Ilbery's early watches were very much in the English style, fitted with full plate movements and duplex escapements. His later movements showed the influence of the Lépine calibre as used in Jaquet Droz's Swiss production signed in London and that of William Anthony, who worked in London. William Anthony (1764-1844), another celebrated watchmaker of his day, was sixteen years senior to Ilbery. He influenced greatly the latter's work and contributed substantially to the development of Chinese watches, however it is William Ilbery who is forever known as the 'father' of the Chinese watch.

Inv. 1317

John Bittleston

Gilt metal, 'en grisaille' painted on enamel and paste-set pair case centre seconds coach watch with regulator dial, lunar calendar, days of the week calendar and flying fifths of a second, made for the Chinese market

Signed Jno. Bittleston, London, no. 1558, circa 1785

Keywound gilt movement with cylinder escapement, chain fusée, profusely chased and engraved backplate, pierced and engraved cock with diamond endstone, dustcover

White enamel regulator-style dial, eccentric mean time dial, two smaller dials for lunar calendar and days of the week, flying fifths of a second, outer seconds track

Circular case, plain inner case, outer case with chased foliate decoration, red and clear paste-set bezel, case back with painted on enamel 'en grisaille' scene of a lady fondly tending her dove symbolizing romantic love, punched with case maker's mark T.H.

72 mm. diam.

John Bittleston worked at 207, High Holborn between 1765-1794 and was made a freeman of the Clockmaker's Company in 1781. He is recorded as being the maker of "a very curious astronomical watch".

Inv. 1454

Attributed to Jaquet-Droz

18K gold and painted on enamel egg-shaped jump centre seconds watch with virgule escapement made for the Chinese market

Unsigned, attributed to Jaquet-Droz, no. 889, circa 1780

Keywound egg-shaped gilt-brass virgule movement, fully engraved 'Chinese' calibre, standing barrel

White enamel dial with Roman numerals

Egg-shaped case, the front overlaid with dark yellow translucent enamel with gold paillomé border, the back decorated with a finely painted on enamel scene of a lady dancing holding a tambourine, another lady observing and a seated boy playing a flute, laurel leaf gold paillomé border over translucent blue guilloche enamel and white enamel outer border

52 mm. diam. 89 mm. overall length.

Although not signed, the style of construction, decoration and quality of this watch are absolutely typical of the work of the celebrated firm Jaquet-Droz. This magnificent watch compares to another similar example in the Jaquet-Droz Museum. Jaquet-Droz was one of the first maker's in Switzerland to introduce oval watches for export to China, the firm was also known for the use of coloured gold paillonés fired into the overglaze over the enamel used to decorate their watches, seen to great effect in the present watch.

Pierre Jaquet-Droz was born in La Chaux-de-Fonds in 1721 and died in Bienne in 1790. He was one of the most brilliant and innovative clockmakers of his era, specialising in musical and automaton

watches and clocks, boxes, fans, singing birds and other ingenious playing-toys. His astonishing creations fascinated nobility, kings and emperors of the world, notably China. Pierre Jaquet-Droz travelled widely, notably in England, France and Spain. In Madrid, he was condemned to death by the Inquisition for allegedly practicing black magic but was saved by the Bishop of Toledo. During the latter part of his life he took his adopted son, J.F. Leschot into business and the company continued to prosper until after his death.

The virgule escapement, first devised by Lepaute but largely used by Lépine, is a variety of the cylinder escapement. The virgule escapement was never widely used because of its extreme delicacy and the difficulty of its construction, therefore watches with this escapement were made in small numbers and even fewer survive today. In the present watch, the use of the virgule escapement enables the centre seconds to move at one-second intervals instead of a sweeping action.

Inv. 1872

Just & Son

18K gold, champlevé and painted on enamel pearl-set centre seconds watch made for the Chinese market

Signed Just & Son, London, no. 3332, circa 1845

Keywound Chinese calibre duplex movement entirely chased and engraved with flowers and scrolls, free standing barrel

White enamel dial with Roman numerals

Circular case, pearl-set bezel, rim, pendant and bow, alternating black and white champlevé enamel decorated band, back decorated with a polychrome enamel bouquet of flowers centred by two courting doves, made by using two different enamel techniques, champlevé and painted enamel,engraved floral and scroll decorated gold cuvette

54 mm. diam.

Distinguished by the beautiful enamel work, imitating cloisonné enamel, the present watch is a fine example of a timepiece made for the Chinese market. This uncommon technique required a highly skilled gold chaser to chase the metal, creating the desired motif by leaving only the fine contour lines, the effect being visually comparable to cloisonné. The cells were then decorated with the desired images by a combination of enamel painting and vitreous enamels.

Leonard Just specialised in making watches for the Chinese market, the company is recorded in London between 1790 and 1825. After Hong Kong was ceded to the British in 1842, Just moved to the island and was running the business there from 1846. Upon his death, the company passed to his son, and carried on as Just & Son.

Inv. 1889

James Morisset & Robert and Charles Lukin

Gold, enamel, diamond, ruby and pearl-set oval watch made for the Chinese market

Signed Morisset & Lukins, London, no. 2635, circa 1790

Keywound gilded three-quarter plate cylinder movement

White enamel dial with Roman numerals, matching white enamel dial below for seconds, oval gold surround overlaid with blue translucent enamel over an engine-turned ground, decorated with diamond-set floral sprays, borders of opaque white and translucent red guillloché enamel

Oval case, the back overlaid with translucent blue enamel over an engine-turned ground, set with a large diamond and ruby-set star, the front and back bezels set with two rows of split pearls, the pendant further set with split-pearls, polished gold cuvette

55 mm. wide. Overall length including pendant 87mm.

This magnificent oval watch is exceptional not only for its richness and beauty, but also for its superb quality and wonderful state of preservation. It was made by James Morisset, one of London's most celebrated goldsmiths, whose name has become synonymous with some of the finest examples of art in enamels, precious metals and stones to have been created in England in the last quarter of the eighteenth century. Morisset excelled in the creation of magnificent gold and enamel objects such as presentation swords and freedom boxes for exalted patrons including the British Admiralty and the Royal family. Three such swords and a box are now in the collection of the Victoria & Albert Museum in London and another sword is in the collection of the Metropolitan Museum of Art in New York (Inv. 26.145.315a, b).

Of Huguenot descent, James Morisset (1738-1815) registered his own maker's mark 'IM' on 31st August, 1770, at Denmark Street, Soho, London. Until that date he had worked with his brother-in-law Louis Toussaint at Parker & Wakelin, the foremost silversmiths in London for most of the 18th century. Morisset was in partnership with the brothers Robert and Charles Lukin between 1780 and 1796 producing watch cases and snuffboxes. Goods made during this partnership are signed "Morisset & Lukins", the "Lukins" being a joint signature for both Robert and Charles Lukin.

Kent's 'Directory for the Cities of London and Westminster, & Borough of Southwark for the Year 1794', lists the firm of 'Morisset, R. & C. Lukin, Jewellers, Goldsmiths & Enamellers, 22, Denmark-Street, Soho'.

The Lukin brothers probably dealt with the retail side of the business with James Morisset being the working craftsman, certainly the superb quality of the pieces produced by the firm at this period would bear this out. In his will, proved for probate on 3rd February, 1815, James Morisset mentions his partners Robert and Charles Lukin (National Archives reference PROB 11/1565/69).

A gold, enamel and pearl set watch signed Morisset & Lukins was in the Frederick T. Proctor Watch Collection and is now in the collection of the Munson Williams Proctor Arts Institute Collection, New York, (Inv. PC. 1023.8).

Literature:

"New Facts about James Morisset and a Revised List of His Known Works, With Others by his Successors John Ray and James Montague." Leslie Southwick, The Journal of the Arms and Armor Society (Sept. 1997), pp. 328–29.

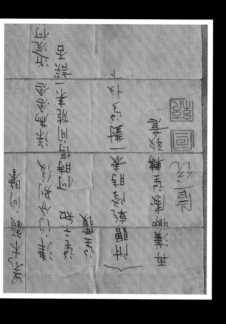

乾隆ノ王冠
（英皇室贈呈）
（黄金の夫婦時計）

Gold and Pearl-Inlaid
"Night King" and "Night Queen"

Glamourous watches Treatured by
Emperor Chien Lung of Tsing Dynasty

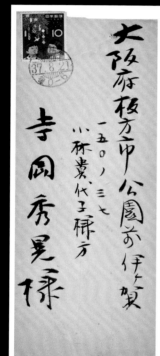

大阪府枚方市公園前伊ヶ賀
一五〇ノ三七
小林貴代子様方
寺岡秀晃 様

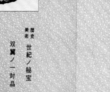

歴史
美術
世紀ノ秘宝
双翼ノ一対品
美術懐中時計
乾隆時表
（英皇室贈呈品）

英
清室
両皇室秘蔵
乾隆時表

双翼ノ王冠
「キング・ローズ花形」
世紀ノ絶品

Gold and Pearl-Inlaid "Night King" and "Night Queen"

大阪府枚方市公園前
伊ヶ賀一五〇ノ三七
小林貴代子様方
秀晃 様

大阪府枚方市公園前
伊ヶ賀一五〇ノ三七 小林貴代子様方
寺岡秀晃 様

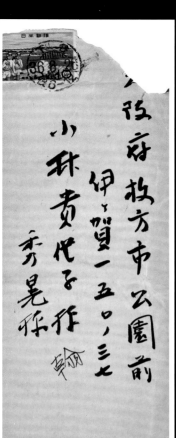

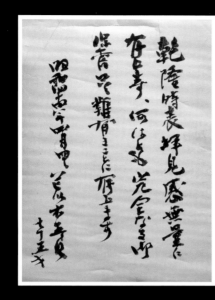

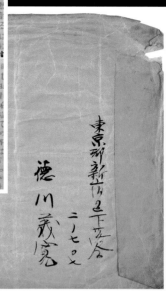

The Imperial Pomegranates

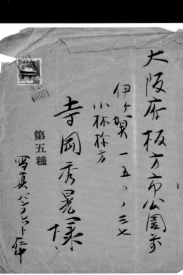

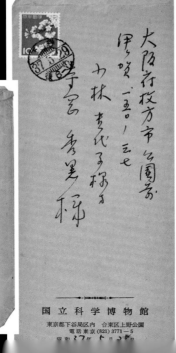

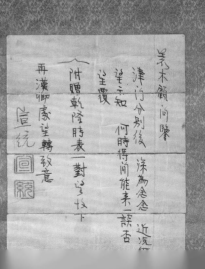

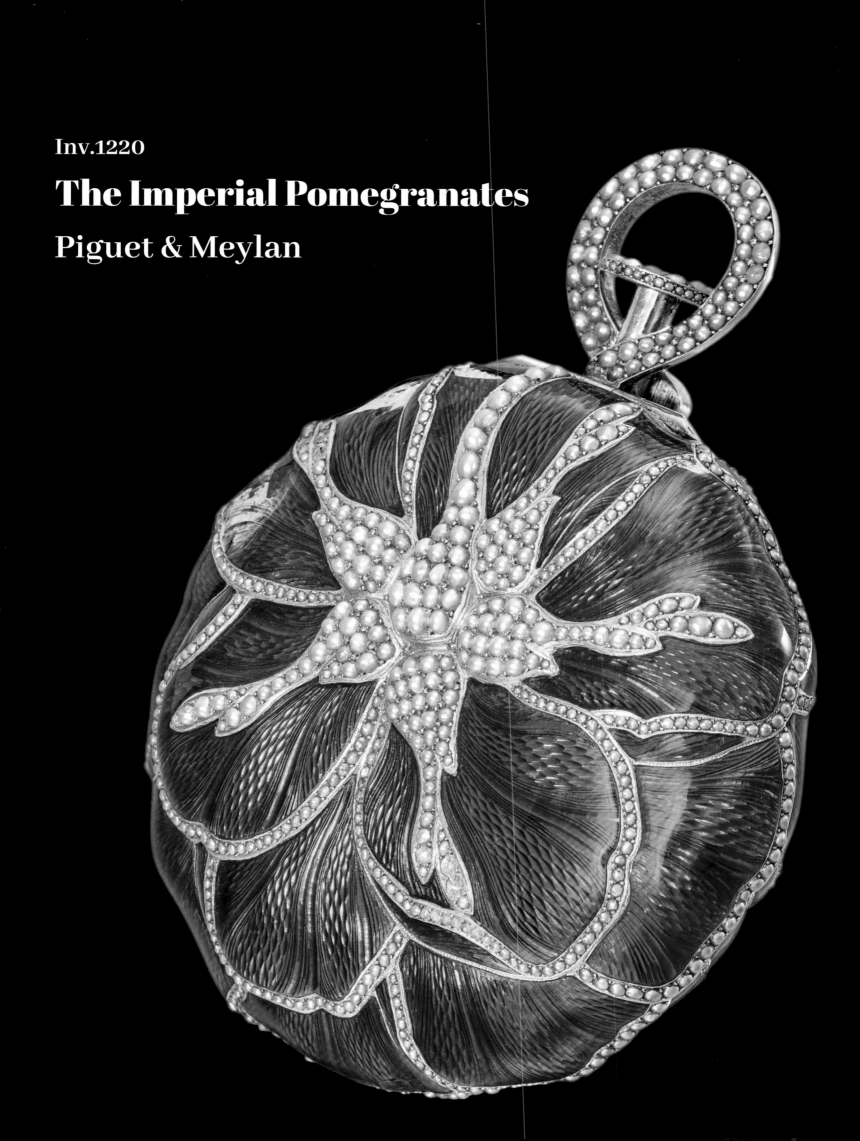

The Imperial Pomegranates

Piguet & Meylan

A highly important pair of gold, enamel and seed pearl set quarter repeating centre seconds watches, with unusual stem winding repeating mechanism.Reputedly presented as an English Royal gift to the Jiaqing Emperor

Signed Piguet & Meylan, no. 7511 & no. 751* (4-indistinct), circa 1820

Keywound identical blued steel duplex movements with polished steel lever and ratchet work, the quarter repeating mechanism operated by turning the flat button at the top of the pendant, this acts as the winding mechanism of the chain that when released provides the power to run the striking of the two steel gongs

White enamel dials with Roman numerals

Cases sculptured as a Pomegranate flower, the stems and edges of the leaves entirely set throughout with graduated seed pearls, the leaves shaped and varied to reflect the movement and uniqueness of each watch, engine-turned ground to replicate the small veins, overlaid with translucent deep ruby red enamel, five-piece hinge, the pendant shaped as the looping stem and set throughout with seed pearls, bezels set with larger pearls, gold cuvette inlaid with painted enamel,

a pastel green ground decorated by a profusion of multicoloured flowers and further engraved with scrolls, the border with pale blue enamel arches, each one centred by an engraved fleur-de-lys style motif, scalloped shaped rim set with pale green enamel and engraved decoration

66 mm. diam.

Provenance:

By tradition, the Jiaqing Emperor (1760-1820), thence by descent to the Emperor

Pu Yi (1906-1967), removed from the Forbidden City and taken with him as he fled in 1924

In the possession of a Japanese family, first certainly documented in 1961

The present owner

Exhibited:'Glamourous Watches Treasured by Emperor Chien Lung of Tsing Dynasty', probably Tokyo,c.1962, as Imperial gold and pearl-inlaid 'Night King' and 'Night Queen'

Legend had it that this spectacular pair of identical watches was reputedly given as a tribute to the

Jiaqing Emperor (r.1796-1820) by King George III (r.1760-1820). It was said that they were taken to China by George Macartney (1st Earl Macartney), who was appointed the first Trade Ambassador of Britain to the Chinese imperial court. However, this story can be discounted because Earl Macartney had visited China in the early 1790s, almost twenty years before the Piguet&Meylan partnership existed.

Notwithstanding, these magnificent watches may indeed have been a royal gift, but instead, from the Prince Regent, later King George IV, via William Amherst, 1st Earl Amherst (1773-1857) who, in 1816 was sent as Ambassador Extraordinary to the court of China's Qing dynasty, with a view to establishing more satisfactory commercial relations between China and Great Britain.

It is recorded that gifts were prepared "magnificent both to their value and their workmanship" but "consist of articles of intrinsic worth, composed of precious metals and stones, than things of mere fancy, being thus intended to suit the supposed taste of the Chinese". Worth the huge sum of £22,005,13s.7p., the gifts were sent with Amherst aboard HMS Alcestein February 1816 with the intention that they be presented at an audience with the Emperor later that year. Amherst arrived in early August 1816 , but due to his refusal to perform the kowtow

(as had Macartney before him) the audience never took place, although the gifts were left at the embassy for the Emperor to select.

The present pair of watches is said to have stayed in the Imperial Collections within the walls of the Forbidden City in Beijing until the Xinhai(Chinese) Revolution of 1911 between the Imperial forces of the Qing Dynasty (1644-1911), and the Chinese Revolutionary Alliance. This conflict ended with the abdication of Emperor Pu Yi (r.1908-1924), known as "The Last Emperor".

Having been chosen by Dowager Empress Cixi (1835-1908) while on her deathbed, Pu Yi ruled as the Xuantong Emperor between 1908 and 1911 and was the last Emperor of the Qing dynasty to rule over China. According to tradition, on the day that Emperor Pu Yi was expelled from the Forbidden City in 1924, amongst the treasures that he took with him into exile was this pair of watches. Supposedly, the minor chips to the enamel work were inflicted on the watches during this tumultuous flight from the palace.

Recently, documents that have accompanied the present watches for many decades have been translated from Japanese to English for the first time. These papers lend some credence to the story that the watches had descended through the Chinese Imperial family. On 26th June, 1961, a Mr. Hideaki Kobayashi and Ms. Kiyoko Kobayashi sent details and photographs of the watches to Yuzo

Sugimura who worked in the Tokyo National Museum. Yuzo Sugimura replied: "I took a look at the pictures of watches, and I guess they were presented to Qianlong Emperor from England. However, I'd like to see the watches by my own eyes for definition. I showed the picture to Mr. Oda who is in the National Science Museum, and he also said he would like to see the movement. And he said they seem to be made in England. Anyway, they are very valuable, so all documents and accessories should be kept together".

A further letter from Yuzo Sugimura to Mr and Ms. Kobayashi dated 4th November, 1961, states that: "I took a look at the picture and letter. The letter was written by Pu Yi (The Emperor) between 1920 and 1930, in the era he run away from (?) to Japanese legation, and then went to (?)".

Another letter from a Mr. Yoshihiro Tokugawa to a Mr. Hideaki Teraoka dated 21st August, 1962, states: "I took a look at the picture of the watches. I have seen Pu Yi at (?) and received his portrait with his signature. Mr. Sigimura said the watches are very valuable. The watches are made for the orient market in late 18th century. In the era, rococo style is popular in Europe, and Chinese art style and Europe style influenced each other. The watch case has curved-shape that is one of the characters of rococo style, and enamel (?) are also beautiful".

These documents would seem to directly link the present pair of watches with the last Chinese

Emperor Pu Yi, therefore pointing to a much earlier Imperial provenance. Significantly, given the Emperor's movements during exile, the letters would place the watches in Japanese hands by the early 1960s at the latest. It also raises the possibility that the author(s) of the letters were not necessarily the owners of the watches, but were perhaps either in the process of attempting to authenticate them in order to acquire them from the former Emperor himself who was still living, or equally possibly, they were asking the Emperor directly to confirm their former Imperial ownership. Indeed, in his letter of 1962, Mr. Tokugawa suggests he has been to see the former Emperor in person, seemingly to discuss with him the pair of watches which are mentioned in the same letter.

The present pair of watches appeared again when they were lent to an exhibition, probably in Tokyo, where they were prominently described and illustrated in the exhibition catalogue as the Imperial gold and pearl-inlaid 'Night King' and 'Night Queen', 'Glamourous Watches Treasured by Emperor Chien Lung of Tsing Dynasty'.

Emperor Pu Yi (1906-1967)

With China in turmoil, the Emperor Pu Yi was forced to flee in 1924, aged 19. He escaped to the international settlement at Tientsin to take shelter with the Japanese. When they took control of Manchuria in

1931, the Japanese proclaimed Pu Yi as Emperor of Manchukuo. There he remained as titular emperor all through the Second World War, but was never really more than a Japanese puppet. After the war, the Russians handed him over to the Communist regime in China where he became prisoner No. 981 and tended the prison vegetable garden.

After some years of "rehabilitation" he was accepted as a genuine convert to Communism and a loyal Chinese citizen and was formally pardoned. He worked part-time as an assistant gardener at the Beijing botanical gardens and in 1962 married his fifth and last wife. He was sometimes brought out to greet visiting foreign dignitaries as a fascinating curiosity until his death in 1967.

Piguet & Meylan

Both watches are stamped with the mark 'PM', for Piguet & Meylan, the makers most associated with the very finest of timepieces made for the Imperial Chinese Market.

Isaac-Daniel Piguet was born in 1755 Switzerland, in Le Chenit in the valley of Joux, Switzerland. At an early age he specialised in the manufacturing of expensive and complicated pieces such as watches with carillons and en passant hour and quarter striking clock watches. He finally settled in Geneva where in 1811 he formed a partnership with Philippe-Samuel Meylan between 1811 and 1828.

Philippe-Samuel Meylan was born in 1772 in Switzerland, a member of a family of renowned watchmakers in Le Brassus. He specialised in the production of very thin watches and became an eminent maker of watches with musical automaton.

Inv. 1892

"Chateau de Chillon"

Piguet & Meylan

Large gold and painted on enamel pearl-set quarter repeating watch made for the Chinese market

Piguet & Meylan, no. 4404, apparently unsigned, the case by Frères Oltramare, circa 1815

Keywound foliate engraved full plate gilt cylinder movement with separate barrels and bridges for the going and repeating trains, repeating the hours and quarters activated by depressing the pendant

Gold dial with Roman numerals on a matted ground, engine turned centre, blued steel serpentine hands

Circular case with translucent royal blue enamel border with red dot decoration, the band set with turquoises and pearls, the pendant decorated with dark blue enamel and gold foliage, pearl-set bow, back cover decorated with twelve curved swept cartouches, each decorated with finely painted on enamel flowers within pearl-set borders, the centre with a finely painted on enamel view of the Chateau de Chillon, the bezel decorated to match, two buttons for opening the covers in the band, hinged and sprung gilt cuvette

60mm. diam.

Splendidly sumptuous, this magnificent watch case was made in the workshop of Frères Oltramare, one of the most renowned makers of gold boxes and watch cases in Geneva in the first quarter of the 19th century. Their mark 'FO' is stamped inside the back of the case. The movement is undoubtedly the work of those most remarkable of watchmakers and mechanicians - Piguet & Meylan.

Made of high carat gold and of large size, it can be placed amongst the very finest enamel watches of the period. One of just a handful of comparable pieces, it represents a pinnacle of the Geneva enamellists and goldsmiths art. The decoration is breathtaking in both design and execution, including champlevé and artist-painted enamel work lavishly set with half-pearls and turquoises. Furthermore, it is the only example of its type known to the author to feature radial curved segmental decoration. Each of the twelve pale blue ground segments is very finely painted with a different spray of flowers and outlined with graduated half-pearls. In the centre is an exquisitely painted on enamel scene depicting the Chateau de Chillon, on the shores of Lake Geneva. The band, bezel, pendant and bow are equally richly decorated.

A very closely related watch by Piguet&Meylan, 'The Marguerite Flower' (Private Collection), decorated in red enamel but with straight florally painted and pearl-outlined segments with a similar central scene probably by the same artist as the present watch was described by Alfred Chapuis as "the ultimate luxury that could be made at the time". Another pair of watches of similar design is in the Patek Philippe Museum in Geneva.

Literature:

The Majesty of the Chinese-Market Watch, The Life and Collection of Gustave Loup of Tientsin and Geneva, Watch dealer and Collector (1876-1961), Ian White, Antiquarian Horological Society, 2019, front slip-cover illustration & pp. 128-129.

Frères Oltramare

Louis-David-Benjamin and Jean-Hughes Oltramare were descendants of the Oltramare family of watchmakers. Originally from Genoa, the family settled in Geneva in the 17th century. The firm registered their punch mark in November 1815 following the liberation of Geneva from French occupation.

CHAPTER 9

BREGUET

The Watches of Abraham-Louis Breguet (1747-1823)

In the oft-quoted words of the great Breguet collector Sir David Lionel Salomons, 'To carry a fine Breguet watch is to feel that you have the brains of a genius in your pocket.' It is indeed quite remarkable that these words still resonate today, almost 200 years after Breguet's death.

It is no exaggeration to say that the watches of Abraham-Louis Breguet were completely revolutionary at the time, both in their technical and aesthetic superiority. His numerous inventions including the tourbillon, equation of time and the first reliable self-winding watches represented a quantum leap in fine watchmaking that provided the benchmark against which the work of all subsequent watchmakers has been measured.

Breguet was born in Neuchâtel, Switzerland, but it was in Paris that he spent most of his working life. No aspect of watchmaking escaped his scrutiny and the ensuing inventions and improvements have become fundamental to horology. His career started auspiciously, with a series of major breakthroughs including the development of the successful self-winding "perpétuelle" watches, the introduction of gongs rather than bells for repeating watches and the first shock-protection for balance pivots.

During the French Revolution, Breguet took refuge in Switzerland, when it was safe to do so, he returned to Paris and started to rebuild his business. Whilst in exile, Breguet had developed some new ideas and he now had the opportunity to put them into practice. These included the Breguet balance-spring, his first carriage clock, which was sold to Napoleon Bonaparte, the "sympathique" clock with its dependent watch, the à tact watch, and perhaps most importantly the tourbillon, which was patented in 1801.

In addition to his watchmaking genius, Breguet possessed another important quality, he was a supremely competent businessman and networker. The exceptional technical ingenuity and avant-garde appearance of his watches meant that the most celebrated figures of the day in Europe and beyond beat a path to his door. To own a Breguet timepiece became one of the ultimate ambitions for the Royal, scientific, military, financial and diplomatic elites of the early 19th century.

The Masis Collection naturally includes exceptional examples of Breguet's work, in particular the spectacular and uniquely complicated gold and enamel cabriolet clockwatch with independent minute repeating with five hammers on five gongs, sold in 1808 and made for the Turkish Sultan. This watch, in common with Breguet's great masterpiece the "Marie Antoinette', is among the most significant and costly of Breguet's complicated watches. One of the earliest known 'montre à tact' watches, sold to the Duke of Bedford in 1794 and a 'montre à tact' once owned by the legendary Sir David Lionel Salomons himself.

Inv. 1820

Signed Breguet

Gold andenamel watch with a painted on enamel map of the Ottoman Empire, made for the Turkish market

Signed Breguet à Paris in Arabic, no. 30083, Swiss, circa 1830

Keywound gilt brass Lépine calibre cylinder movement

White enamel dial with Turkish numerals

Circular scallop-edged case, the back decorated with a map of the Ottoman Empire of the period with Turkish characters, on the outer and the bezel, a translucent red enamel border over engine-turning decorated with flowers painted en grisaille, pendant and bow with champlevé enamel, gold hinged cuvette engraved with a view of a chateau

55 mm. diam.

Three other very similar and related watches signed "Breguet à Paris" in Arabic and with cases decorated with an enamelled map of the Ottoman Empire are known publically:

The first, with the same map, is illustrated in: Orologi Nel Tempo,Luigi Pippa, p.179.

The second, a cabriolet watch, no. 30450, was formerly in the collection of The Lord Sandberg CBE and is illustrated in the book of the Sandberg collection, Terence Camerer Cuss, pp. 284-285.

The third, in the Topkapi Palace collections in Istanbul is illustrated in: Topkapi Palace, Editions Akbank, 2000, p. 272.

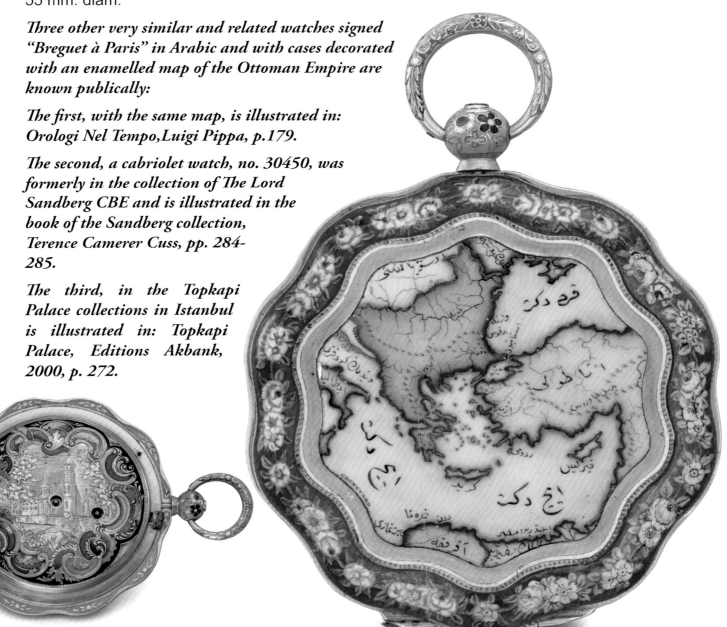

Inv. 1832

Breguet No. 852

18K pink gold, enamel and diamond-set hunter case à tact watch with original key and chain

Signed Breguet, no. 852, sold to Monsieur Tambu on January 3, 1803 for 1680 Francs

Keywound gilt-finished 'souscription' caliber ruby cylinder movement with central barrel, plain three arm brass balance, flat blued steel balance spring, blued steel regulation arm

Eccentric silvered dial withBreguet numerals, blued steel Breguet hands

Circular case with rose-cut diamond-set hour markers on the coin-edged band, the translucent royal blue enamel front over striped engine-turning decorated with an applied white gold and rose-cut diamond-set monogram, the reverse with white gold and diamond-set arrow-shaped pointer on translucent royal blue enamel over engine-turned sunburst decoration, rose-cut diamond-set pendant, stamped P.B.T. for Pierre Benjamin Tavernier, gold cuvette

40mm. diam.

Provenance:

Sir David Lionel Salomons, collection no. 41.

Literature:

Daniels, George. The Art of Breguet, p. 182, pl. 146 a-c.

According to the archives of Montres Breguet the present watch was sold to Monsieur Tambu of Poland on 14 Nivose, an 10 (January 3, 1803) for the amount of 1680 francs.

This watch once formed part of the world's greatest collection of Breguet watches assembled by Sir David Lionel Salomons(1851-1925) in the late 19th and early 20th centuries. Furthermore, it is illustrated in George Daniels' definitive book 'The Art of Breguet', 1977.

The montre à tact or 'tactful watch' was invented by Abraham Louis Breguet in the late 1790s during an epoch when it was unseemly to read the time in public. The 'à tact' system helped to tell the time in polite society without taking the watch out of your pocket and possibly offending your host or hostess. It is also referred to as the watch for the blind as the exposed pointer and markers on the band allow the wearer to determine the time by touch.

Breguet's tact watches were fitted with a variation of the so-called souscription movement, classified as petite (small), moyenne (medium) and grande (large). It is thought that a total of around 915 of these movements were made, out of which about 35 petites, such as the present watch, are known.

These exclusive watches, first introduced in 1799, were quite costly, priced between 1,000 and 2,000 francs. Those fitted with a jeweled case would cost as much as 5,000 francs.

Sir David Lionel Salomons, 2nd Baronet

Sir David had a great interest in horology throughout his life and became the leading authority on the work of the legendary watchmaker Abraham-Louis Breguet, generally acknowledged as the most brilliant watchmaker of all time. In 1921, Salomons published the first major book on Breguet's life and work, including illustrations of important pieces from his own collection.

Sir David Salomons put together the world's largest private collection of Breguet watches and clocks, comprising 124 pieces, including the two watches considered to be the zenith of Breguet's achievement, the so-called 'Marie Antoinette' collection no. 160 and the 'Duc de Praslin', collection no. 92. Upon his death in 1925, Salomons left fifty-seven Breguet pieces to the L.A. Mayer Institute for Islamic Art in Jerusalem. He left the remainder of his collection, including the present watch, to his wife who later sold them at auction for considerable sums. The Christie's dispersal of 'The Celebrated Collection of Watches by Breguet, formed by the late Sir David Salomons, Bart.' over three auctions held in 1964 and 1965, were among the most memorable auction events of the 1960s.

Inv. 1862

Breguet

18K gold and enamel quarter repeating pair case cabriolet watch, made for the Turkish market

Signed Le Roy, Élève de Breguet, the dial signed with Le Roy's Turkish signature, no. 5021, cases numbered L 5021, circa 1815

Keywound gilded brass ruby cylinder movement, plain three arm brass balance with pare-chute suspension on the pivot, blued steel flat balance spring with bimetallic compensation curb on the regulator, quarter repeating on two polished steel hammers on a gong

White enamel dial with Turkish numerals

Circular case, both cases decorated with gilt foliage and translucent scarlet champlevé enamel over an engine-turned background, both backs decorated with very finely painted polychrome enamel scenes depicting fantasy harbour views in the Ottoman Empire, the pastel-coloured sky with translucent enamel sunray effect over engine-turned background, quarter repeating pull-twist push-piece in the pendant, gold cuvette

53.4 mm. diam.

Literature:

Prominently illustrated and described in:Breguet - Watchmakers since 1775, Emmanuel Breguet, 1997, pp. 231 & 374, pl. 57, and pp. 359 & 378, pl. 55.

Exhibited:

Musée International d'Horlogerie, La Chaux-de-Fonds, 'L'Oeuvre d'Abraham-Louis Breguet', 15th May-20th September 1976.

Signed 'Leroy Élève de Breguet' and displaying the same style elements as Abraham-Louis Breguet's Turkish watches, the present watch is a wonderful example of one of Breguet's timepieces sold under the name of his representative in Constantinople. There are a few other watches made by Breguet for the Turkish market and signed Le Roy.

Leroy became Breguet's agent in Constantinople from 1811, from then onwards, all of Breguet's sales for the Turkish market were handled by him. Leroy was so highly regarded that Sultan Mahmud II asked him to look after the maintenance of all his clocks and watches.

The lavishly decorated cases and finely painted enamel scenes demonstrate the superb craftsmanship that established Geneva as the centre of enamelling and watchmaking excellence in the 19th century. The two cases are conceived for the watch to be used either 'open' and showing the dial or 'closed' showing the back of the inner case, hence the designation 'Cabriolet'. The case and frame are of such outstandingly high quality, allowing the inner case to fit so perfectly into the outer case, that the two sides show virtually no difference, neither visible nor tangible, when used as hunter case.

Inv. 1115

Sold to the Duke of Bedford

Breguet No. 1099

18K gold, enamel and diamond and pearl-set hunter case à tact ruby cylinder watch

Signed Breguet, No. 1099, case nos. 1865 and B 1975, sold to Monsieur le Duc de Bedford le 2 Floreal An II (21 April 1794) for 1500 Francs

Keywound gilt-finished souscription calibre ruby cylinder movement with central barrel and plain three arm brass balance

Small silver dial with Breguet numerals and blued steel Breguet hands

Circular case with pearl-set hour markers to the coin-edged band, the translucent light grey enamel front on engine-turned decorated background depicting a rising sun over waters, the reverse with a gold and pearl-set arrow-shaped pointer on translucent light grey enamel on engine-turned sunburst decoration, pearl-set pendant, case numbered B 1975 and 1865 and stamped P.B.T. for Pierre Benjamin Tavernier, cuvette signed and numbered 1099

42 mm. diam.

The copy of the Breguet Certificate no. 3283 dated 21 June 1971 accompanying the watch confirms the sale of the present 'Montre en médaillon à tact' with grey enamel case, hour markers and arrow with pearls and cylinder escapement to Monsieur le Duc de Bedford on 2 Floreal An II (21 April 1794) for the amount of 1,500 Francs. It is also accompanied by a gold ratchet key and short length of chain and later Breguet red leather presentation box numbered 1099.

The 'montre à tact' or 'tactful watch' was invented by Abraham Louis Breguet in the late 1790s during an epoch when it was unseemly to read the time in public. The 'à tact' system helped to tactfully tell the time in polite society without taking the watch out of your pocket.

The present watch, sold in 1794, is one of the earliest examples of a 'montre à tact', which Breguet officially introduced in spring 1799 only. These watches were also called 'médaillon à tact' and destined to be worn on a chain around the neck.

Breguet's *à tact* watches were fitted with a so-called variation of the 'souscription' movement, classified as "petite" (small), 'moyenne' (medium) and 'grande' (large). It is thought that a total of around 915 of these movements were made, out of which about 35 'petites', such as the present watch, are known. These exclusive watches were quite costly, priced between 1,000 and 2,000 francs, those fitted with a jewelled case would cost as much as 5,000 francs.

Pierre Benjamin Tavernier

The case of the present watch is stamped PBT for Pierre Benjamin Tavernier. The renowned case maker located in Paris supplied his exceptional cases to the most famous watchmakers of the time, notably Breguet, Lépine, Ferdinand Berthoud and others.

Duke of Bedford

The present watch was sold to the Duke of Bedford, the Dukedom of Bedford is one of the greatest English aristocratic titles, dating back to the 15th century. Based on the year of its sale, it must have belonged either to Francis Russell, 5th Duke of Bedford (1765-1802) or his brother John Russell, 6th Duke of Bedford (1766-1839).

One of the faithful British aristocratic clients of Breguet, the name of the Duke of Bedford is mentioned on several occasions in Emmanuel Breguet's book: Breguet - Watchmakers since 1775, pp. 197, 201 and 291.

A similar watch, No. 2627, was sold by Sotheby's New York, Masterpieces from the Time Museum, 13th October, 2004, lot 578.

Made for the Sultan of the Ottoman Empire

Breguet No. 1950

22K gold and enamel 'cabriolet' pair case two-train Grande and Petite sonnerie striking ruby cylinder clockwatch with independent minute repeating, striking with five hammers on five gongs, Breguet gold chain and ratchet key

Signed Breguet et Fils, no. 1950, 'Montre a Grande et Petite Sonnerie Répétition a Minutes, boîte et étui d'orgravés et émaillés formeTurque', case no. 2563, sold to Ottoman diplomat and statesman Galip Effendi on 6th May 1808, for 4000 Francs

Keywound gilt movement with third series ébauche, ruby cylinder escapement, two barrels, three gear-trains, monometallic balance with parechute suspension on the top pivot, striking and repeating with five hammers on five gongs, striking clockwatch mechanism on the backplate, repeating mechanism beneath the dial, repeating activated by a pull-and-twist piston in the pendant

White enamel dial by Master dial-maker Borel no. 258, with Turkish numerals, Breguet hands

Circular case by Master case maker Pierre-Benjamin Tavernier, the double-body outer case decorated with polychrome champleve red and blue enamel border and matching bezel, the back overlaid with translucent red guilloche enamel with gold paillone decoration and central Turkish emblem of the crescent moon and star. Four-body inner case, the bezel and back overlaid with translucent red guilloche enamel and gold decoration of palmettes and a central sunray. Hinged gold cuvette with winding apertures and levers for Grande/Petite sonnerie and silence

63 mm. diam.

With Breguet Certificate No. 3736 dated 16 March 1982.

"Your reputation in the capital here is at its peak. All the great princes admire your work" –Turkish Ambassador Esseid Ali Effendi to Breguet in 1805"

This exceptional, highly important and probably unique clockwatch is one of the most splendid watches ever made by Abraham-Louis Breguet for the Turkish market. Collected from Bregue tin Paris by the Turkish diplomat and statesman Mehmet Said Galip Pasha, known as Galip Effendi in May 1808. At a price of 4000 Francs, it is one of Breguet's most expensive watches of the period and almost certainly made as a special order intended for the Sultan of the Ottoman Empire himself. Interestingly, the period 1807-1808 encompasses the reigns of three Sultans. As this watch would have taken up to two years to complete, it can be assumed that it was probably originally ordered by Sultan Selim III (reigned 1789-1807) but ultimately delivered to either Sultan Mustafa IV (reigned 1807-1808) or his successor Sultan Mahmud II (1808-1839). A previous owner of the watch stated that by family tradition the watch had been given to his forebear directly by Sultan Abdulaziz (1861-1876), the son of Sultan Mahmud II. In fact, Mahmud II had the distinction of owning one of the most expensive objects ever made by Abraham-LouisBreguet - a 'Sympatique' clock covered in precious stones, worth 35,000 Francs, (see Breguet - Watchmakers since 1775 by Emmanuel Breguet, p. 234), chosen in 1813 by Napoleon as a gift to mark the installment of the Sultan. Mahmud II was so delighted that he assigned Breguet's representative Leroy with the maintenance of all the timepieces in his palace.

In October 1980, the present watch was cleaned and returned to working order by the legendary English watchmaker George Daniels, the undisputed authority on the work of Abraham-Louis Breguet.

The movement is constructed using a third-series ébauche made in 1796 and one of only six examples made. Of those six movements the present watch is the only one with the striking and repeating mechanism constructed with five hammers and five gongs. The finishing of the movement is recorded in the Breguet archives as being started at the end of 1805 (French Revolutionary Calendar year 13) and was completed on 31st December 1807.

The two lavishly decorated cases exemplify the best craftsmanship of 19th century watchmaking and enamelling in Geneva. Abraham-Louis Breguet's timepieces made for the Turkish market captivate by their opulently enamelled, brightly coloured decoration, ostentatiously contrasting with the neo-classical, often almost understated design of his traditional watches. The two separate cases are conceived for the watch to be used either 'open' and showing the dial or 'closed' showing the back of the inner case, hence the designation 'Cabriolet'. The cases are of such outstandingly high quality, allowing the inner case to fit so perfectly into the outer case, that the two sides show virtually no difference, neither visible nor tangible, when used as hunter case.

Today such 'survivors' of this rarefied category of the famed watchmaker's production are always justly admired amongst collectors of these exceptional timepieces.

Galib Effendi – Mehmet Said Galip Pasha

Born in 1763, the diplomat and statesman Mehmet Said Galip Pasha represented the Turks during negotiations of the Treaty of Paris between France and the Ottoman Empire signed on 25th June, 1802, which ended the French campaign in Egypt and Syria.

Between 1806 and 1812, against the background of the Napoleonic Wars, the Ottoman Empire declared war on the Russian Empire. Galip Pasha again used his diplomatic skills to negotiate the peace treaty of 1807.

Galip Pasha became Grand Vizier, the effective head of government, between 1823 and 1824 and died in 1829.

Breguet and the Ottoman Empire

The Ottoman Empire became concerned about the Revolution in France after 1797, when Napoleon sent agents to spread anti-Ottoman propaganda in the Balkans. The French possession of territory in the Ionian archipelago brought about a break in Franco-Turkish relations. The Ottomans joined the Second Coalition against France in the wake of Napoleon's Egyptian expedition. The evacuation of French forces from Egypt led to the renewal of relations between France and the Ottoman Empire. A preliminary treaty of peace was signed in October 1801. Relations between the two countries were close due to Turkish fears of Russia.

The relationship between Breguet and the Ottoman Empire began in the early 19th century, at the time when trade relations between Breguet and his main markets, notably England, Spain and Russia, were suspended by the Napoleonic wars. The success of his watches in Turkey was largely due to the Esseid Ali Effendi, nicknamed 'The Sublime Portal', who had been sent to Paris as the Ottoman Ambassador in response to the arrival of Marshal Sebastiani as French Ambassador in Constantinople. In Paris, Ali became acquainted with the famous diplomat Talleyrand, friend and faithful client of Breguet, who introduced the two men. The friendship between Esseid Ali and Abraham-Louis Breguet contributed to the latter's early awareness of the importance of the Ottoman market, especially since Turkey was the only major power still allied with Napoleonic France.

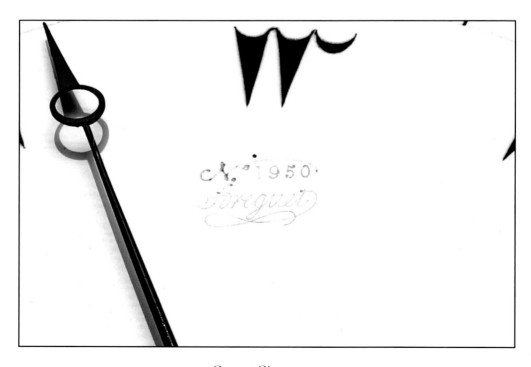

Secret Signature

In 1798, Esseid Ali bought his first watch from Breguet, followed by a continuous stream of orders after his return to Turkey four years later, ranging from highly complicated watches to simple models as well as thermometers and barometers. In his letters, Ali described in detail the aesthetic features required to appeal to clients in his country, including lavishly decorated and enamelled inner and outer cases in vivid colours, such as scarlet or 'Turkish' red, and as of 1803 white enamel dials with Turkish rather than Arabic or Roman numerals, radically different from the neo-classical style which Breguet had so successfully introduced into the watch industry.

In 1804, Esseid Ali had become the Minister of the Navy and commissioned the finest possible repeating watch for the Ottoman Emperor Selim III. Highly pleased by the watch, the Emperor requested a second watch identical to the first. With his growing popularity in the Ottoman Empire, Breguet decided to send Leroy (or Le Roy), a skilled and trustworthy watchmaker, as his representative to Turkey. Leroy settled in Constantinople and, as of 1811, he received a yearly average of six to eight extremely valuable pieces. Geneva-based workshops specialising in opulently enamelled watches and familiar with Ottoman motifs enabled Breguet to meet the strong demand from Turkey.

Istanbul's Topkapi Palace Museum owns several of Breguet's finest creations specially made for Turkey, including the magnificent 'Sympathique' clock. These masterpieces impressively emphasize the successful symbioses of avant-garde watch technology introduced by Breguet and the evocative, splendidly decorative style elements of the Ottoman Empire.

Selected Bibliography

Jürgen Abeler. "Meister der Uhrmacherkunst", Wuppertal, 1977

Emmanuel Breguet & Martin Chapman. "Breguet – Art and Innovation in Watchmaking", DelMonico, 2015

Britten, F.J. "Old Clocks and Watches and Their Makers - A History of Styles in Clocks and Watches and their Mechanisms", Bloomsbury Books, London, 1986

S. Bull &F. Sturm. "Geneva Watches", exhibition catalogue for the Muséed'Horlogerie, Dr. E. Gschwind Foundation, Basel, 1978

Hans Boeckh. "Emailmalerei auf Genfer Taschenuhrenvom 17. biszumbeginnenden 19. Jahrhundert", 1982

AdolpheChapire. "La Montre Française", Les Editions de l'Amateur, 1991

Alfred Chapuis. "La Montre Chinois", Attinger Frères, Neuchatel, 1919

Chapuis&Gélis. "Le Monde des Automates", 1928, Vol. II

Cecil Clutton and George Daniels."Watches", Sotheby, Parke, Bernet, 1979

Genevieve Cummins & Nerylla Taunton. "Chatelaines, Utility to Glorious Extravagance", Antique Collector's Club, 1994

Brian Loomes. "Watchmakers and Clockmakers of the World", N.A.G. Press, London, 2006

Osvaldo Patrizzi. "Dictionnare des Horlogers Genevois", Antiquorum Editions, 1998

Sir David Lionel Salomons. "Breguet", 1921

Tardy. "Dictionnaire des Horlogers Francais", 1972

Ian White. "The Majesty of the Chinese Market Watch, The Life and Collection of Gustave Loup of Tientsin and Geneva, Watch Dealer and Collector (1876-1961)", AHS, 2019

Index

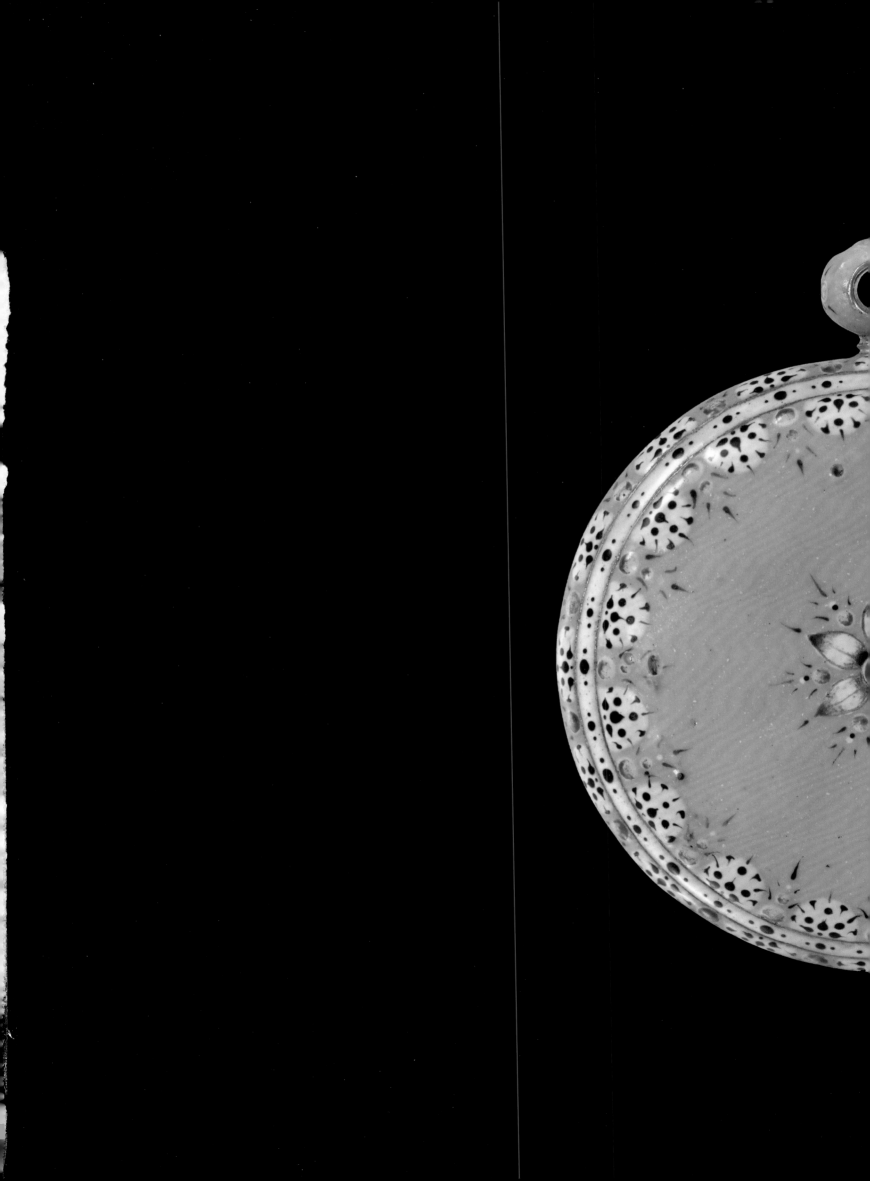